Innovate or Die!

Innovate or Die!

ANDRES OPPENHEIMER

Innovate or Die!

First published in Spanish: September 2014

All rights reserved © 2014, Andrés Oppenheimer

All rights reserved © 2015, worldwide publishing rights:
Penguin Random House Grupo Editorial, S. A. de C. V.
Blvd Miguel de Cervantes Saavedra No. 301, 1er piso,
colonia Granada, delegación Miguel Hidalgo, C. P. 11520,
Mexico City

www.megustaleer.com.mx

D. R. © Juan O. Tamayo, por la traducción

ISBN: 978-1-941999-95-0

Printed in the US

Penguin
Random House
Grupo Editorial

For Sandra

Index

Prologue 11

1. The Coming World 17
2. Gastón Acurio: the chef who gives away his recipes 64
3. Jordi Muñoz and the "makers" movement 85
4. Bre Pettis and new Industrial Revolution 104
5. Rafael Yuste and the brain manipulators 125
6. Pep Guardiola and the art of innovating while winning . . . 144
7. Branson, Musk, Kargieman and the art of reinventing
   oneself 165
8. Salman Khan and "flipped schools" 194
9. Zolezzi, Von Ahn and the social innovators 220
10. The five secrets of innovation 249

Notes 283
Acknowledgments 293

Prologue

When Apple founder Steve Jobs died, I wrote a column that has kept me thinking to this day. In that column, I posed several questions that should be at the core of our countries' political agendas: why have no Steve Jobs emerged in Mexico, Argentina, India, South Korea, or other countries that have people just as talented or more so than the Apple founder? What made Jobs succeed in the United States, like Microsoft founder Bill Gates, Facebook founder Mark Zuckerberg and so many others, while thousands of talented people in other parts of the world could not do it in their own countries?

That is a fundamental question, which should be at the heart of any political analysis of our countries, because we live in a global knowledge economy, where nations that generate technological innovations grow faster, and reduce poverty faster, than those that don't. Today, the prosperity of countries increasingly depends less on their natural resources or manufacturing capacity and more on their education systems, their scientists and innovators. The most successful countries are not those that have more oil, more water, more copper, or produce most basic manufactured goods. A successful computer program, a new medicine or a popular clothing brand are worth much more than huge outputs of raw materials or manufactured products.

It's no coincidence that as I write this, a company like Apple is worth 20 percent more than the entire Gross Domestic Product (GDP) of Argentina, and more than twice the GDP of Venezuela. And it's no accident that many of the wealthiest nations, in capita income, are countries like Luxembourg and Singapore, which have no natural resources (Singapore has long imported its food, and even its water, I learned during a visit there) while countries rich in oil and other natural resources, like Venezuela or Nigeria, have obscene levels of poverty.

The question, then, is how can our nations produce innovators like Steve Jobs. In my previous books, I pointed out that the quality of education is one of the keys to the knowledge economy. And that's still true. As Gates himself told me in an interview, he never would have been able to create Microsoft and revolutionize the world with his computer programs if he had not received an excellent education in high school, which had a late-model computer that sparked his curiosity for the information sciences. And, as Gates said in another interview, far from being proud of the fact that he dropped out of Harvard University, he always lamented leaving the school before he graduated. He said, "I left college because I thought I had to move quickly on the Microsoft opportunity. I had already finished three years and if I had used my AP credits properly I would have graduated… I am as fake a dropout as you can get."[1]

But it's also clear that a good education, without an environment that fosters innovation, produces a lot of cultured taxi drivers, yet little personal or national wealth. It's clear from the stories of Jobs, Gates, Zuckerberg, and so many others, that much more than just a good education is required to foster creative minds. But what exactly are those requirements? The search for the answer to that question led me to write this book.

Before starting my research, I had heard various possible answers from several experts, and listed them in a *Miami Herald* column. I didn't find them very convincing. One was that excessive government interference asphyxiates any potential culture of creativity. A Twitter message that a Spanish reader sent me just hours after I published that column on Jobs, in October of 2011, put it this way: "In Spain, Jobs would never have been able to do anything, because (in Spain) it's illegal to start a business in your garage, and no one would have loaned you a cent." The message suggested that the biggest hurdles to innovation in our countries are excessive government regulations and a shortage of venture capital to finance projects of talented people. There was some truth to that, but that explanation didn't satisfy me.

It's true that Jobs would have had to be very patient —and lucky— to launch a computer company in Spain or most Latin American and Asian countries. One World Bank study shows that Argentina requires 14 legal steps to start a business —even if it's a home-based car repair shop—, Brazil requires 13, Venezuela 17, India 12 and China 13, while the United States and most of the industrialized nations require only six.[2] Yet the same study also showed that a number of countries, like Mexico and Chile, significantly reduced their bureaucratic obstacles in recent years and currently require the same number of procedures as the United States for opening a business. If government bureaucracy was the principal impediment to creative productivity, then Mexico and Chile already would be producing global entrepreneurs of Job's caliber.

Another explanation that I listed in that column, coming from the opposite side of the political spectrum, was that more state intervention is needed to produce innovation. According to this theory, most countries do not produce more innovators because their governments do not invest enough in science and technology. In recent years, presidents of many middle-income countries have inaugurated huge science and technology parks with great pomp and circumstance, that they insist will turn their nations into world-level research centers. Brazil already has 22 of these technology parks, Mexico has 21, Argentina and Colombia have five each and several more are under construction in those and other countries. And all were created under the argument, which emerged in the United States and Great Britain in the 1950s, that close links between private corporations, universities and governments facilitate the transfer of knowledge and innovation.

But recent studies have shown that these technology parks are little more than real estate ventures, which generate political profits for the presidents that inaugurate them but few advances in innovation. A recent report by the InterAmerican Development Bank (IDB)

13

concluded that in Latin America, "the policy of the science and technology parks is far from achieving its objectives."[3]

Finally, another widespread explanation for why world-class innovators such as Jobs have not emerged from most developing and middle-income countries is cultural. According to this theory, Hispanic and Asian cultures have a long tradition of top-to-bottom control, obedience and lack of tolerance for diversity, all of which tend to limit creativity. This argument of cultural determinism didn't fully convince me either. If verticality and obedience are the problem, South Korea —a small Asian country that produces 10 times more patents of inventions than all of Latin America and the Caribbean put together— would be producing far fewer patents.

In my column about Steve Jobs, I suggested a different theory: that the main reason why no innovators of Steve Jobs' stature have emerged in other parts of the world is that most countries lack a culture of tolerance for failure. The world's most creative entrepreneurs fail many times before they succeed, I wrote, and if that's to happen in our countries, we need societies that tolerate failure.

Indeed, Jobs, who died at the age of 56, co-founded Apple in the garage of his home at the age of 20. But he was fired from the company 10 years later, when he was barely 30, after losing a corporate battle inside Apple. His fall from grace made the front pages of the main newspapers around the world. In many other countries, Jobs' career would have ended there. The reaction of the business community would have been, "he fell into disgrace," or "his 15 minutes of fame are over," or "he's finished." But in Silicon Valley, after he was fired by Apple, Jobs began what he later described as the most creative period of his life.

He launched new companies and found investors to finance them. In the innovators' culture of Silicon Valley, where failure is something that the majority of successful people have experienced many times, Jobs made a quick comeback. Would the same have happened in Spain, Latin America, or many Asian countries? Would someone who fell into disgrace repeatedly, like Jobs, have been able to make a comeback and succeed?

After writing that column, I traveled to Palo Alto, in California's Silicon Valley, and several countries to interview some of the most creative minds on the planet and find out what distinguishes creative people and innovative cultures. In other words, how can we become more creative, at the personal and national level, and turn our ideas into profitable projects that will help to improve our lives, and our countries' economies. In my travels and interviews, I found some surprisingly auspicious answers. Far from being condemned to underdevelopment, emerging countries can use their talent —and most countries have it, as we will see in this book— to boost and channel our creativity. Innovation is becoming more democratic, and it is increasingly within most countries' grasp.

In the following pages, I will try to share with you what I learned during my trips and interviews with some of the world's most prominent innovators.

1

The Coming World

We are entering a period of radical transformations

Palo Alto, California. The first place I visited when I started to write this book was Silicon Valley in California, the undisputed heart of global innovation and home to Google, Apple, Facebook, eBay, Intel and thousands of other high-tech companies. I wanted to figure out the secret to Silicon Valley's success and learn what other countries can do to follow in its footsteps. I had a thousand questions in my head.

Why is there such an impressive concentration of globally innovative enterprises in that part of northern California, near San Francisco? Has the U.S. government designated this area as a center for technology development and does it provide technology companies with enormous benefits to settle there? Is it that the state of California gives them tax breaks? Or are technology companies attracted by defense industry contracts or its proximity to Stanford University, one of the world's best in science and technology research?

My first stop after renting a car at the San Francisco airport was Singularity University, one of the key centers for the study of technological innovation. I had an appointment with Vivek Wadhwa, a vice president for innovation and research at Singularity, a professor at Duke and Emory and an innovation guru who writes regularly for *The Wall Street Journal* and *The Washington Post*. Wadhwa had suggested that I visit that week to take part in a conference that was to attract entrepreneurs from around the world to listen to several presentations on the latest developments in robotics, nanotechnology, space exploration, cyber-medicine and other topics of the future. But my main interest was to interview Wadhwa. He had studied the issue of innovation like few others, and had a global vision that put him apart from many other experts in the United States.

When I arrived at Singularity University —which is not a typical university because it does not grant degrees and only offers courses for qualified business people and entrepreneurs—, after driving south of San Francisco for 45 minutes, the first thing that caught my attention was that its building was not very impressive. Far from a glass tower or an ultramodern building, the university is housed in an old military base. It was built in the 1940s, became part of NASA's Ames Research Center in 1958 and now rents to all sorts of technology companies. Nearly all its buildings are two-story military barracks, all painted the same color. Singularity University was just another building, with a small sign identifying it stuck on the lawn.

Wadhwa received me cordially and led me to a small conference room where we could talk quietly. He was middle-aged, wearing a white shirt open at the collar and no tie, like almost everyone else around him. He told me he was born in India and raised in Malaysia, Australia and various other countries where his father, a career diplomat, had been posted. At the age of 23, when his father was transferred to the United Nations, Wadhwa moved to New York City and obtained a masters' degree in business administration at New York University. After graduation he worked as a computer programmer and joined up with colleagues to launch several companies, one of which was sold for $118 million after a few years. Some decades later, after suffering a heart attack that led him to seek a less stressful life, Wadhwa dedicated all his time to teaching and research on innovation.

THE SECRET IS THE PEOPLE

When I asked him for the secret of Silicon Valley, he gave me a three-word answer that was not at all what I expected. "It's the people," he said. "The secret of Silicon Valley has nothing to do with the government, or economic incentives or science and technology parks, which are a useless waste of money. The secret is the kind of people who concentrate here."

I looked at him with a certain skepticism, not really understanding what he was trying to say. What's the difference between the people in Silicon Valley and other parts of the United States, I asked him. Wadhwa replied that Silicon Valley has a peculiar agglomeration of creative minds from around the world, attracted by the climate of acceptance of ethnic, cultural and even sexual diversity.

At least 53 percent of Silicon Valley residents are foreigners, and many of them are young engineers and scientists from China, India, Mexico and other parts of the world who find the area conducive to developing their own ideas, Wadhwa explained. "The California mentality, the open mind and the worship of what is 'different,' has a lot to do with the success of Silicon Valley," he said. "The presence of Stanford University, and its excellence in research and development, no doubt contributed to so many technology companies coming here."

"But the number one factor is the people," Wadhwa insisted. "You can see it for yourself. Take a walk on Castro Street, the main street of Mountain View, and you will see what I'm telling you with your own eyes. The cafes are full of young people with their laptops, totally immersed in their startup projects, going from table to table to figure out how to fix software problems even if they don't know each other. All these young people want to be the next Mark Zuckerberg."

After our chat, we went to Mountain View, a small city a five-minute drive from Singularity University, to see for ourselves what Wadhwa was talking about. Along Castro Street, the main street, there were Chinese, Indian, Vietnamese and Mexican restaurants, together with acupuncture clinics, macrobiotic food markets and an unusual number of bookstores. That was interesting. At a time when the main U.S. bookstore chains were closing —victims of the crisis in the book publishing industry and the growth of e-books— in Silicon Valley, birthplace of the Internet, stores that sold paper books were proliferating. In one block of Castro Street alone I spotted three big bookstores packed with people —Book Buyers, East and West and Books Inc.

Nearly all the tables at the nearby Olympus Cafe were taken up by youths with long hair, pony tails or shaved heads. Just as Wadhwa had told me, they were hunched over their laptops, many of them using earphones, totally focused on God-knows-what software they were trying to develop. If any of them were having fun on video games, they managed to hide that pretty well, because none of them had the idle look of someone who is just killing time. But the most significant image was the racial hotchpotch: at nearly all the tables, young people from the United States, China, India, Latin America and other countries sat together. And on the streets, nearly all the couples were mixed: Americans with Chinese, Indians with Mexicans, Chinese with Indians, etc. The diversity in ethnicity, culture and relationships that Wadhwa had talked about was visible everywhere, and much more so than in multicultural cities like New York or Boston.

As we had a coffee on Castro Street, and I tried to digest everything that Wadhwa was telling me, I could not stop thinking that what I was seeing and hearing was good news for many countries trying to create their own Silicon Valleys: if the secret of innovation lies in talented people more than resources or economic incentives, then many Latin American and European countries, where niches of creativity are flowering, have an excellent chance to stand among the leaders of innovation in a future world.

THE EMERGING WORLD'S POTENTIAL

Contrary to the belief, widespread in academic and business circles some years back, that the key to boosting innovation is to offer economic incentives, reduce bureaucratic hurdles or have a good business climate, Wadhwa told me that what's most important today is having a critical mass of creative minds backed by good educational systems. And he assured me that he had seen an enormous pool of creative talent in São Paulo, Buenos Aires, Mexico City, Bogota, Santiago de Chile and other Latin American or Asian cities with enclaves of artists, inventors and entrepreneurs —what used to be called "bohemian quarters," which perhaps without realizing it have a lot in common with the "California mindset."

But can technology companies succeed in countries with laws that make any sort of enterprise difficult? There's no doubt that a bad business climate, hellish bureaucracies and corruption are huge hurdles. It's difficult to create an innovative company in Venezuela, where the World Bank study we mentioned in the prologue showed that 17 legal steps are required to register a new company, 14 in Argentina and 13 in Brazil and Colombia. And they generally take months to complete the process.[1]

It's also difficult to start a company that has a high degree of business and financial risk —like nearly all high technology companies— in countries with laws that don't tolerate failure. They condemn business people who are forced to close or restructure their companies to many years of ostracism and economic ruin, as shown by the World Bank studies. Nevertheless, the experience of Silicon Valley and the most recent research on innovation show that the concentration of creative minds is by far the principal driver of collective creativity, even more important than the economic environment.

INNOVATORS WANT TO LIVE IN VIBRANT PLACES

One of the first to call attention to this fact was University of Toronto economist Richard Florida, who over the past decade has radically changed theories of innovation that used to point to a favorable business climate as the principal requirement for innovation. In his book, *The Rise of the Creative Class*, Florida argues that in the future, companies will not attract creative minds but rather the other way around —concentrations of creative minds will attract companies. As Florida himself explained it to me over several interviews, this is good news for Latin America: the region has in its favor several cities with unusual dynamism, which act as magnets for creative minds and can become centers of innovation.

What generates creativity? More than anything else, the presence of other creative people, Florida says. The idea that creativity is linked to individual genius is a big myth. The truth is that creativity is a social process. Our greatest achievements come from people from whom we learn, from our competitors and from our collaborators. And cities are real centers of creativity. It was always that way. The Athens of the classics, the Florence of the Renaissance, the Vienna and Paris of the late 19th Century, New York after World War II, all experienced an incredible flowering of genius in several fields, in good measure because of their condition as cities. They generated new ideas thanks to the diversity of their populations, large social networks and public spaces where people could meet and exchange ideas. And, with their financial, organizational and commercial infrastructures, they could turn those ideas into reality.[2]

Florida reached these conclusions when he was a visiting professor at Harvard. One day, he read a report in *The Boston Globe* newspaper that caught his attention. The story said that the Lycos company had decided to move from Pittsburgh to Boston. Florida, who until then had lived in Pittsburgh and taught economics at Carnegie Mellon University, was dumbstruck. Lycos was the pride of Carnegie Mellon. The Internet company had been founded by Carnegie Mellon professors, recruited graduates of the university and received many economic incentives from the city of Pittsburgh. Why had Lycos decided to move to Boston, a city with a much more adverse economic climate, which offered no fiscal incentives and where taxes and labor costs were much higher?

"That report made me realize that everything I thought I knew about innovation was wrong, and forced me to radically change my thinking," Florida recalled.[3] The professor began to research the issue. When he returned to Pittsburgh, he asked his students in the masters' program in economics if they planned to stay in Pittsburgh after graduation. "None of the students raised their hands," Florida said. "And when

22

I asked where they wanted to live, their answers were the same. 'I want to live someplace that has energy,' or 'I want to live in a vibrant place' or 'I want to live in a place with a good vibe.' And I told myself, 'Wow. There's something here that I have to look into.' "[4]

Florida began to study the movement of cutting-edge companies and discovered the Lycos case was not unique. Companies were migrating to places with creative minds. "Lycos had moved to Boston for only one reason: to have access to a permanent source of innovative people, not only on its technology side but also for its marketing, business development and other functions. Those people were in Boston," he said.[5]

And where do creative people gather?, Florida asked himself. The answer he found is that innovative people don't always gather around the best universities or the biggest companies. After studying the case of Silicon Valley, he concluded that innovators tend to gather in places that allow them to work "outside the rules of traditional corporations, outside the bureaucracy, in those spaces where they can control the means of production and which offer them venture capital that is capital and not just debt."[6] In the following years, Florida told me in an interview he found several promising places in Latin America.

MANY COUNTRIES CAN HAVE A SILICON VALLEY

Florida said that he is much more optimistic than many of his colleagues about the possibility of innovation flourishing in Latin America, or other parts of the world. Although universities in Buenos Aires, Mexico City or São Paulo don't rank among the best in the world, and those countries don't offer the best business environment, they have vibrant cities full of creative people. After studying the geography of innovation like few others, Florida said he "reached the somewhat controversial conclusion that the most fertile places for innovation are those where the arts and new musical expressions flourish, where there is a big gay population, where there's good food, as well as universities that can transform creativity into innovation."

23

Florida dedicated many years to the study of innovation in the world of music —he's a rock fanatic— and discovered a number of lessons that can be applied to science and technology. "What's interesting about our research on music is that we found that the ecosystems that support innovation are those that allow for a constant combination and recombination of people. Rock bands constantly come together, break up and reform with other people. Jack White, the musician who founded White Stripes, said it better than anyone else when he defined success as the result of a constant mixing and remixing. You fail, and you look for a new combination. Success is the ability to find a new member for your team, who helps you to get where you want to go," Florida said.

His research led him to the final conclusion that the places where innovation flourishes celebrate talent more than money. And that's good news for Latin America because that is one of the characteristics of many cities in the region, Florida added. "Steve Jobs was revered in Silicon Valley not because he was wealthy, but because he was good at what he did," Florida noted. "That's one of the characteristics of places that generate innovation. In New York City, for example, you are going to find innovation not in Wall Street but in the artists' enclave of Chelsea. The same happens in almost all innovation centers. In Latin America, and especially Brazil, Mexico and Argentina, I see a very creative ecosystem, especially in music and the arts, and I see that characteristic of admiring the talented more than the rich."

THE WORLD OF THE FUTURE

If a number of Latin American countries already have large pools of creative minds, which are the essential requirement for innovative societies, their great challenge will be to improve the quality and global connections of their education systems and to create legal systems that are much more tolerant of business failures. Doing nothing will be enormously risky and will condemn the region to lagging permanently behind, because in the next few years there will be an extraordinary acceleration of scientific and technological advances that will widen the gap between countries on the leading edge and those on the periphery.

Most scientists agree that in the next decade we will experience technological advances more revolutionary than all those produced by humans since the invention of the wheel, around 3500 B.C. The reason is that science and technology are growing exponentially —at a faster clip each day. Today, an indigenous person in southern Mexico or the Bolivian Altiplano with an iPhone can access more knowledge than the president of the United States or NASA had two decades ago. And that's only a hint of what is to come. According to the so-called Moore's Law —based on an article by Intel co-founder Gordon Moore in 1965— the capacity of computers is doubling approximately every two years. And technology is changing at the same pace.

Thousands of companies in Silicon Valley —many of them headed by 20-something entrepreneurs like Gates, Jobs and Zuckerberg when they started— are launching surprising innovations that will change our lives as much as or perhaps more than the arrival of the Internet. During my visit to Singularity University and a number of Silicon Valley companies, I had the opportunity to see some of the innovations coming down the pike, and they surprised me more than I had expected.

I was shown 3D printers that will allow the home-based and individualized manufacture of any object, and threaten to wipe out industrial production across the world. I saw robots that we have seen only in science fiction movies, that will become our assistants, bodyguards, companions or sex partners. There were self-driving cars that will slowly replace current vehicles and allow us to work, read or sleep while the vehicle takes us to our destination. There were computerized glasses, like Google Glass, that will allow us to look at a garden and see the names of each plant, or to look at a plate of food and see the calories in each item, or to walk into a party and see the names of each person we greet. All these inventions already exist, and some have been under development for years. But the price and legal barriers that blocked their massive use are coming down, and their widespread use in turn will generate new industries, just like it happened with computers.

3D PRINTERS THAT MAKE SHOES

Printers that until very recently printed only on paper now have 3D versions that can reproduce shoes, clothes, auto parts, tableware, jewelry, toys, food and even human organs. And this, I was told by industry leaders, will bring with it a new Industrial Revolution that will transform manufacturing as we know it, allowing each of us to produce what we want, to our own measure and in our own homes. A good part of mass production will be replaced by individualized production. The 3D printers were spotlighted in 2013, when President Barack Obama mentioned them in his State of the Union address to Congress —the most important U.S. presidential speech of each year— as an invention that "has the potential to revolutionize the way we make almost everything."[7] Although a number of U.S. inventors had been experimenting with 3D printers since the 1980s —and some already had been producing some models— Obama was referring to the National Additive Manufacturing Innovation Institute, which operates out of an old warehouse in Youngstown, Ohio, and has been cooperating with several companies to turn the 3D printers into everyday hardware, much like personal computers.

Today, 3D printers are used mostly by architects, engineers and designers to create scale models of their projects. While an architect working on a project once had to order the model from a specialized maker —a process that could cost thousands of dollars and take weeks— a 3D printer today can produce the model in 30 minutes and for less than $10. And if the architect does not like the result, it can be produced again with whatever changes he wants.

3D printers are also being used to produce items needed instantly. If the oven knob, a car part or grandma's dentures break, or you lose a button, or you want to produce a machine part that has been discontinued, you could quickly fix those problems with your home 3D printer. Just take a photo of the object with your cellphone, send it by e-mail to your computer, specify the measurements and the materials to use, press the PRINT button and the desired object will be produced.

I saw these devices work for the first time during a program on 3D printers that we did on CNN, when a distributor brought one to the studio and explained how it worked. The printer was no bigger than a desktop computer and looked like a combination of a sewing machine and a dentist's drill, or a laser ray pistol. The center of the printer had an open space, and above it a needle that dropped layer after layer of a plastic material as it formed the desired object. I can't say I was thunderstruck, but I felt I was seeing a rudimentary and slow-motion version of a machine that could soon be as essential as personal computers or smartphones.

During a visit to the San Francisco headquarters of Autodesk —the giant company that makes software for the auto industry, architects and others— I was shown a motorcycle made totally with plastic pieces produced by a 3D printer. The motor was a plastic replica, but it's only a matter of time until the parts for a real motor can be made at home, I was told. Gonzalo Martínez, director of research at Autodesk, said there are already 75 materials that can be used with 3D printers, and various companies are working on new "multi-materials" (combinations of plastics and other materials) that will completely change the production capabilities.

"NASA is putting 3D printers in space vehicles so that when something breaks we can can reproduce it in space. Instead of calling and saying 'Houston, we have a problem,' we will say, 'Houston, send us the design in 3D and we will print it here,' " said Martínez.[8] "We will do the same in our homes when something breaks in the refrigerator, the car or anything else."

The production of almost everything we buy will also be less massive and more individualized. MakerBot, one of the companies selling 3D printers to the public —it opened its first store in New York City in 2013— already sells low-cost Replicator 3D printers that can produce eyeglasses in any desired shape, size and color, depending on the day's mood.

When I visited the MakerBot store in New York's SoHo neighborhood, it was already selling watches and jewelry made in 3D. And the Japanese, German and other tourists who arrived by the busloads to check out the store could walk out with a bust of themselves made by a

27

3D printer. In what could be the future of photography, sales persons at the store put visitors in front of a computerized camera, scan their faces and *voilà*, a printer generates a bust that the tourist takes home as a hint of things to come in the future. I couldn't resist the temptation. I was scanned and a little while later received a small bust that, I have been told, looks surprisingly like me.

Many people predict that 3D printers will eclipse mass production as we have known it since Henry Ford began the assembly-line production of automobiles. Developed countries will export fewer products and more plans and designs for products. The new mantra of some manufacturing industries will be "sell the design, not the product." That means we will buy the designs for our clothes, furniture and even food on the Internet, make whatever changes we want and then —if we don't have a 3D printer at home— order them from the 3D shop in our nearest shopping mall, where we will be able to pick them up within minutes.

The manufacturing industry will have to reinvent itself. The 3D printers, with the capacity to produce our products, to our taste, with our computers and in our homes, will force manufacturing companies to develop new products or disappear along the way. The rallying cry for companies, and for countries, will be "Innovate or Die."

DRONES THAT DELIVER PIZZA

The unmanned aircraft, or drones, that the United States has used in Iraq and Afghanistan to attack Al Qaeda terrorists will revolutionize the transportation industry. Commercial drones already are being used for police surveillance, monitoring cattle and the rescue of swimmers. Soon, they will be used to deliver pizzas and FedEx packages. The Federal Aviation Administration (FAA) planned to open all U.S. airspace to drones by the end of 2015, and to have more than 10,000 civilian drones flying over the country in 2018. Commercial drones must fly at less than 100 meters of altitude and remain at least five kilometers away from airports, FAA officials have said.

"Just about anything you do with aviation today... you can do with unmanned aerial vehicles in the future," said Andrew R. Lacher, a researcher at Mitre Corporation, which advises the U.S. government on drones.[9] Some experts, like Benjamin M. Trapnell, a professor at the University of North Dakota, predict that unmanned aircraft will even replace piloted aircraft on commercial flights.

Experiments are already under way in Great Britain, with regional flights operated by remote control, although they carry a pilot aboard 'just in case,' and for now they do not carry passengers, said Trapnell.[10] But airlines will soon begin to replace their two pilots per cabin with one pilot in the cabin and another on the ground, and later will put both pilots on the ground. It will be a transition much like when elevators stopped being operated by human beings, he added.

Jordi Muñoz, the 24-year-old Mexican who heads 3DRobotics and has become one of the world's leading entrepreneurs of commercial drones —we will detail his amazing story later in this book— says that the first to use commercial drones on a daily basis will be farmers, police, firemen and the Coast Guard —for example, to deliver a life preserver to someone drowning. In the agricultural industry, farmers today don't have all the information they need on what's happening with their fields, which means they may put too much water in some areas or too little pesticide in others. But drones are solving that problem. Jordi Muñoz' company is already selling $500 drones that operate with a GPS and monitor farms for water and pesticide levels. In comparison, farmers can pay about $1,000 per hour for piloted airplanes that perform the same tasks.

But that's only the beginning. Students at the Freie Universität Berlin in Germany already created an unmanned helicopter that delivered pizzas. The creators named their pizza-delivering drone Leonardo and posted a video on YouTube showing its flight from a pizza shop to the university, where a professor and students were waiting at an outdoor table. The video ends with the professor, Mexican researcher Raúl Rojas González, and his students celebrating the arrival of the unmanned aircraft and getting ready to eat their airlifted pizza.

When I first saw that video, I thought it was just a bit of entertainment. But Rojas González, who teaches artificial intelligence at the university, told me that the technology for delivering pizzas, medicines or other light products already exists and is being used. The only obstacles to the daily use of drones are legal questions, he said, such as who would be responsible if one crashes and causes damages. Some companies are working on a system for delivering pizzas to rooftops, and Federal Express and UPS, among several home delivery companies, are waiting for the green light from authorities.

When I did a CNN program on drones, I invited Jordi Muñoz, the young president of 3DRobotics, and asked him if the delivery of pizzas by drone wasn't too expensive to be commercially viable. Wouldn't it be cheaper to deliver the pizza by car, even by limousine, than by unmanned aircraft? "Not at all," he replied, "because the drones use rechargeable batteries, so they don't need fuel. And you don't have to pay the salary of a driver or a pilot. A drone is a very simple device that uses very simple parts, and can fly 30 to 40 kilometers on its batteries to deliver the pizza and return." He added that whenever laws and regulations on the mass commercial use of drones are put in place, "their uses will be limitless."[11]

CARS WITHOUT DRIVERS

If I had not seen the Google Self-Driving Car with my own eyes, I would not have believed it. But the demonstration I watched in Silicon Valley —a Toyota Prius with a small control tower on its roof and Google technology— persuaded me that it's quite possible that in the next decade we will see increasing numbers of these kinds of vehicles on our streets. Some Mercedes Benz, Audi and Cadillac models already have automatic pilot systems that allow them to brake or accelerate and even park themselves. But all these models still require the driver to be alert and ready to react when required. However, the Goggle Self-Driving Car and others under development around the world, with sensors that measure the distance to the nearest vehicle, do not require the driver to pay attention. As I witnessed during the demonstration, a few blocks from Google headquarters, the drivers no longer drive. They can sleep, work or turn to chat with passengers as if they were on a train.

Brad Templeton, a member of the team developing the Google Self-Driving Car, told me that the vehicle will be a success primarily because it is much safer. Auto accidents in the United States today cause 34,000 deaths and 240,000 injuries per year, and the World Health Organization (WHO) estimates they cause 1.2 million deaths and 50 million injuries worldwide. And the majority of accidents are caused by drivers who drink too much, fall sleep at the wheel or become distracted while texting on their cell phones, according to WHO. "Robots generally don't drink", Templeton joked. "And they don't fall asleep at the wheel. Self-driving cars are a lot safer than the ones we use now."[12]

Google estimates that driverless cars will reduce the number of fatalities by 90 percent, significantly decrease the number of vehicles on the streets and generate huge savings in gasoline. They will be used more efficiently, because they can be shared by several people, and therefore will help to ease traffic congestion. They will be able to drop off different people at their respective jobs, then park themselves, perhaps somewhere outside the city, and return later in the day to pick them up. And cities will be able to turn parking lots into recreational and green areas. "The car will drop us off at work at 9 am and pick us up at 6 pm. In between, we can send it to the dry cleaners to pick up our laundry, to school to pick up our kids or to park itself somewhere outside the city," Templeton predicted.

Engineers working on the Google vehicle say that in the United States alone, the cars will save nothing less than $400 billion a year in auto accidents avoided, not counting the time that people lose driving every day.[13] A report quoted in *Forbes* magazine showed that traffic congestion in the United States —often caused by accidents— is responsible for the loss of 4.8 billion work hours and 1.9 billion gallons of gasoline every year.[14] But we will soon be able to work, read or relax while the car takes us to our destination. Several states like Nevada,

Florida, Texas and California, anticipating the many savings that driverless cars will generate, already have approved legislation authorizing their use on state highways.

Of course, not everything will be as simple as the Google engineers paint it. The first crash of a Google Self-Driving Car, near the company's headquarters in Mountain View, California, was reported in mid-2011. The company said a human being was driving the car at the time, but another accident a few months later —another Google test vehicle was rear-ended when it stopped at a stop sign— raised new doubts about the safety of the driverless vehicles. But a video posted by Google on YouTube in March of 2012 showed a blind man with a cane getting into the driver's seat and happily cruising the city, stopping at a fast food restaurant and a dry cleaners while the car drove itself. Shortly afterward, Google announced that its experimental driverless vehicles —about a dozen— already had racked up about 500,000 kilometers without an accident. And the demonstration I witnessed in Palo Alto seemed to prove that the driverless vehicles works.

Skeptics argue that several factors can delay the spread of the driverless cars, such as their high costs and the legal problems that could arise if victims of a crash —with no driver to fault— file a lawsuit against the vehicles' manufacturers. Nevertheless, most experts believe that the price of the self-driving cars will fall steeply, as it happened with computers, and that possible lawsuits against the automakers will not be a problem because legal frameworks will be established to make owners at least partially responsible for their vehicles. Soon, perhaps in the next 10 years, self-driving vehicles will change the face of big cities, opening the way for new uses of parking lots and maybe helping to fix most traffic problems.

SELF-HEALING MATERIALS

Aside from the 3D printers and the "multi-materials" being produced for their use, we will soon see "self-healing materials" on the market. In other words, materials that can repair themselves, and therefore prolong the useful life of many products and reduce the need to replace them or send them out for repairs.

Do you remember the Terminator movies with Arnold Schwarzenegger, when the robots' synthetic skin was destroyed by gunfire but immediately healed itself? A group of researchers led by Zhenan Bao at Stanford University has created a flexible material based on polymers for use in robot frames or human prosthesis like artificial legs. More basic versions of self-healing materials are already on sale, such as layers of anti-corrosion materials that regenerate themselves when damaged.

Joe Giuliani of Autonomic Materials, a company working on the self-healing layers of anti-corrosion materials developed at the University of Illinois, said his products are already used in the shipping industry, mostly on ships, docks and oil platforms. The anti-corrosion layer has two microcapsules, one containing a self-healing component and the other a catalyzer. When the layer is damaged, the microcapsules break open and their contents mix, repairing the damage. This technology prolongs the useful life of marine and underwater platforms, for example, and is just starting to be used in remote places where maintenance is difficult or enormously expensive.[15]

Could we be too far from vehicles with self-healing paint that can repair their own scratches, or self-healing body panels that can return to their original shapes after crashes? Everything indicates that day is not too far away. Several companies in fact are predicting they will soon produce self-healing glass for the military and automotive industries. This new type of glass will contain a liquid that will immediately fill any cracks in a windshield after a crash, allowing the driver to maintain visibility and survive a suddenly risky situation. The same technology could be used on our cell phones and many other products. From there to the robots whose skin can heal itself —like cyborgs in Terminator movies— is just a short step, according to experts.[16]

THE INTERNET OF THINGS

Almost every object around us, from kitchen appliances to clothes, will soon carry microchips and connect with each other through a new ecosystem known as "the Internet of things." In the same way that the Internet connects people, this new system will connect things with each other so that, for example, a refrigerator whose filter has expired can order a replacement from the computer at the filter factory —without any human participation. The Starbucks chain of coffeehouses is already planning to connect their refrigerators to the new ecosystem, so that they can reorder products automatically when they run low. The next step will be when our own refrigerators can decide that our milk or vegetables are running low and either let us know or order directly from the supermarket. The billions of sensors that will be put into objects will become a $9 trillion industry in 2020, when there will be more than 212 billion objects connected to the new ecosystem, according to the International Data Corporation, a technology research company.

Some aspects of "the Internet of things" will be unquestionably positive. There will be sensors in clothes, for example, that can automatically call an ambulance when an elderly person faints and there's no one else to call for help. Airplane accidents also are likely to decrease because each aircraft part will have a microchip that will alert a central computer when it is approaching the end of its useful life, and can be replaced before they break. And savings in energy and water will be enormous because the microchips will control lights and home appliances. In Barcelona and other cities around the world, microchips are already alerting to leaky water pipes.

The 2014 Consumer Electronics Show in Las Vegas saw the first smart tooth brushes, tennis rackets and beds. Sensors in smart tooth brushes register the frequency and other details of how we brush our teeth, and send the data to our cell phones along with tips on how to improve our dental hygiene. Tennis rackets with sensors register the way we grip the racket and hit the ball, and send the information to our cells

34

along with video lessons on what we're doing wrong and how to fix it. What will happen to tennis instructors, many of us wonder. The smart beds will monitor our breathing, our movements and how many times we wake up during the night, and send us e-mails with suggestions for a better night's sleep.

But other possible effects of "the Internet of things" are more worrisome. Some pharmaceutical companies are planning to put microchips on the lids of medicine bottles, which will alert doctors when their patients have not taken their medicines for a few days. We could wind up being monitored by the objects around us. And there's the danger that the system will not work as designed. We could receive an avalanche of phone calls from the refrigerator of an unknown person, reporting that it's run out of milk. Even worse, in a world where we will have sensors on our bodies and our clothes, cyber-terrorism could be a worse threat than ever. What will happen if a hacker gets into a computer that is regulating the pacemaker of a patient? Or when a hacker wants to have fun by changing the program on our smart clothes to make us hotter or colder? The consequences can be chilling. As with the Internet, however, it's unlikely these risks will stop the expansion of the "Internet of things."

BIG DATA: 21ST CENTURY GOLD

Information, more than ever, will be a source of power and money in the 21st Century. The expansion of the Internet, social networks and "the Internet of things" will generate more data in cyberspace about each one of us than ever —what we buy, what we like to read, what movies we watch, what we eat, what kind of clothes we wear, where we travel, who our friends are and our political and sexual preferences. Each and every time we buy something on the Internet or with a credit card, or when we write something on Twitter or Facebook, or we type an address into a GPS device, we are leaving a fingerprint with personal details on the Internet. And the ownership and processing of this mass of details, known as Big Data, will have enormous value to anyone who wants to sell us something, from a car to a political party.

According to one report by the World Economic Forum, the growth in the volume of data available and its processing will produce a boom that will rival the gold rush in San Francisco in the 19th Century and the Texas oil boom in the 20th Century. Data has become the equivalent of gold or oil. And the countries best prepared to gather, process and analyze that data —to establish not just current consumer habits but future preferences— will prosper the most.

The good news is that Big Data will allow us to detect epidemics at an early stage, for example by alerting governments when unusually high numbers of people are searching the Internet for flu symptoms or buying certain medicines. It can also ease big-city traffic, by using street sensors to improve the synchronization of stop lights, according to the number of vehicles crossing intersections. "We should be able to collect, measure and analyze more and more information about everyone and everything, in order to make better decisions, individually and collectively," the World Economic Forum report noted.[17] The bad news, of course, is that the proliferation of information in cyberspace could lend itself to government spying even more intrusive than we can imagine, like the recent revelations about the National Security Agency in the United States, and a significant loss of privacy

WATCHES THAT MONITOR HEARTBEATS

Medicine as we know it today, where a doctor diagnoses our ailment and prescribes a medicine based on his studies and experience, will soon be a thing of the past. The new medicine will be digitized and personalized, and flesh-and-bones doctors will become supervisors of computer systems that will make the diagnosis and prescribe the medications most adequate for our DNA.

Hundreds of companies already sell sensors in watches or bracelets that constantly monitor our hearts, and can transmit the information to a databank which then sets off an alarm when it spots an anomaly. The information from the new sensors also will not just alert us to possible emergencies, but will allow us —thanks to artificial intelligence— to receive better diagnoses and more efficient cures than what traditional doctors can offer us today. Instead of a doctor prescribing a medicine for us based on his experience with his patients, powerful databases in the Cloud —massive computer servers that allows us to store almost limitless quantities of data and process it individually for each of us— will prescribe medicines known to have worked most effectively in cases like ours, following a statistical analysis of the data from millions of people treated for the same ailment.

"While the medicine of the past was episodic and reactive, the medicine of the future will be continuous and proactive," I was told by Daniel Kraft, a physician, inventor and entrepreneur in new medical technologies at Stanford University in Silicon Valley. "In the old days, we went to a doctor when something hurt, and he prescribed something to cure the pain. Now we can monitor our health constantly, thanks to sensors that we carry in our watches, or on our cell phones, or on our clothes, and we can take action before something hurts. On this very day, I am checking my health all day because I see my vital signs on the screen of my cell phone every time I check my e-mails."[18]

Kraft showed me his watch, with sensors that monitor the heart and alert his primary doctor to any problem. Dozens of companies already sell this type of watch for less than $45 on the Internet, he said. He then pulled his iPhone out of his pocket and asked me to place my fingers on a thin metal strip, attached to the back of the phone, which he had bought on the Internet from the AliveCor company. In a few seconds, he had taken my blood pressure and e-mailed me the results.

He later showed me a blood pressure cuff, made by the Withings company that connects to a smartphone. The phone immediately e-mails the results to you, your doctor or anyone you designate, or a databank that holds your medical history. The blood pressure monitor, like another sold by the iHealth company, is one of several that have been on sale for many years on the Internet and now costs less than

$100. Kraft was carrying around an entire hospital, just in his watch and his cell phone. "Before, the doctor prescribed medicines for us. Now, he will prescribe iPhone apps that will determine what medicines we should take," he said, smiling but only half-joking.

Soon, even the watches that Kraft showed me will pass into history and be replaced by mini sensors implanted in our bodies. These mini sensors will report our body temperature and the functioning of our organs to supercomputers, which will give us very early warning of any developing problems. Several companies, like Biohack, are already developing implants that will constantly transmit data from various parts of our body and shift medicine —today mainly focused on curing ailments, often when it's too late— toward a more preventive approach.

THE SUPERCOMPUTER THAT PRESCRIBES MEDICINES

At U.S. medical conventions, the big superstars are increasingly not the flesh-and-bones eminences of medicine but rather machines like IBM's Watson supercomputer, which appeared at the 2012 conference of the Healthcare Information Systems and Management Society in Las Vegas. Watson was already famous. Much like the IBM supercomputer Deep Blue that defeated chess champion Gary Kasparov in 1997, Watson had conquered two finalists in Tv's Jeopardy game in 2011, and walked off with the $1 million first prize.

But the most notable part of Watson's victory on Jeopardy was that it answered questions without a connection to the Internet. Watson's hard drive contained about 200 million pages of all kinds of information, including various encyclopedias, and answered the questions by searching its internal memory. In 2013, shortly after its presentation in Las Vegas, IBM launched its first commercial application for Watson for medical use, processing information for lung cancer patients. After that, many people started asking if we are approaching the day when we go to a doctor's office and a nurse tells us, "The robot will see you now."

Although hundreds of Internet sites already focus on medical issues, like WebMD, Watson's developers claim their supercomputer can process much more information more quickly, and has the capacity to analyze data —including the medical records of millions of people— and make diagnoses based on much more experience than a human doctor. While a human doctor diagnoses and prescribes based on his personal experience, which in most cases is limited to a few thousand patients, Watson can diagnose and prescribe based on data collected from many millions of patients.

Marty Kohn, one of the doctors who "train" Watson for health services, said many cases of mistaken diagnoses are caused by the doctors' very human tendency to put too much emphasis on a small part of the facts at their disposal[19]. Kohn told *The Atlantic* magazine that doctors in hospitals routinely diagnose patients based on two or three symptoms, and unconsciously dismiss other symptoms that could lead to different conclusions. Watson, however, can offer doctors a much more varied menu of options and allow them to consider new possibilities. Pretty soon, doctors will carry Watson around, in a laptop, tablet or a robot just like they now carry their stethoscopes, Kohn said.

Does this mean that Watson will replace human doctors? Probably not. But this supercomputer and its competitors are extraordinary tools that will help doctors make better-informed decisions. Kohn himself describes Watson as "technical support" that will surely —and soon— become indispensable to any doctor. With the information received from the censors that we will all carry —in our watches, our bracelets or our bodies— these supercomputers will alert us when we're developing a disease and advise us on what to do long before we become ill.

PERSONALIZED EDUCATION

Thanks to technology, but especially thanks to the growth of online education, the schools of the future will function exactly the opposite way of schools today: instead of children going to school to study and doing their homework at home, they will study at home —on their computers with videos and interactive programs— and work later at school, with groups of other students and the help of their teachers. In other words, our children will do at home what they now do in school, and in school what they now do at home.

These "flipped schools" are already spreading in the United States because children can learn much more if they study alone while watching videos, which they can stop and rewind when they don't understand something. They can then do practical exercises on their computers, and later go to school and ask their teachers any questions they may still have.

The "flipped schools" started to get noticed amid the boom in free online classes offered by Salman Khan, a young hedge fund employee who started posting short lessons on math and algebra on YouTube to help a cousin who was having problems at school. After a while, he found that millions of young people around the world were looking at his classes. As Khan told me —we will see the details of his story in Chapter 8— he was swamped by e-mails from young people who thanked him for helping them figure out math and algebra problems they had been unable to solve. They also told him they were learning much more with his videos than in regular classes. In 2008, he founded the Khan Academy for free online videos, and in 2014 he was already offering free courses in 28 languages to about 10 million students each month. Shortly afterward, similar courses started popping up for university students, such as Coursera and Udacity, which like the Khan Academy are revolutionizing education around the world.

"The flipped classroom is a strategy that nearly everyone agrees on," *The New York Times* wrote in a front-page article.[20] The newspaper quoted Justin Reich, an educational technology researcher at Harvard's Beckman Center, who said that the flipped schools were "the only thing I write about as having broad positive agreement."[21]

In some specific cases, like the Clintondale High School in Detroit, one of the worst in its district, flipping the times and functions of the classrooms led to a significant reduction in the number of failing students in barely one year. While 30 percent of the school's students were failing to move on to the next grade before the change, the rate dropped to 10 percent one year after flipping the functions of the classrooms. The number of graduates who went on to college also rose from 63 percent to 80 percent, according to the article.

Khan confessed to me during an interview, however, that the most important parts of his academy are not the videos, but the new technologies that allow education to be personalized, so that it can be adapted to the needs of each child. The Khan Academy already offers, aside from the videos, practical exercises so that students can advance at their own pace. Thanks to an algorithm developed by Khan, similar to the one Netflix uses to recommend movies based on previous preferences, the lessons advance at the speed of learning of each student. And teachers can check on their own computers to see how each student is doing, which allows them to tailor their work to the rhythms and preferences of each student.

All of this will force education, which has barely changed since the King of Prussia in the 18th Century introduced what we today call the "Prussian model," to change in radical ways. The Prussian model was designed to require all children to learn to read and write and — although not explicitly declared— to create a docile working class of people who would be accustomed from childhood to wake up early, go to work and accept the authority of their bosses. Almost nothing has changed since then. Most of our schools are still grouping children by age in classrooms where they all face the teacher, for lessons that begin and end with a bell ringing. At the end of the school day, they take home assignments to be completed for the next day. Even the summer vacations, created by agrarian societies so children could help their parents with farm chores, remain in place as though the world had not shifted toward urban societies.

Khan and most experts on the future of education say all of that will end soon, however. The school of the future will be totally unlike the school of today, because there's increasing agreement that each of us learns in a different way. Some of us study better in the morning, some of us at night. Some of us learn more visually, and others by hearing. Some of us prefer to study in one-hour blocks, and others prefer to study for 20 minutes at a time. The new education technologies will allow each of us to study at our own pace, in the manner we prefer. And what we used to know as "going to class," to listen to a teacher's lecture, will become a series of supervised tasks in which the teacher will help the students solve the problems they were not been able to solve at home.

TRAVELS TO THE STARS

Space exploration, which faded into the background in the nearly 50 years since the first manned trip to the Moon by Apollo 11 in 1969, will soon be in the news again and generate lots of talk in the next few years. Although Barack Obama announced in 2010 that NASA's new managers will focus on a manned voyage to an asteroid by 2025 and a manned trip to Mars by the mid-2030s, several space industry leaders predict these voyages may well take place before then. Some experts, as we will see in the following chapters, told me that they expect important announcements by the U.S. government in 2019, on the 50th anniversary of the first manned voyage to the Moon.

The emergence of private industry in space exploration —with space tourism companies like Virgin Galactic, led by the eccentric British magnate Sir Richard Branson, and the SpaceX company of Elon Musk, founder of PayPal— is already revolutionizing the space industry. With the help of NASA, which earmarked $6 billion to help develop the private space industry, Virgin Galactic, SpaceX and other companies have been building spacecrafts that can be reused many times, like airplanes, instead of being lost with each mission. These vehicles will transport cargo to space stations, deliver satellites that will slash the cost of the Internet and telephone communications, and transport space tourists —expected to become an increasingly important industry as the costs of the voyages drop— and to launch public-private missions to other planets.

Branson smiled, as if he'd been waiting for the question, when I asked him during an interview whether Virgin Galactic and other space tourism companies are not just fun for millionaires —trips of two or three hours cost $200,000 per passenger— that will generate few scientific contributions. He told me that throughout history, many technological innovations, like the airplanes invented by the Wright brothers, were developed for wealthy people. "Look, when people started flying across the Atlantic, it was rich people who did it," Branson told me. "Thanks to these wealthy people who pioneered air travel, prices have come down and many more people can afford air travel today." The British mogul went on to say that his private space tourism company "will not only be taking people into space, but we will be carrying out a great number of scientific research projects. We can put satellites in space for a fraction of what it costs today, which will significantly reduce the cost of your telephone calls, the cost of your Internet connection, your WI-FI."[22]

Musk, on the other hand, is already working on even more ambitious plans, like a manned voyage to Mars. The businessman has said publicly, and in all seriousness, that he plans to begin building the infrastructure for a permanent colony of 80,000 people on Mars. And he wasn't just talking, because he has been investing tens of millions of dollars on the project.

TECHNO-UTOPIANS AND TECHNO-SKEPTICS

Will the quality of our lives improve with all these technological innovations? Or, on the contrary, will the 3D printers, the self-driving cars, the super computers that will replace doctors and the space voyages take us into a world with an increasingly larger gap between rich and poor, more dependent on technology and less humane?

For innovators in Silicon Valley and other centers of world innovations, those questions were settled a long time ago. There's no doubt at all that technological advances are the main engine for reducing poverty and improving our quality of life, they assert. Poverty in developing countries has fallen by more than half, from 52 percent of the population in 1980 to 20 percent in 2010, according to World Bank reports. That's thanks in large part to the "green revolution", the body of technologies developed since the 1960s to maximize grain harvests, which has allowed countries that once suffered from famines, like India, to become net exporters of food. Statistics on life expectancy show that the global average rose from 31 years at the beginning of the 20th Century to nearly 70 years today, and that people live longer now even in the poorest nations, thanks to medical advances.

And we don't just live longer today. We live better. Not even in the poorest countries do the majority of the people go barefoot or lack proper winter clothing. As optimists like to say, just imagine the difference between going today to a dentist, who gives us a shot of local anesthetic that we don't even feel before he works on a tooth, to a dentist 100 years ago who used pliers to yank out a tooth without anesthesia.

Bill Gates, the richest man in the world, who today is supporting the fight against polio and other diseases in the poorest nations, said recently that thanks to new vaccines and other technological advances, "we've had more progress in the last decade than ever before." Gates added that in the 1960s, "a third of the world was rich and two-thirds was very poor. Now the biggest block of the world's population is middle-income: Brazil, Mexico, Thailand, China. The size of the very poor world is much smaller."[23] And this is fundamentally due to technology advances in agriculture and public health, the principal factors that allowed those countries to emerge from poverty, he argued. By 2035, "there will be practically no poor countries," Gates predicted in his annual public letter in 2014.

A TIME OF PLENTY?

Techno-utopians believe that the last decade saw only a hint of the progress that is to come. In his book, *Abundance: the future is better than you think*, Peter H. Diamandis, president of Singularity University and co-founder of the International Space University, and co-author

Steven Kotler argue that humanity "is now entering into a period of radical transformation, in which technology has the potential to significantly raise the basic standards of living for every man, woman and child on the planet. Within a generation, we will be able to provide goods and services, once reserved for the wealthy few, to any and all who need them. Or desire them. Abundance for all is actually within our reach."[24]

Many skeptics regard Diamandis and other champions of future technologies as peddlers of utopias, however. Pessimists go further, arguing that although there's no doubt that medical advances such as the vaccines against polio and smallpox, or more recently the treatments for HIV-AIDS, have saved hundreds of millions of lives, the fact remains that all the technological advances of the last 200 years have not managed to eliminate world poverty, and that millions of people still die each year from diseases relatively easy to control, such as diarrhea and pneumonia.

"The tech gurus, like so many evangelists of earlier eras, are wildly overoptimistic about what their gadgets can accomplish in the world's poorest places," wrote Charles Kenny and Justin Sandefur of the Center for Global Development, an independent think tank in Washington D.C. "The weak link between technology's advance and global poverty reduction shouldn't come as a surprise. Most technologies were invented in the rich world to tackle rich-world problems," they added.[25] The iPhone, the iPad, the 3D printers and the self-driving cars by themselves will not change the lives of the billions of people who still live in poverty, they noted. Skeptics also caution about the dangers the new technologies bring with them, such as the possibility that anyone with a home 3D printer will be able to manufacture a gun. Or the day when commercial drones can deliver not just pizzas, but bombs.

Who's right, the techno-utopians or techno-skeptics? Both have valid arguments, and the debate seems at times like it hinges on whether they see the glass as half full or half empty. But what is certain is that whether we like it or not, advances in technology are unstoppable. As much as some governments may try to stop them —as the George W. Bush administration tried to do with stem cell research— they will prevail. As University of California professor Susan Fisher explained it, "Science is like a stream of water, because it finds its way."[26] The big challenge is how to channel these new technologies to benefit the largest number of people possible.

FROM "MANUAL LABOR" TO "MENTAL LABOR"

Scientific advances in coming years will not only change our lives but will also determine which countries will increasingly move forward and which will increasingly lag behind. That's because we are in the age of knowledge, where countries that develop products with high added-value will grow increasingly rich, and those that continue producing raw materials or basic manufacturing will fall further behind. As I wrote in my previous books, *Cuentos chinos* (2005) and *Basta de historias* (2010), the world had changed, and Latin American presidents who say that their countries will prosper by selling oil, soya or metals or by assembling manufactured goods are fooling themselves or their people. While 50 years ago agriculture and raw materials accounted for 30 percent of the world's economic activity, today they represent a far smaller share, and everything indicates that it will continue to shrink. According to World Bank figures, agriculture today accounts for 3 percent of global production, industry accounts for 27 percent and services add up to 70 percent.[27] We are increasingly moving from a global economy based on manual labor to one based on mental work.

That's why it is no coincidence that companies like Google or Apple are worth more than the GDP of many Latin American countries. It's also no accident that small countries with no raw materials, like Singapore, Taiwan and Israel, have much more prosperous economies than oil-rich countries like Venezuela, Ecuador and Nigeria. Or that the richest men in the world are businessmen like Bill Gates, Carlos Slim or Warren Buffett, who produce technology or services but no raw materials. This trend will accelerate even more during coming years because technology grows exponentially.

THE DEVELOPING WORLD'S TECHNOLOGY LAG

The clearest evidence of Latin America's technology lag is the insignificant number of patents for new inventions registered from countries in the region, especially when compared to Asian countries. According to those numbers, one of the main measurements of innovation and technology advances, Latin America ranks among the world's worst performing regions. Contrary to the fairy tales that many Latin American presidents spout every time they inaugurate a technology park, or when they welcome a new technology company, the region's lag in technology is alarming. Even small countries like South Korea and Israel produce more patents each year than all the countries in Latin America and the Caribbean combined, according to United Nations (UN) reports.

South Korea, a country that 50 years ago had a lower per capita GDP than almost all Latin American nations, today registers about 12,400 international patent applications each year with the U.N.'s World Intellectual Property Organization (WIPO), while Israel registers about 1,600. In contrast, all the countries of Latin America and the Caribbean together apply for barely 1,200 patents —660 by Brazil, 230 by Mexico, 140 by Chile, 80 by Colombia, 26 by Argentina, 18 by Panama, 13 by Peru, nine by Cuba and one by Venezuela, according to WIPO.[28]

The numbers for Latin America are even more worrisome when compared to the international patent applications from the more powerful countries: the United States registers about 57,000 applications for international patents with WIPO each year, Japan 44,000, China 22,000 and Germany 18,000.[29]

Another major indicator of innovation —the number of patents that each country registers with the U.S. Patent and Trademark Office— shows similar results. According to a UPSTO report in 2014, about 148,000 patents were registered from the United States in the previous year, 54,000 from Japan, 17,000 from Germany, 16,000 from South Korea, 12,100 from Taiwan, 6,600 from China and 3,200 from Israel. In contrast, 290 patents were registered from Brazil, 200 from Mexico, 80 from Argentina,

60 from Chile, 20 from Colombia, 13 from Cuba, nine from Costa Rica, eight from Ecuador, three from Peru and two from Bolivia.[30]

Why don't Latin American nations, with all the human talent that we have, register more patents for new inventions? There are many reasons, including the absence of a "culture of registering patents" among universities and companies, and a shortage of loans and venture capital for the research and development of new products. Another reason is the lack of respect for intellectual property. Why should they spend their time and money patenting their inventions when their idea is certain to be stolen, many inventors ask themselves.

When I asked Carsten Fink, the chief economist at WIPO, based in Geneva, Switzerland, why Latin America registers so few international patents, he told me that "the challenge that Latin American countries have is creating an environment in which innovation can flourish." That means, he added, "having a good education system, having fiscal incentives to encourage research and development, having financial mechanisms to support venture capital, and policies that favor the mobility of highly skilled people, to bring talents from other places."[31] Most of those problems can be fixed relatively quickly, however, as shown by South Korea, Singapore and other countries that until recently suffered from the same problems as Latin America.

THE CAPITALS OF SCIENCE

Scientific Reports, a research publication of Nature and one of the most prestigious magazines in international academic circles, published a map in 2013 of the world's most important cities for scientific research. When I saw it, I could not avoid feeling a mixture of frustration and sadness. Although I did not expect to find many Latin American cities in the map, I hoped to see some. But Latin American countries and their cities were conspicuously absent. Despite all the talk about the rise of the developing nations and the chest-thumping boasts of many Latin American leaders about the technological advances achieved by their governments, the map showed the Northern Hemisphere of the globe full of lights, and the Southern Hemisphere in darkness. The map was especially significant because it was not based on the subjective opinions of the magazine's editors, but on a study of more than 450,000 scientific articles and citations, from more than 2,000 cities around the world, published in magazines of the American Physical Society over the previous 50 years. According to the article that accompanied the map, the physics studies that are originated in the United States have fallen from 86 percent of the world's total in the 1960s to less than 37 percent today, although the United States continues to lead the world in that category. Boston, Berkeley and Los Angeles continue to be the most important production centers for physics, followed by Tokyo and Orsay in France. The list of the 20 top cities in the world includes Chicago, Princeton, Rome, London and Oxford.

But there's not a single Latin American city among the world's top 100 producers of scientific knowledge, according to the magazine. A chart published with the map showed that 56 percent of the top 100 cities are in the United States and Canada, 33 percent are in Europe and 11 percent in Asia. Did they forget to include Latin America?, I asked myself.

After reading these numbers, I called Dr. Nicola Perra at Northeastern University in Boston, one of the authors of the report, to confirm that I had read the chart correctly. "Yes, we did not forget anyone. Indeed, there are no Latin American cities among the top 100," he told me.[32] The map shows that not only by the number of patents, but by the number of scientific publications, Latin American countries and their principal cities do not show up in the main measurements of scientific research.

THE WORST UNIVERSITIES?

The situation has not changed much since we started, in *Cuentos chinos* in 2005, and its English version *Saving the Americas* in 2007, to call attention to the fact that Latin American universities rank at the bottom of the lists of the best universities around the world. In 2013, not one Latin American university made the top 100 in any of the three main international rankings, even though some countries in the region are part of the G-20 —the group of the world's 20 biggest economies— and Brazil was the sixth largest economy that year, while Mexico was the 14th largest.

The three rankings —which measure, among other categories, the percentage of professors with doctorates, the number of academic papers published in international science publications and the number of patents registered— agree in placing U.S. universities among the top 10, and place several institutions of higher education in Singapore, China, South Korea and other developing countries in Asia among the first 50. Latin American universities, however, begin to show up only after the 100th place, and those can be counted on the fingers of one hand.

In the Times Higher Education World University Rankings, a pioneer in this kind of report, the first Latin American university to appear is the one in São Paulo, Brazil, in the group of institutions that rank from 226 to 250.[33] In another ranking, known as Ranking QS, the first university to appear is also the one in São Paulo, in 127th place.[34] The third ranking, by the Jiao Tong University in Shanghai, China, puts the São Paulo university in the group of 101 to 150 places, and the Universidad Nacional Autónoma de México and the Universidad de Buenos Aires between 151 and 200.[35]

WE ARE ALL PHILOSOPHERS, SOCIOLOGISTS AND POETS

One of the reasons for the sad showing of Latin American universities in international rankings is the fact that our countries invest relatively little in scientific research and have little participation by the private sector in the investments, which translates into fewer scientific publications and registered patents. In Latin America, we are producing too many philosophers, sociologists, psychologists and poets, and too few scientists and engineers.

According to statistics from the Ibero-American and Interamerican Network on Science and Technology Indicators, 63 percent of the 2 million young people who emerge each year from universities in Latin America and the Caribbean graduate with degrees in social sciences and liberal arts, and a mere 18 percent graduate with degrees in engineering, exact sciences and natural sciences. The rest graduates with degrees in medicine, agriculture and other areas.[36] In some countries, like Argentina, the big public universities have three times more students of psychology than engineering, which means the country is creating three psychologists to heal the "coconut" (that's what Argentines call the head) of each engineer.[37] In contrast, universities in China and most Asian countries are producing far more engineers and technicians than graduates in social sciences or humanities.

Investments by Latin American countries in research and development is also pathetic. Barely 2.4 percent of the total global investment in research and development takes place in Latin America, according to data from the Organization of Ibero-American States, based in Madrid. In contrast, 37.5 percent of global investment in research and development takes place in the United States and Canada, 32.1 percent in the European Union and 25.4 percent in Asia.[38] With so little domestic or foreign investment in research, and such a small percentage of the investment coming from the private sector, it's no accident that Latin America registers so few patents for new inventions at the international level.

LAST IN PISA TESTS

A big part of Latin America's gap in technology comes from the primary and secondary schools, where the quality of education has fallen increasingly behind the rest of the world. According to the Programme for International Student Assessment (PISA), an international test for 15 year-olds that measures knowledge in math, science and reading, Latin American students rank toward the bottom of the 65 participating countries.

Students in China and other Asian countries have the best scores in all the PISA categories. In math, students from Shanghai ranked in first place, followed by Singapore, Hong Kong, Taipei in Taiwan, South Korea and Japan. Lower down on the list were Switzerland (9), Finland (12), Germany (16), Spain (33), Russia (34), United States (36), Sweden (38), Chile (51), Mexico (53), Uruguay (55), Costa Rica (56), Brazil (59), Colombia (62) and Peru (65). The results for science and reading were similar.[39]

The lack of a good education in math, science and reading has contributed to the technology lag in Latin American countries, to their excessive dependence on the export of raw materials and to their economic slowdowns in the second decade of the 21st Century, when the prices of raw materials stagnated. Latin American countries now need to create nationwide obsessions with education, with a special emphasis on math and science, in order to diversify their sources of revenue and insert themselves into the new economy of knowledge.

Does this mean that Argentina and Brazil should stop producing soybeans, or that Chile should forget about copper, or that Mexico should abandon basic manufacturing to dedicate all their time to high technology? Of course not. What they must do is to add value to their raw materials and assembly lines —which means they will need more engineers, scientists and technology experts— while at the same time developing innovations in areas where they might have competitive advantages.

THE EXAMPLE OF COFFEE

Coffee illustrates this issue extremely well. When I wrote *Cuentos chinos*, I quoted a Harvard professor who estimated that from the $3 spent buying a cup of coffee in the United States, barely 3 percent returned to the coffee grower in Colombia, Brazil, Costa Rica, Vietnam or any other coffee exporting country. The remaining 97 percent went into the pockets of those responsible for the genetic engineering of the coffee, the processing, marketing, distributing, publicity and other areas that form part of the economy of knowledge.

Five years later, when I wrote *Basta de historias,* I argued that the drop in the importance of raw materials, compared to the rise in the importance of high value-added products, was gaining speed. In that book, I wrote that one of the largest coffee producers in El Salvador had approached me at the end of a conference in San Salvador and told me, "You're wrong Andrés. The percentage for the grower is not 3 percent. The real number is closer to 1 percent."

Since then, the gap has grown even wider. The countries that added value to coffee —producing coffees with exclusive tastes, medicinal coffees, coffee cookies, coffee liqueurs, the single-cup packages known as pods, or expanding their distribution and sales abroad— benefited enormously while those that stuck to selling the raw material fell increasingly behind.

According to a report by Bain & Company, "Coffee is an example of how a 'low-tech' product can be 'improved' to create more economic value." While a cup of basic coffee may sell in the United States for 50 cents, a cup of a premium coffee sells for up to $4 at a chain like Starbucks. If we now add other innovations like espresso machines —selling for an average of $300— or the new market in coffee pods, the coffee industry has truly exploded in recent times and turned into a $135 billion a year business. While worldwide consumption of coffee grew by 21 percent, innovation increased the value of the industry by 80 percent, according to the report.[40]

ENGINES OF INNOVATION

What makes some countries more innovative than others? As we noted in previous pages, there is a broad range of factors —what experts call an "ecosystem"— that makes innovation possible. For this ecosystem to exist, there must be quality education; companies and universities that invest in the research and development of new products;

study centers that attract talent from all parts of the world; a constant interaction between companies and universities; an economic environment that stimulates risky investments; legislation that encourages the creation of new companies; and a concentration of creative minds in the same city.

But the key factor, which is spoken about less frequently, yet is critical to the creation of innovative societies, is a culture of social tolerance for people's failures. Social tolerance for individual failure is a common factor that I found in the principal world centers for innovation like the United States, Great Britain, Germany, France, Finland and Israel. Japan was one of the very few exceptions. Former British Prime Minister Winston Churchill's definition of success, "going from failure to failure without losing your enthusiasm," is one of the key common characteristics of innovative societies.

SILICON VALLEY PEOPLE BRAG ABOUT THEIR FAILURES

One of the things that caught my attention during my visits to Silicon Valley was how candidly people talked about their failures. Many of the entrepreneurs I met there happily volunteered to talk about both their failures and successes, with the same smile on their faces. In some cases, they spoke about their failures almost with pride.

On one of my first nights in San Francisco, during a reception at the Autodesk design company, I asked a young entrepreneur what he did. He said he created software and immediately added —without my asking— that he had started five companies, four of which wound up in bankruptcy. When he saw the surprise on my face, he quickly assured me that, luckily, one of his companies was doing very well. The admission of failure, I confirmed during that and other conversations that night, was a typical tale of Silicon Valley entrepreneurs.

"People here brag about their failures," I was told with a shrug of the shoulders by Wadhwa, the professor who had received me at Singularity University and alerted me to the importance of the human factor in inno-

vation. "In Silicon Valley, when you list your failures, it's as if you are list-
ing your university diplomas. Everyone here understands that with each
failure you learn something, and you are therefore wiser than before."[41]

Palo Alto in California has the world's largest concentration of
innovators. More than 50 percent of the people in the area was born in
another country, Wadhwa told me. "There is a culture here that is very
different from the majority of other countries, and from much of other
parts of the United States. In New York City, bankers wear suits and ties
and boast about their real or imagined successes. Here in Silicon Valley,
the richest businessmen and the most prestigious scientists walk around
in jeans or shorts and flip-flops, and talk very candidly about their failures. It's another world."

Wadhwa was right. A few days before, I had personally confirmed
that when I interviewed New York real estate mogul Donald Trump
in Miami for CNN. His constant promotion of his successes —and his
denials of his failures— contrasted sharply with the candor I found
among the most successful entrepreneurs in Silicon Valley. The innovative businessmen in California and the big businessmen from New York
really did seem to come from different worlds.

MINE WERE NOT FAILURES

Trump had come to Miami to promote his plans to purchase a ram-
shackle hotel and golf course for $200 million, renovate them and
turn them into an exclusive destination. During the interview, about
the collapse of the real estate bubble that the United States was just
emerging from, I asked Trump what he had learned from his failures.

Before the interview, I had read several articles about Trump's history, which was full of failures. A number of his companies had declared
bankruptcy. Trump Airlines had failed dismally, and a brand of vodka
did not survive long after its launch. But to my surprise, he became
angry when I asked him what he had learned from his failures. Shaking
his head and the blond mane that he always insisted was not a toupee,
he told me, "I never failed at all."

"But you declared bankruptcy three times," I said, as cordially as I could. His answer: "Those were not failures. What I did was to take advantage of the legal system."

Obviously, I was disappointed by his lack of candor and intellectual sophistication. But it wasn't until the following week, speaking with Wadhwa in Palo Alto, that I could fully appreciate the big difference between innovation tycoons in California, Seattle and other parts of the West Coast of the United States —like Gates, Jobs and Zuckerberg— and the real estate and financial moguls of New York.

The former dressed in jeans, t-shirts and sandals, tried to save the world with their innovations and charity foundations and spoke proudly about their failures. The latter, like Trump, wore starched white shirts with stiff ties, paid little attention to social causes and denied their business failures as if they were shameful defeats. And while many of the former played down their fortunes, the latter tended to magnify them. Trump once filed a $5 billion lawsuit against *The New York Times* —eventually thrown out by a judge— for a 2006 report that his fortune totaled only $150 million to $200 million, instead of the billions he claimed. In New York's business culture, in contrast to California's, the key was appearances.

THE THOUSAND FAILURES OF THE INVENTOR OF THE LIGHT BULB

The societal tolerance for individual failure that so impressed me in Silicon Valley, as I learned later, has been one of the constants of innovation throughout history. Almost all of the greatest inventions were preceded by great failures. Thomas Alva Edison, the entrepreneur who invented the commercial light bulb and patented more than 1,090 products —including the phonograph and the movie camera— failed in more than 1,000 attempts to develop a light bulb for mass use before he succeeded, according to his biographers. That's why he is widely credited with having said that he "did not fail 1,000 times, but the invention of the light bulb required 1,000 stages."

Alexander Graham Bell, inventor of the telephone, was rejected by the Telegraph Company, today Western Union, when he tried to sell it his patent for $100,000. According to a story in the 1919 book *The History of the Telephone*, by Herbert N. Casson, the executive of the Telegraph Company who received Bell's proposal asked pleasantly, "What use... could this company make of an electrical toy?" [42] Another version of the story, probably apocryphal but used in top business schools around the world, has the company committee in charge of studying Bell's proposal concluding that the idea of a telephone was "idiotic." According to the alleged text of the report from the committee, company executives had decided that the voice quality of Bell's contraption was so bad that it was worthless. "Why would any person want to use this ungainly and impractical device when he can send a messenger to the telegraph office and have a clear written message sent," one member of the committee was quoted as asking.

Aviation pioneers Orville and Wilbur Wright made 163 failed attempts before their first successful manned flight in December 1903.[43] Some of their predecessors had less luck: they were killed in their attempts. And auto industry pioneer Henry Ford, produced more than a dozen auto models before the Ford Model T, the first mass-produced car. His biographers wrote that he called it the Model T because he had started with the Model A and needed 19 attempts, to the letter T, to go from prototypes to the finished vehicles.

Practically all stories of success are the culmination of stories of failure, and not just in the world of technology but also in commerce, politics and art. British Prime Minister Winston Churchill constantly reminded his audiences of the importance of not being discouraged by failures. The statesman had been a bad student who repeated a year, attended three schools and twice flunked the entry exams for the Royal Military Academy Sandhurst. In a famous speech during an Oct. 29 1941 visit to the Harrow school, where he had distinguished himself as one of the worst students in his class, he told the students, "Never give in, never give in, never, never —in nothing, great or small, large or petty— never give in except to convictions of honor and good sense."

IS CREATIVITY GENETIC?

Perhaps it's no coincidence that so many inventors and innovators throughout history have been persistent, obstinate, eccentric and often insufferable, like Apple founder Steve Jobs. Several studies on the psychology of creativity have shown that innovative people tend to be extroverted, open to experimentation, not very concerned about pleasing others and somewhat neurotic. In other words, the stereotype of the "mad genius" is not far from the truth.

Shelley Carson, a Harvard psychology professor and widely recognized researcher on the psychological characteristics of creativity, wrote that Albert Einstein used to pick up cigarette butts from the streets to fill his pipe. Composer Robert Schumann believed music was transmitted by Beethoven and other dead composers from their tombs. And writer Charles Dickens used his umbrella to drive off imagined juvenile delinquents as he walked the streets of London. "It isn't just average Joes who perceive highly creative individuals as eccentric. These individuals often see themselves as different and unable to fit in," Carson wrote. "The latest findings in brain imaging, creativity research and molecular biology suggest that these perceptions are not just based on a few anecdotal accounts of 'weird' scientists and artists. In fact, creativity and eccentricity often go hand in hand, and researchers now believe that both traits may be a result of how the brain filters incoming information." [44]

Carson quotes the 1966 research of Leonard Heston —who showed that the children of mothers diagnosed with schizophrenia tend to go into more creative careers than the children of mothers who did not suffer from the disease— and other studies showing that creative people have a special personality that amounts to mild versions of psychiatric disorders. That's nothing new. In ancient Greece, Plato warned that poets and philosophers suffered from "divine madness," a disorder granted to them by the gods yet madness nevertheless, Carson noted. Aristotle also suggested that there was a connection between poets and melancholy, which today we label as depression.

A BIT OF MADNESS AND MUCH AUDACITY

So, is it true that creative people have a dash of madness? Carson wrote that her research at Harvard did not indicate that these genetic characteristics by themselves promote creativity. But she added that these types of personalities have fewer mental filters, which helps to explain the "eureka" moments that geniuses have when they make a discovery. The minds of these special personalities, with fewer filters, allow more ideas to pass from the unconscious to the conscious world —hallucinations as well as ideas or intuitions that turn out to be brilliant— according to Carson.

That was the case of John Forbes Nash, the Nobel prize winner in economics portrayed in the Hollywood movie *A Beautiful Mind*. Asked how he made his scientific discoveries, he replied candidly that they came into his mind in the same way as his visions of supernatural or extraterrestrial beings. All these discoveries about creativity, Carson wrote, mean that "even in the business world, there is a growing appreciation of the link between creative thinking and unconventional behavior, with increased acceptance of the latter."

For that reason, as companies put more value on creative minds, the more advanced countries, cities and companies are increasingly allowing more exemptions to their rules in order to accommodate and assimilate eccentric people. As a result, there's been an increase in the number of communities with high concentrations of artists, writers, scientists, cyber-nerds and entrepreneurs who take risks, she adds. And there's been an increase in the value placed on originality and boldness. "Managers within these communities tolerate bizarre clothing choices, disregard of normal social protocols and nontraditional work schedules, in the interest of promoting innovation," she wrote.

GREAT SUCCESSES AND RESOUNDING FAILURES

Some of the most successful innovators I interviewed told me that innovation requires, aside from a tolerance for failure, an enthusiasm for risk. Almost all of them, at some time in their lives, were at the point of bankruptcy or took on risks that many of us would not have accepted. Sir Richard Branson, the founder of Virgin Records, the space tourism company Virgin Galactic and hundreds of other companies, told me that successful companies promote a culture of tolerance with employees who launch failed projects, and offer incentives to those who take risks. Fear of failure destroys innovation, he insisted, and one must constantly embrace the risks.

Branson's life, as we will see later in this book, has been a rollercoaster of great successes and resounding failures. As a child, he was told that he would either wind up in prison or a millionaire. In fact, he admits that he spent at least one night behind bars. He always attacked his much more powerful business rivals, whether they were music recording companies or Coca-Cola. And at one point, he rented a battle tank, parked it on Times Square in New York and pointed its canon at a huge Coca-Cola sign to make his point before the news media.

Even in his private life, Branson loves risky sports. As we will see in more detail in Chapter 7, he broke navigation records by crossing the Pacific Ocean on a balloon, crossed the Atlantic aboard a small sailboat and kite-surfed from one side of the English Channel to the other. When I asked him what drove him to such high-risk sports, he answered, "Being an adventurer and a businessman is not that different. In both cases you set out to overcome apparently huge problems, you prepare to overcome them and at the end you close your eyes and say 'It's in God's hands.'" In sports as in business, one tries to turn dreams into realities, and that requires taking some risks, he added.

Elon Musk, one of Branson's main competitors in the private sector race for space, has been on the edge of bankruptcy a number of times after betting his first $100 million on his SpaceX project to reach Mars and —no joke— create a colony there with 80,000 people. When a reporter for the cbs program *60 Minutes* asked him if, after various failed flights, he did not consider taking back the rest of his money and retiring to an easy life, Musk answered, "Never... I never give up." [45] A short while later, Musk risked his last $40 million on the Tesla electric car company.

Branson and Musk are the archetypes of the innovative business-men who take risks, but most successful innovators have something in common with them. Professor Florida, the economist who argues that companies do not attract creative minds, but rather the other way around, likes to joke that top male innovators usually have three qualities that begin with the letter "T" —technology, tolerance and… testicles.

ENVIRONMENT CREATES GENIUSES, NOT THE OTHER WAY

The most important part of the research on psychology and creativity, however, is the evidence that although geniuses are born with an extraordinary intelligence, they don't produce transformative inventions by themselves. They do that only when they were surrounded by mentors, collaborators and competitors, and when they are supported by families and have the right kind of education. As we will see in the following pages, innovation is increasingly a collaborative process and less the product of an individual act of genius. Even Albert Einstein, the first name that comes to mind when we think about genius, was the product of a collaborative environment.

Einstein started to talk at age four, was a mediocre student and only managed to write down his early scientific works thanks to the help from his uncle, Jacob, and other mentors who helped and stimulated him in his youth. Professor Vera John-Steiner, author of the book *Creative Collaboration*, has argued that there are strong indications that Einstein's first wife, Mileva Maric, was a tremendous help in his initial research. The love letters between the two show that Einstein and Maric, who studied together at the Swiss Polytechnic Institute, shared "a dream of common interests and scientific collaboration," according to John-Steiner.[46]

Like Einstein, most of the leading scientific, technology and artistic innovators have emerged through a collaborative process. Picasso, another genius generally seen as a solitary painter who broke all the rules of his time, emerged through a process of interaction with peers. Although history regards him as the father of the cubist movement, Picasso benefited enormously from his close friendship and collaboration with the artist George Braque. Picasso himself confessed many years later that "almost every evening I went to Braque's studio or Braque came to mine. Each of us *had* to see what the other had done during the day. We criticized each other's work. A canvas wasn't finished until both of us felt it was," John-Steiner wrote.[47]

The same or more has happened with the technology innovators of our era, like Gates, Jobs or Zuckerberg. Most of us admire Zuckerberg for inventing Facebook, but his company was an innovative variation of previous companies, like Friendster and MySpace.

As John-Steiner, Florida, Wadhwa and other students of creativity point out, the idea of a solitary genius is a myth. The grand innovations are not sparks of genius that come out of nowhere, but the result of creative minds that take nourishment from other creative minds in cities or neighborhoods full of creative energy, who experiment tirelessly, tolerate failure and have the necessary audacity to impose their will over thousands of obstacles.

THE NUMBERS GENIUS

The world is full of people with extraordinary intelligence who make no notable contribution to humanity because they lack a favorable environment. Shakuntala Devi, a woman born in 1919 in Bangalore, India, was one of the smartest people in the world. Her father, who worked on-and-off in a circus, realized early on that his little girl had an extraordinary gift for math calculations, and soon put her to work before audiences. First in India and then around the world, Devi became famous. In one of her demonstrations in London, she took only 30 seconds to mentally multiply 7,686,369,774,870 times 2,465,099,745,749 and come up with the correct answer: 18,947,668 ,177,995,426,462,773,730. She was a human computer.

But after her death in 2013 at the age of 83, *Time* magazine noted that despite her supernatural intelligence, Devi "made no lasting contribution... The child prodigy turned into an admirable but not influential adult." "What would have become of Devi if her father, instead of being a circus performer, was a Google engineer?" the magazine asked. And what would have happened if, instead of growing up in Bangalore at the beginning of the 20th Century, she had grown up in Silicon Valley in the 21st Century? The answer is obvious: Her life probably would have been very different.[48]

A recent study by U.S. and German psychologists, published in the *Journal of Personality and Social Psychology*, confirms that geniuses —and creative minds in general— tend to flourish in the same cities or in the same spaces within the same cities.[49] The study examined the creativity and the propensity to launch companies of more than 600,000 people in the United States, and concluded that innovators tend to get together with each other. The "entrepreneurship-prone personality profile is regionally clustered," the study reported. It added that the same studies in Germany and Great Britain produced the same results.

The same thing is happening in Latin America, where enclaves are emerging inside cities, with large agglomerations of young people attracted by the tolerance for extravagant life styles, where creativity and innovation are flourishing, just as Wadhwa and Florida had told me. In earlier times, these bohemian areas were at best seen as tourist attractions. Today, they should be seen as valuable hotbeds of productive innovation, with enormous economic potential, and probably far more important to the future of countries than the costly science and technology parks created by many governments. From these neighborhoods in São Paulo, Buenos Aires, Mexico City, Santiago de Chile, Bogota and many other Latin American cities, top global entrepreneurs will emerge, according to Wadhwa and Florida.

As I learned when I started to travel around the world to interview some of today's top innovators, that's already happening.

2

Gastón Acurio:
the chef who gives away his recipes

A chef who doesn't share his recipes disappears

One of the main lessons I learned when I started to interview many of the leading business, technology and science innovators was that collaboration with rivals, rather than competition, was one of the keys to their success. In contrast to what is still taught in business schools about the virtues of competition and "might makes right," today's innovators increasingly achieve success by following a different road: collaborating with competitors under the premise that growing the cake benefits everyone, especially the best. And there are few better examples to illustrate this phenomenon than Peruvian chef Gastón Acurio.

Acurio is the Latin American chef best known around the world. He has built up a chain of 37 Peruvian restaurants in 11 countries —including some of the best-known in New York, San Francisco, Miami, Madrid, Buenos Aires and Bogotá— with sales of more than $100 million per year.[1] He is a visionary who converted something as simple as food into an economic and social phenomenon, as well as an industry that today accounts for 9.5 percent of Peru's Gross Domestic Product (GDP). As Nobel laureate Mario Vargas Llosa wrote, Acurio triumphed thanks to his success as a chef and businessman, but "his achievement is social and cultural."

Acurio invented, or discovered, the new Peruvian cuisine in the mid-1990s, and started to spread it with the passion of an evangelist.

Thanks to him, Peru went from having no culinary school in 1990 to more than 300 today, with about 80,000 students.[2] Just in Lima, the capital city, 15,000 chefs graduate each year, according to the Peruvian Gastronomy Association (APEGA).[3] Today, thanks to the boom in Peruvian cuisine sparked by Acurio, Peru has more people studying cooking than many traditional careers. And Lima —until recently so gray and boring that poet César Moro called it "Lima the ugly"— has turned into an international city that aims to become the gastronomic capital of the world by 2021, overtaking Paris and Rome.

Many travelers —including myself— now go to Peru largely attracted by its restaurants and the originality of its food, an amalgam of Amazon and Asian flavors that always surprise diners with new ideas and tastes found nowhere else in the world. Peru has added value to Andean products like native peppers and potatoes, the ulluco and manioc roots, quinoa, a type of beans known as pallares, guinea pigs and fish of all types. And it has converted them, and the new Peruvian cuisine, into pillars of national pride. When Peruvians are asked today what makes them proud of their country, gastronomy winds up in second place, after Machu Picchu but well ahead of culture, art, geography or history.[4]

Overnight, gastronomy also became a pillar of economic development for the country, employing 380,000 Peruvians. With the boom in gastronomy, the number of restaurants in Peru soared from 40,000 in 2001 to about 80,000 in 2012. There are also more than 300 Peruvian restaurants in Argentina, 105 in Chile, more than 500 in the United States and at least 47 in Tokyo, according to APEGA. The prestigious *Restaurant Magazine* in Great Britain, aimed principally at luxury restaurant chefs and owners, recently ranked seven Lima restaurants among the top 15 gourmet spots in all of Latin America —seven out of 15!

IF YOU TAKE YOUR RECIPE TO YOUR GRAVE, YOU DON'T EXIST

Perhaps the most interesting part of Acurio's story, however, is neither the cuisine he invented nor his professional success —today he has the Astrid & Gastón chain, which he founded with his wife, and another nine restaurant chains— but the way in which he built his gastronomic empire. Contrary to what business school textbooks preach, Acurio never hid his recipes from competitors. In fact, he shared them with everyone, thinking that if other restaurants spread the news about the new Peruvian cuisine, they would all benefit.

When I met him in Miami and he told me the story of his success, he described it as the result of a collective effort. "The chef who does not share his recipes is condemned to disappear," he told me. "The image of the chef has changed. Before, it was 'the chef who took his secrets to the grave.' But that's in the past. Today, you exist only if you share your recipes —on the social networks, in the media."

Acurio must have perceived my skepticism, and before I could ask he started to explain his reasons for such generosity. "Today, your recipe is ephemeral by its very nature. If you insist on taking your recipes to the grave, you are an isolated event, and you disappear. In the world of innovation, in the area of gastronomy, you have to create a movement. Peruvian chefs do not compete. We share. We are building a brand that belongs to all of us and that benefits all of us," he told me. I looked at him with a mixture of surprise and admiration, although I was not totally convinced. Before asking for more details on his recipe for success, I wanted to hear more about his start as a chef, at a time when being a chef in Peru was viewed as a very lowly career.

"MY FATHER WANTED ME TO BE A LAWYER"

Acurio comes from a well-off family. He was raised on Los Laureles street in San Isidro, one of Lima's most elegant neighborhoods. His father, Gastón Acurio Velarde, was an engineer who came from a land-owning family and dedicated his life to politics. In 1965 he was named minister of development and public works under President Fernando Belaúnde Terry. He was elected to the nation's senate in

1980 and was re-elected in 1985 and 1990. At the Acurio home, politicians walked in and out all the time. Politics was always in the air.

Sen. Acurio Velarde had one son and four older daughters. As a boy, Acurio was vaguely interested in but not passionate about his father's conversations with politicians. He was a bit chubby, a kid who liked to eat, and eat well. "When I was six or seven, I would go out on my bike and buy squid in the supermarket," he told me. "In my house, no one cooked. Not my mother, not my sisters. So I bought my squid, grabbed my grandmother's recipe books, read them, made up the recipes and cooked them for myself. And my father looked at me from a distance, out of the corner of his eye, like he thought that the boy was 'playing at something strange.'"

Acurio said he does not know where his love for cooking comes from, but believes that maybe it was a refuge from the world of politics or the many women in his home. "Since my sisters had their own lives, I spent a lot of time in the kitchen. I could hide there a little bit from the world of my sisters. Maybe that's where the relationship with the kitchen came from. Maybe I isolated myself in the kitchen," he said.

Senator Acurio Velarde did not appreciate the time his son was spending in the kitchen. "My father wanted me to be a lawyer, and a politician. As a child, he took me to meetings, to see the debates in Congress, I imagine with the hope of creating a future politician in his party's new generation," Acurio recalled.

"I WAS THROWN OUT OF THE UNIVERSITY"

As his father expected, Acurio graduated with good grades from the Colegio Santa Maria, one of Lima's most traditional schools, and enrolled at the Universidad Católica to study law even though he now confesses that he did everything possible to make the university turn him away. Instead of studying day and night for the entrance exam, he barely attended the academy where he had enrolled to study for the exam. "I took the sample tests, and that's all. But it turned out that the entrance exam for the Universidad Católica included a lot of questions on the humanities, and I had been hammered with politics at home every day. As a boy, I was forced to read all the books about the protestant ethic, the spirit of capitalism, all those things," Acurio recalled. "So, when the day came for the entrance exam, I obviously answered what I knew, and I passed. I almost had a heart attack, because I was admitted to a place where I did not want to be. I messed up," To the great pride of his parents, the son of Sen. Acurio Velarde had one of the top scores in the exam, and was ranked in 70th place among 4,000 applicants.

But when he started to study law, Acurio quickly realized it was not for him. Classes were boring, and the studies even more so. Although he had been a very good student in high school, he began to flunk some classes. "Truthfully, I forced them to throw me out. It's the same university that expelled Jaime Bayly. I flunked all the classes. And if you flunk all your classes in one year, they throw out out," Acurio recalled. "When my father heard I had been expelled, he almost had a heart attack. I told him, 'I am going to Spain.' Trying to straighten me out, he sent me to continue my law studies at the Universidad Complutense in Madrid."

CHANGE OF COURSE IN MADRID

In his first year at the Universidad Complutense, Acurio received excellent grades in all his classes, perhaps out of his sense of guilt toward his father. "But I ended up totally burned out," he recalled, "because studying Roman law, Canon law, Common law, is horrible in Spain, where it's all memorization."

That's how he started to work nights in restaurants, and to cater dinners at the Peruvian embassy and other social events. And in his second year, without telling his parents, Acurio changed schools and started to study cooking at the Escuela de Hotelería, a top hospitality school in Madrid. "I did that for three years, studying hospitality without saying anything to my parents," Acurio said.

And what did you tell them when they visited you in Madrid, I asked him.

"When they came to visit me, I hid the cooking books, brought out the law books and told them that everything was going well, that there were no problems, that everything was fine," he answered. "After I graduated, I had to tell them."

Like the joke about good news and bad news, Acurio told his father that he had finally graduated —but as a chef, not as a lawyer.

"Obviously it was a scandal, but I think they already suspected something. They later confessed to me that they smelled something because friends would say to them 'Hey, your son makes great dinners for the embassy,' or things like that. But they didn't really want to know," he told me. Faced with the facts, however, "my parents supported me. I told them my dream was to continue my training in France, because at that time France was the mecca in cuisine, and they helped me," Acurio recalled. "After my studies in Spain, they helped me to go to France and study at Le Cordon Bleu in Paris."

"WE MADE WONDERS IN PARIS"

At the age of 21, Acurio enrolled in the prestigious Le Cordon Bleu institute in Paris, where he quickly began receiving some of the best grades in his class. He also worked nights at a nearby restaurant, where he had become friends with the owner. "I finished my studies and went to work there at night. I had clearly found my love, because my routine started at 7 am and ended at 2 am the next day. But it was an absolutely perfect and happy world," he said.

He eventually rose to the rank of head chef. "It was fascinating. I was Peruvian and a head chef in Paris at the age of 23. It was a dream come true. We made wonders in the kitchen. We invented dishes con-stantly," Acurio recalled. It was in Paris where he met his future wife, Astrid, a German also studying at Le Cordon Bleu. Astrid spoke Span-ish, as well as German and French, and was fascinated by Peru. The two student chefs had much in common, and after a short while they decided to live in Peru.

RETURN TO PERU

Acurio and Astrid married and decided to start a restaurant in Lima, while at the same time helping to establish a Le Cordon Bleu school in Peru. "I didn't have to do a lot to persuade her. She already had decided to come with me, and we came," he said. "My parents were very annoyed. I was 24, my wife was pregnant and we did not have one cent. And we were returning to a world totally different from gastronomy in Peru today." Being a chef was a low-status job, especially for someone raised in San Isidro.

The owner of the Le Cordon Bleu school in Paris, a descendant of the Cointreau family, had taken a liking to his Peruvian student and asked him to find someone who might want to open a school in Peru. Acurio found a candidate, helped to establish the school and meanwhile searched for a locale for his own restaurant. At the time, Acurio and his wife had no intention whatsoever to open a Peruvian restaurant. They wanted a French restaurant. "The good restaurants at that time were all French. And chefs were trained to be French chefs. So our dream was to have a French restaurant," he said. While Gastón helped to establish Le Cordon Bleu and Astrid worked in a pastry shop, they searched for a place for their own restaurant. After a year, they opened a French restaurant and called it Astrid & Gastón.

"I ASKED ALL MY RELATIVES FOR MONEY"

Acurio asked to borrow money from his parents, his in-laws, his uncles, just about everyone, to open the restaurant. Some people loaned him money, seeing it almost as an act of charity. As Acurio remembers it, "At the time, everyone loaned me money, almost resigned to losing it, like saying 'poor boy, he wants to be a chef, we have to help him,' but convinced they would never see their money again. They gave it to me, like a donation." Today, those same relatives must be regretting not having loaned him more money, as an investment in Acurio's future. As he recalls it, his lenders had so little faith in his project that none of them thought to ask for a share of the business. Had they done that, they would have earned millions of dollars.

Astrid & Gastón opened Mondays through Saturdays. Acurio got there at 7 am and went home at 2 the next morning. "And Sundays, when we were closed, I went in at 9 am to do the bookkeeping I couldn't do during the week because I was cooking and my wife was taking care of the clients. We did everything. But we were able to quickly repay all the loans we had received. And because we were very successful with our French restaurant, other offers started to come in," he said.

At first, Acurio rejected the offers to open new restaurants. He wanted to have the best French restaurant in Lima, and did not want to spread himself too thin on new projects. But soon, influenced by what was happening in gastronomy outside Peru, Acurio and Astrid started to experiment with a new type of cuisine.

Barcelona chef Ferran Adrià and others had revolutionized the world of gastronomy in the late 1990s, moving away from French cuisine to create their own styles based on local flavors and colors. Chefs in Spain were creating the "Taste of the Mediterranean." Some called it "molecular gastronomy," others called it "deconstructionist cuisine." Regardless of the name, it signaled that some European chefs had started to abandon the dogmas of French cuisine and change the ingredients, forms and textures of their dishes. And the young Peruvian chefs, who followed those trends closely, decided they wanted to do the same thing with Peruvian food.

"We realized that when we opened the French restaurant, we were desperate for the dehydrated mushrooms that I had been taught to use in France. My eyes could not see the things around me, and I could not understand that Peru is a country with more than 500 different fruits with the most unbelievable flavors." Acurio recalled. "I was looking for green pepper from Madagascar, when I had roots, herbs and barks all around the Amazon with flavors just as strong, or better."

Inspired by the possibility of using products from the Peruvian jungle, Acurio spent part of 2002 traveling throughout his country in search of new ingredients. Leaving Astrid in charge of their restaurant for three months, he went from town to town in the Amazon and the Andes, discovering what was available in warehouses and restaurants. He wound up writing a book he titled *Perú, una aventura culinaria* (Peru, a culinary adventure). As he recalls it, "That's where I came full circle... I said, OK, this is the road."

TRANSITION FROM *FOIE GRAS* TO GUINEA PIGS

The couple started to innovate at their Astrid & Gastón restaurant, replacing the butter and creams that flavored their French dishes with peppers and herbs from the Amazon. Astrid & Gastón began a transformation from a restaurant that offered *foie gras* as its top dish, to a place that offers guinea pigs, a traditional dish in Peru and now the restaurant's top seller.

But how did you manage to transform that into a multi-million dollar business?, I asked Acurio. I told him that there's a restaurant in the historic heart of Mexico City, Don Chon, that offers pre-Hispanic dishes like grasshoppers, cayman meat, maguey worms, mosquito eggs, ant larvae and pupae, and other exotic dishes once favored by the Aztecs. I told him that when I visited Don Chon and wrote a story about it in the 1990s, European tourists were arriving by the busloads, eating some worms, laughing as they had their photos taken and then going away. Two decades later, the restaurant remained a small place, a curiosity more than anything else. Mexico's pre-Hispanic cuisine, unlike Peruvian food, had not won over the rest of Mexico or the world.

What did you do differently?, I asked Acurio.

"The difference is that we did not just open a restaurant, but rather we started a movement," he answered. "In a movement, you are part of an activity. The difference is that we did not just open a restaurant. We started a much larger economic movement."

What does that mean, in practical terms?, I asked.

"In practical terms that means that as the movement develops, it's not just one chef but many chefs who start to talk among themselves. In personal terms, we realized that when we opened the restaurant we used 30 kilos of butter and 50 liters of cream, but years later we didn't use any of that because they were not appropriate for the style we were creating," Acurio said. "From the 'Frenchified' style, we went to a style where the Peruvian peppers, the herbs, provide the flavors. And the new ideas came out of local culture."

You're saying you created a movement that benefited all the chefs, I noted.

"And more than the chefs. Because we were also starting to talk to local producers, to understand a little more about what was going on the countryside, what was available from the local biodiversity. And we were starting to try to attract the diners," Acurio added.

"WE DON'T COMPETE, WE SHARE"

Acurio said he did not create the new Peruvian cuisine movement by himself, and that other chefs in the country were simultaneously heading in the same direction. One of them was Pedro Miguel Schiaffino, who studied at the Culinary Institute of America in New York City, worked five years in Italy, returned to Peru in 2001 and lived in the Amazon city of Iquitos for one year to study the regional food. In 2004 he founded his famous Malabar restaurant, today one of Lima's best.

Another was Rafael Piqueras, the young founder of the Maras restaurant, who studied at Le Cordon Bleu in Peru and the Piamonte region of Italy. Piqueras worked in the legendary El Bulli restaurant in Barcelona before he returned to Peru and started to experiment with fusions of foreign dishes and typical Peruvian ingredients. Acurio and the other young chefs returned to Peru about the same time, and set out to revolutionize Peruvian gastronomy. The three chefs, and others, soon began to exchange ideas and host television shows where they frequently invited each other and promoted the culinary innovations the other chefs were offering in their restaurants.

Listening to Acurio talk about this idyllic movement of young restaurant owners who helped each other, I could not help but feel a bit skeptic. Common sense told me that far from helping each other, restaurant owners —in Peru and the rest of the world— try to destroy each other. You were competitors, I said. Why should I believe that you helped each other?

"The fact is, we did not compete, we shared. We were building a brand for all of us," Acurio said.

From the start?

"Yes".

How did that happen?

"We started to meet, between 2000 and 2003, to chat. Most of us were about 30 years old, we already had high-cuisine restaurants, we were published in magazines, we were interviewed and were starting to gain some prominence on television. I started a television program. We started to have a voice, and something of a media influence on the dining public that benefited all of us," he replied.

Why did you start to meet?

"We used to say that we need to come together, we need to do things, we need to promote our products, we need to develop our own language, we need to have the same line, the same principles, the same common values. We have a priceless environment that only 10 or 12 other countries can match, and we must take advantage of it. Because if we don't, we will always be Peruvians who do French cuisine in Peru —in other words, nothing," Acurio said.

Did you meet spontaneously, to have coffee, or was it something organized?

"Both. We met, and above all we communicated, trying to articulate what would later become a single discourse and then a movement," he said. "But basically it was accelerating the process of transforming our cooking. In other words, 'de-frenchifying' our own restaurants."

But what did you agree on, specifically?, I asked. Things like sending a representative to food fairs abroad?

"Yes, things like that, and many others. For example, agreeing to foster more of an environmental conscience among our clients. In Peru, for example, the season for shrimp closes in January. And, until our time, when the shrimp season was closed, diners would go into a restaurant and ask for shrimp, because what is illegal is more attractive. And the chef, afraid of disappointing, would give in to the request," Acurio replied. "So we met and decided, OK, from now on, we are joining hands and we tell the clients, 'Gentlemen, it's horrible, illegal and immoral to sell shrimp. As chefs, we have the responsibility to protect them during this closed season, and we will be very vigilant in complying with it and trying to make sure that other chefs comply.' We asked our waiters to say, 'Gentlemen, the shrimp season is closed, and it's important to comply because the oceans are threatened throughout the world. And if we don't comply, we'll have no shrimp next year.'"

Did it work?

"That was the acid test, and the diners backed us. We already had a media presence, beyond the people who would tell us after dinner, 'Congratulations. Delicious dishes!' And the campaign was successful, because we also brought in the other chefs. And today everyone complies with the closed season. That's fantastic!" he said.

But how did you avoid fighting each other, I asked. Because it's obvious that the restaurant that decides to sell shrimp in January would beat the others.

"At the beginning, it was difficult," he replied. "What's the main attitude? Mistrust. Ego. Vanity. That creates a wall that makes dialogue impossible… Then you begin to isolate yourself, to make your own world. But when we were all preaching the same message in the media, it was difficult to say one thing on television and then offer shrimp in our restaurants."

"THE CHEF WHO DOES NOT SHARE HIS RECIPES DISAPPEARS"

At this point in our interview, I was still having problems believing Acurio's tale of the young chefs who started the new Peruvian cuisine movement, not only agreeing to promote their Amazon dishes but even exchanging their recipes.

Don't chefs take their recipes to their graves?, I asked Acurio. He smiled and told me again that "those were other times" and that today, the chef who fails to share his recipes and makes them transcend his immediate environs is condemned to disappear.

"If you keep the recipe to yourself, it does not exist. There is an almost crazy drive to share anything you do, because it is the only way to make it transcend yourself. That's what is happening today in the world of gastronomy, in the world of innovation," Acurio said.

Interesting, I told him, because perhaps you have intuitively done what scientists and technology innovators are increasingly doing around the world. Great innovations, such as drones and 3D printers, are increasingly developed through collaborations open to everyone on the Internet.

Recipes "have to be open, shared. Because that's how you become an icon, you are a model to imitate, you start trends. If you dream up a new ceviche, and the next year that ceviche is all over Miami, then you exist: you have an urgent need to do that, and that others do that," he added.

And what happens to competition?, I asked.

"What we had before our movement was a competition for crumbs. Our premise was, we either fight for crumbs or we try to build a new environment that benefits all of us. That was the argument," he said. "If Chinese, Japanese, Italian and French cuisine already exist in the world, why not Peruvian? That was our starting point."

HOW TO AVOID THE INTERNAL WARS

Aside from the threat of competition among the innovative restaurants, there was the danger of a silent war by the traditional restaurants against the young chefs, like Acurio, who were inventing a new cuisine.

How did you keep some competitor from launching a dirty war against you, I asked, for example leaking to the news media information that could damage you, like negative reviews, or suggesting that some of your ingredients were unhealthy.

"From the beginning, we tried to knock down that absurd fight between tradition and innovation. The traditional chef felt threatened by those of us who were doing innovative dishes. That always happens, and all over the world. We identified that problem from the start. We were appearing too often in the magazines. Innovation is what draws, and that frustrated them. But I personally think the television program helped a lot with that problem. I brought the traditional chefs to the program all the time so they could tell their stories, to help them succeed, so that they would be recognized. And that generated trust," Acurio said.

And today?

"There came a moment, in 2003, when all the barriers we talked about at the beginning had been knocked down," he explained. "Then the traditional chef felt respect and affection for the haute cuisine chef. And vice versa. We saw each other as equals, as an industry. And together we will build up this industry, including more sectors each day."

What sectors?

"Like producers. Right now, we have managed to move from the stage of the anonymous producer to the producer as a key player. Today, the city finally applauds the producer in the countryside. It recognizes its labor, because the producer is very important for generating new commercial links. Since 2007, we have been organizing a gastronomy fair in Lima, called Mistura, and already the biggest in Latin America, where we reward not only the restaurants and the chefs but also the producers. And about 500,000 people turn up every year," Acurio said.

How do you reward the producers?

"The most important part of the Mistura fair are the awards for excellence. Two years ago, we decided to award prizes to a dozen producers of typical Peruvian items like coffee, cacao, quinoa, potato and pepper. Producers who had distinguished themselves in various ways,"

Acurio noted. "Before, because of our ignorance, we believed that the producers came to the fair just in search of new markets, thinking that the fair could generate new sales for them, and that was the only thing important to them. But I remember an anecdote that changed everything. A producer of quinoa came up to me and told me about how emotional he became when the people, the public in Lima that had never thought about the producers, had applauded him at the fair. And this man told me that he was shaking my hand 'in the name of my people, because we have waited 500 years for this moment.' I was stunned. That's when we understood that we had to re-establish the trust between the city and the countryside."

Returning to the question of how all the chefs managed to work together instead of fighting "over crumbs," Acurio said the Mistura fair is an excellent example of how everyone —young and innovative chefs as well traditional chefs, producers and consumers— benefited from the culinary boom in Peru. During the 10-day fair, dishes from all regions of the country are highlighted, along with food from Europe, China, Africa and other parts, and the best chefs from around the world are invited. The event has turned into a national happening, where participants unveil new dishes and ideas that turn into front-page news and fuel the curiosity —and the hunger— of diners. "We all win," Acurio concluded.

THE ROLE OF GOVERNMENT

Curious to know how much help the Peruvian government had provided for the movement that revolutionized the country's gastronomic industry, I asked Acurio about the government's role at the start of the project. Did they receive subsidies from the federal or local government, or any other entity, to create the movement? Was government assistance a key factor in promoting the innovation?

Acurio said the government "joined" when the movement was already working, not before, but did help to promote it. "We founded APEGA in 2007. We were all together. The photo is memorable, because it shows the minister of commerce and tourism, the potato farmer, the woman who sells chicken skewers on a corner and the vanguard chefs. The government help was limited to promotion, supporting the participation of Peruvian chefs in food fairs abroad, that's all. In other countries, the government participation is much higher," he said.

Give me an example, I said.

"In Sweden, you go to the government's Web page and see that they have a 20-year plan. They want to be the most important country in the world in gastronomy," Acurio replied. "The case of Sweden is very interesting because it has little diversity and a meager food culture. Nevertheless, they have decided that through innovation they must become a gastronomic power."

How do they expect to do that?

"Sweden already has cut taxes on restaurants by 50 percent, as long as they devote the savings to innovation. What's the objective of that policy? To generate top chefs. They have an interesting plan," Acurio said.

"DID I FAIL? OF COURSE! ALL THE TIME"

Like other successful visionaries, Acurio is not ashamed to admit that he failed a number of times during his career. When I asked him if he had ever failed, he shot back, "All the time." Then told me about his abortive attempt to compete with McDonald's with a chain of fast Peruvian food.

"In the middle of this madness about focusing on everything 'Peruvian,' we created a sandwich chain, called Los Hermanos Pascuales, in 2007. We said we were going to compete with McDonald's. But we did it wrong. Instead of creating a new world, our mistake was to start a Peruvian sandwich shop with a U.S. look, thinking that all fast food should have that same format, with neon lights and people ordering the food at a counter. We opened seven restaurants in one year. It was a mistake, madness," he recalled.

What did you learn?

"Based on our failure, others corrected those mistakes and are developing an industry," Acurio said. "Peruvian sandwiches are now fighting an incredible and beautiful battle against American fast food. They are selling Peruvian sandwiches, but in ways that are in line with local culture. They have created their own style. That's super."

But at that time, how did it affect you?

"Failure should not defeat you. You have to take risks. We've done it other times, and done well," he declared. "When we opened our San Francisco restaurant in 2008, for example. At a time when many U.S. banks were going bankrupt, we inaugurated a seafront restaurant that cost us several million dollars. The rent alone was $60,000 a month. That day, the United States was going bankrupt. And we were planting our Peruvian flag there."

How did it go?

"Well, that restaurant, named La Mar, is the top seller of all our restaurants. It sells $10 million a year," he said.

"INNOVATION MUST BE CONSTANT"

I had heard that the chefs in every one of Acurio's restaurants are expected to constantly create new dishes, but I didn't know that it was a requirement, not just a suggestion. As Acurio told me, the chefs in each of his restaurants must change the menu every six months and create five new dishes per week —an even bigger challenge.

I asked if that was five dishes to be tasted by the staff, or five dishes to offer to the public.

"For the public, of course. Each new dish is put on a blackboard. How do you create new dishes at Astrid & Gastón? Well, I get new type of bean, a purple bean. With that purple bean, for example, I make a cracker that I use in a dessert. That's how I create something new —taking the bean, which is on the salty side, into the sweet side. Each chef has to create all the time. Innovation must be constant," he explained.

And what's your role in all this process?

"My job is to make sure that the chefs understand their turf. Because we cannot make an Astrid & Gastón dish in La Mar. They are totally different culinary languages and styles. And all the chefs, when they are young, want to be chefs at Astrid & Gastón, because they are thirsty for creativity. What I have to do is to explain them that there's creativity everywhere, but that each restaurant has a different turf," Acurio said. "In some, the creativity is in the traditional cuisine, looking through old cook books, checking out recipes from 50 and 100 years ago and then giving them a modern language. That's how you innovate from the very heart of tradition. In other restaurants, you have to do other things."

"OUR FIRST OBJECTIVE: TO GROW THE PERU BRAND"

Perhaps the most surprising part of the gastronomic phenomenon sparked by Acurio is that it has led Peruvian chefs not only to work better and feel proud of their labor, but to do so with patriotic fervor, as if they are fighting for a larger cause. "The first mission of our enterprise is to develop Peruvian cuisine throughout the world. If you join our company and ask what's our mission, the answer you'll get is this: Develop Peruvian cuisine around the world," Acurio said.

Are you sure?, I asked. The main goal of a restaurant, or any other company, is to make money.

"Yes, but our first objective is to promote the Peru brand, because as Peruvian cuisine becomes better known, we will open more restaurants and develop our company, and we will fare better," he answered. "Now, if the question is why our mission is to promote Peruvian cuisine around the world, we have three goals. The first is to promote the Peru brand and what Peru produces: that's to say, Peruvian gastronomy as a tool for promoting national products, strengthening the country's image and generating other positive effects around the world."

How's that?

Acurio's answer: "If I generate trust through the Peru brand, then all of Peru's products and activities generate trust. I always tell an anecdote about the time we opened our restaurant in Madrid. A guy approached me and said, 'I want to thank you.' When I asked why, he said, 'Because your restaurant is on the Paseo de la Castellana and says 'Peruvian cuisine' on the door. I have a Peruvian silverware shop near the Puerta del Sol, and I sold nothing until you opened.' Do you see how it's all related?"

What are the two other objectives?

"The second is to attract more people to Peru, boosting tourism. That's promoting 'destination Peru' through gastronomy. Peru competes with the rest of America to bring tourists from Europe. Why did people come to Peru before? Machu Picchu. Why do people come to Peru now? Because they want to visit Machu Picchu and because they want to eat well. That's two reasons," he said. "And there's one more. Peru also competes for tourists at the regional level. Where am I going? Am I going to go from Latin America to Europe, or am I going to go to a neighboring country? So that's why we Latin American chefs have started to look for common standards."

And the third objective?

"The third objective is to bring Peruvians together through the food, to turn Peruvian cuisine into a vehicle for the integration of all Peruvians, through the different activities that we carry out," he answered.

"NO NEED TO FIGHT OVER CRUMBS"

For Acurio, "making money is the result of the success promoting the Peru brand. If that's not working, we don't make money, and instead of growing the business for all of us, we will go back to fighting for crumbs. I want Peruvian cuisine to have value, the same value around the world as Italian cuisine. Do you know what's the global value of Italian food? It's $500 billion. That's the value of Italian cuisine. The Italian pizzerias in Miami, the Italian brand tomatoes in the supermarket, and an international pizza brand have a combined brand value of $500 billion."

But Italian food has centuries of tradition, I said. It's not a brand that established itself in just one generation.

"Italian food has 100 years of tradition," he answered. "Japanese food, which has 40 years, has a market value of $200 billion. Forty years ago, there were 500 Japanese restaurants in the world. Today there are 50,000. Forty years ago, kids in the Western world knew nothing about Japanese food. If you told a kid that you would pay him to eat seaweed, wasabi or raw fish, he would have said, 'You're crazy!' But people eat that today everywhere."

So?

"So, based on that argument, you can really develop national cuisines in a few years. Peruvian food today has a market value of $10 billion, including food exports. We have a long way to go," Acurio added.

"THE BOOM INCREASED THE SELF-ESTEEM OF PERUVIANS"

Toward the end of our interview, when I asked Acurio what makes him most proud of the movement he created, his answer was swift: "The best is that it has been one of the most important engines for recovering our pride in being Peruvian, the confidence that we have in ourselves —as a culture and as a nation— to play leading roles," he said.

Acurio added that every time Peruvian food wins an international prize —such as when a British publication named Lima as the gastronomic destination of 2012, or when the World Travel Guide listed Peruvian cuisine among the five with the best future— it's as if the country had won an Oscar. It's a prize for all Peruvians.

"When Peruvian food, as part of Peruvian culture, is recognized around the world, that's like a scream of freedom. And since self-confidence is a key to almost anything, then that may well be the biggest contribution of Peruvian food, to be able to look to the future with confidence, with common goals," he told me. "In the latest polls on self-confidence and pride in Latin America, we have clearly moved from the bottom to the top, surpassing Mexico. You can see that when you go to Peru. People greet you with pride. Twenty years ago, they would have taken you to a French restaurant, and they would have tried to tell you that Lima looks much like Miami. Not today. Gastronomy has contributed enormously to changing all that."

Months after this interview, during a trip to Peru, I confirmed just how highly Peruvians value the role that Acurio has played in raising the self-esteem of the people. There was serious talk in political circles about the possibility that the chef could become president of Peru at some point. Acurio was telling reporters that he was not interested, but many leading politicians were seriously considering the possibility: none of them had the high popularity ratings of the chef who gives away his recipes.

3

Jordi Muñoz and the "makers" movement

The explosion of collaborative innovation on the Internet

What Peruvian chef Gastón Acurio did with his cooking recipes —sharing his secrets and collaborating instead of fighting with competitors— is something that technology innovators in Silicon Valley have been doing more and more. One of the fastest-growing phenomenons in that part of California is the "makers" movement, whose members publish their projects and inventions on the Internet, arguing that it's better for them to share their work with everyone, and get feedback from everyone, than to keep it secret. This seemed to me like a very romantic and somewhat unrealistic concept until I met Jordi Muñoz, a 26-year-old Mexican who already had been president for three years of one of the top civilian drone companies in the United States.

If anyone had told Muñoz when he was 19 years old that by the age of 23 he would be the president of 3D Robotics, a California company with more than 200 workers, 28,000 clients and projected sales of $60 million in 2015, he would have died laughing. He would have taken it as a cruel joke, a jab designed to push him to stop being an aimless young man and settle down. But at the age of 23 he was CEO of 3D Robotics and was rubbing shoulders with leaders of the U.S. aerospace industry. His story was Hollywood material.

NO PAPERS, NO JOB, NO DEGREE

Muñoz came to the United States at the age of 20 from Tijuana, Mexico. He had no papers, no job, no university degree. He was one of the many "ni–nis," the Spanish-language slang for the millions of young people who neither work nor study. And his girlfriend, Priscila, had just had a baby.

The young couple, afraid of their parents' anger and without a clear future in Mexico, decided to abandon their studies and move to the United States, taking advantage of her U.S. citizenship. Once in Los Angeles, Muñoz could not work while he waited for his U.S. residency papers. He spent his days at home, taking care of the baby and writing in amateur blogs about computing, robotics and drones —all topics that had fascinated him since childhood. His future prospects were not very bright. At best, he confessed to me much later, he expected to work as a salesman in the computer section of a Best Buy store, and probably earn minimum wage for the rest of his life.

But that's not how it turned out. Muñoz' obsession with aviation technology, his participation in the "makers" community —the growing world of cybernauts who publicly share their projects and discoveries— and a pinch of luck transformed him overnight into one of the most promising entrepreneurs in the United States. His business godfather and partner, Chris Anderson, a former editor-in-chief of the magazine *Wired* who resigned in 2012 to co-found 3D Robotics with Muñoz, described his young partner in his book, *Makers: The New Industrial Revolution,* as "one of the world's leading aerial robotics experts."[1]

The first time I interviewed Muñoz, 3D Robotics was already a well-established company regularly mentioned in many civil aviation magazines. Among other products, the company was selling unmanned aircraft for police surveillance, recording videos for television stations, delivering medicines to remote places, flying over farm fields to detect plagues and dropping life preservers to people drowning. But that was just the beginning. The civilian drone industry was set to explode in 2015, when the U.S. Federal Aviation Administration planned to unveil regulations that would allow companies like Domino's Pizza, Amazon or FedEx to use drones to deliver all kinds of goods.

How did Muñoz go in a few months from a jobless immigrant to president of a company that might soon be at the cutting edge of the aerospace industry? His story, as he told me in three separate interviews, is gripping and illustrates the rise of the "makers" communities in the world of technology.

"I HAD PROBLEMS IN SCHOOL"

Far from being a good student, Muñoz was a mediocre student. As a child, he was diagnosed with Attention Deficit Hyperactivity Disorder (ADHD). He attended five schools before graduating from high school. The only child of middle-class professionals —his father is a neuropsychiatrist, his mother an accountant— Muñoz spent his childhood in Ensenada and Tijuana, in Baja California, Mexico. His memories of primary school are not very happy. "I had problems in school," he told me. "I could not focus. The teachers talked about something and I was always distracted, thinking about something else. In the nuns' school, I was a problem, very rowdy. I was a distracted and unruly kid that teachers did not like."[2]

His father, concerned about Jordi's grades, moved him to a Montessori school. "But the change backfired. Montessori is supposed to be a school where children do whatever they want, but it turned out that I was difficult even for Montessori," a smiling Jordi recalled. In one of the many times he was reprimanded, he opened the doors of a cage with white doves, which flew away immediately. "My father was told several times to medicate me, but he resisted and I was never medicated," he said. While the teachers lectured, he was thinking about little airplanes, robots and even bombs.

His mother, Rosa Bardales, told me that as a child Jordi loved to play with Legos and take apart and put back together everything in his reach. "Even the neighbors brought their blenders for Jordi to fix," his mother recalled. "His passion was Legos. We gave him a Lego Learning set when he was a baby, when he was one year old, and that's where his creativity was born. He used to spend all day playing with Legos."[3]

The child probably got the habit of repairing old things from his father, Dr. Jorge Muñoz Esteves, whose long-time hobby was to repair old mechanical things he bought in flea markets. "I was always buying electronic gadgets, which I found for a cheap price and fixed them. That was my therapy, to get away from my job as a psychiatrist. That's what Jordi saw as a child. I never imagined that he would go that route, but that's what happened."[4]

Dr. Muñoz studied languages with the hope of practicing in the United States or Europe. After finishing his post-graduate degree in Mexico City, he won a scholarship to polish his English in Philadelphia. He was ready to travel to the United States when the Mexican government canceled his scholarship at the last minute, as part of the drastic budget cuts that followed the economic crisis of 1982. His study plans were cut short. Curiously, or perhaps not so much, Jordi years later wound up doing the two things that his father did not: dedicating himself full time to innovation and moving to the United States. "The sons always try to compensate for some deficiency in their parents, real or imagined," Dr. Muñoz told me, speaking both as a father and a psychiatrist. "Perhaps unconsciously, Jordi perceived some degree of frustration on my part for being unable to study in the United States, and possibly wound up compensating for my deficiency."[5]

"I MADE A BOMB AT THE AGE OF 11"

As a child, Jordi Muñoz dreamed of having a computer. But his parents, afraid that he would spend all his time playing with it and become even more distracted from his studies, did not buy him a used computer until he was 10 years old. At first, he didn't even know how to turn it on. But after a few days he was fascinated with his new machine. "I spent 18 hours a day stuck to the computer," he recalls.

And when he was not stuck to the computer, the boy had fun with experiments that did not always amuse his parents. "One time, when I was 11 years old, I made a remote-controlled bomb," a smiling Muñoz remembered. "I took some fireworks, took out the powder, put it in a tube, added an electronic circuit and exploded it in a big field far from everything," he recalled. His parents didn't know if they should be proud or alarmed with their son's experiments. "My father looked at me like I was some sort of strange creature," Muñoz added.

At the age of 14, Muñoz was already designing his first Web page and exploring anything that had to do with aeronautics. Like many children with ADHD who manage to control or overcome their problem in their teenage years, Muñoz started to earn better grades in school and get along better with his teachers. "I started getting good grades at 16 and finished senior high school at 18. It's a miracle I never had to repeat a year", he said.

After he finished high school and his parents divorced, Muñoz moved to Mexico City to enroll in the Instituto Politécnico Nacional (IPN), the only university in Mexico that offered aeronautical engineering. His father was not too happy with that idea, because Mexico City was not very safe at the time. Despite his father's objections, and perhaps annoyed by the fact that his father had started a new family with a woman who had a young daughter, Muñoz moved to the capital to try to get into the institute.

"THE IPN DID NOT ACCEPT ME"

Muñoz took the institute's entrance exam twice, but was rejected both times. The quotas for students from the provinces were smaller than for students from the institute's own high schools, and he did not have enough points to win admittance. "I lost two years trying to get into the IPN, and I did not get in. In the end, I went back to Tijuana with my tail between my legs," he recalled.

In Tijuana, frustrated by his failure to win admission to the one university where he could study aeronautical engineering, Muñoz decided to change course and open a taco restaurant. He sold his mother a Volkswagen car that had been given to him by his father, and invested the money in a locale for his taco shop. When his father found out, he went crazy. "I told him, 'So much hard work, to wind up making tacos?'" the father recalled. Jordi said his father "was angry because he wanted me to study a career in a university." Soon afterward, Jordi started studying computer engineering at the Centro de Enseñanza Técnica y Superior (Cetys), one of the most prestigious private universities in Baja California.

Muñoz studied at Cetys for 12 months, until his girlfriend and fellow student became pregnant. The young couple, afraid and knowing that their parents would not approve, decided to leave their studies and try their luck in the United States. It was 2007. "It was really stressful for both of us," Muñoz recalled. "The baby was on the way, I had no papers and we had no money. I couldn't work for seven months, until I received my green card. On top of everything, the economy was failing, and in 2008 the economic crisis exploded. It was very hard to find work."

"I STARTED TO WRITE IN BLOGS"

In 2008, staying at home to take care of the baby boy while his wife worked, Muñoz started to write on the Internet blogs of open-source innovation communities. The groups of "makers" were creating more and more Web sites and discussion forums to share their ideas on innovation, hoping to benefit from the experiences of others and advance more quickly in their own projects. Some of these sites, such as Wikipedia, the free Internet encyclopedia created by a community of people who volunteer their time to manage an alternative to commercial encyclopedias, are known around the world. But thousands of new sites were emerging every day for communities interested in all sorts of different issues.

That's how Muñoz found a blog by Anderson, then editor-in-chief of the magazine *Wired*. It was a recently created forum called DIY Drones —Do It Yourself Drones. At that time, the blog had just 14 members, all people who had been experimenting by their own with toy drones, he said. Like most of these types of blogs, most of the participants wrote under pseudonyms.

Muñoz' first post in the Anderson blog started out apologizing for his English. "English is not my first language, so I apologize for my mistakes when I try to explain this project," he wrote. He went on to offer his answer to a query posted by Anderson on how to cut the costs of the automatic autopilots for homemade drones.

Muñoz wrote in the blog that he had created an automatic autopilot from parts he took out of video games. Using a toy helicopter that his mother had given him, a cheap Arduino electronic micro controller board and pieces from his Nintendo Wii video game, Muñoz built a cheap version of a device that Anderson and other technology buffs in Silicon Valley were producing at much higher costs. While a normal platform was costing $500, Muñoz' home-made version cost barely $30. Muñoz explained in his post how he had flown his helicopter with parts of a video game, and a few days later began posting photos and videos of his helicopter in flight.

Anderson, the blog's creator, recalled that readers started to take notice. Another blogger wrote, "Your English is very good; don't worry too much about translations. A picture is worth a thousand words, and we're excited to see (the) video. That's an excellent helicopter you put together," another blog member wrote. "I was impressed too," Anderson wrote. "I'd never used Arduino, but this prompted me to look more closely at it".[6]

COOPERATION WITH ANDERSON STARTS

Anderson contacted Muñoz by e-mail to ask more questions about the Arduino board, and they started to exchange ideas. "I liked his energy and was impressed by his fearless experimentation and effortless grasp of software concepts that I had struggled to understand. I had a feeling that he was on to something," he wrote.[7] As the months went by, the *Wired* editor and the young Mexican wrote each other more and more frequently. "His instinct kept leading him to more and more exciting technologies, from sensors he found to figured out how to use to algorithms he tracked down in obscure papers," Anderson added.

Muñoz and Anderson started new projects on the DIY Drones blog, such as electronic circuits for piloting the aircraft. They published everything they knew on the blog, loyal to their belief that the benefits of the contributions from other members of the blogging community would be bigger than the risks that some of them would perfect the ideas and obtain a patent for commercial use. "I wrote posts on my blog describing our progress, and documented the projects with online tutorials, showing how to do them," Anderson wrote.[8]

After three or four months, Anderson sent Muñoz a check for $500 for his collaboration, designed to keep him interested and, perhaps, lay the groundwork for starting a joint commercial project sometime in the future. Shortly afterward, Muñoz and Anderson met for the first time when the *Wired* editor gave a conference in Los Angeles. From then on, Muñoz' erratic life would take a more well-defined course.

OPEN-SOURCE INNOVATION

Twenty years earlier, before the birth of the Google search engine, what would have been the chances that the editor of *Wired* —the most popular magazine among nerds, with a circulation of 800,000— would resign to launch a new company with a 20-year-old, recently arrived in the United States and with only a high school diploma? Very few. "But today that's very normal," wrote Anderson, one of the most enthusiastic proponents of the open-source movement on the Internet, made up of people who generally have other jobs but whose hobby is technology.

"The Web allows people to show what they can do, regardless of their education and credentials. It allows groups to form and work together easily outside of a company context, whether this involves 'jobs' or not," Anderson noted. Many of them have other jobs and contribute "for no money at all, as global volunteers in a project they believe in."[9]

After leaving *Wired* to launch 3D Robotics with Muñoz in 2012, Anderson continued to publish his technology recipes, to take advantage of the talent of technology fans around the world. Explaining his philosophy, he noted that because the company does not operate in a traditional way, hiring employees already working in the field, 3D Robotics has been able to recruit far more creative minds.

If 3D Robotics was a traditional company, "we would have a cake maker, the graphics artist working for the Brazilian ad agency, the guy who runs the Italian ambulance radio company, the retired car dealership owner, the Spaniard working for an energy company in the Canary Islands, and all the others who followed their passions into the project, even though their careers had taken them elsewhere," he explained.

"WE MANAGED TO HAVE MORE PEOPLE, MORE TALENTED"

Thanks to the collaborative innovation allowed by the open-source community, "we've got more and smarter people working for us," Anderson wrote "A social network is our common roof. Skype is 'the next cubicle.'[10]

The author added, "Why turn to the person who happens to be in the next office, who may or may not be the best person for the job, when it's just as easy to turn to an online community member from a global marketplace of talent?"[11]

Anderson argues that traditional companies "are full of bureaucracy, procedures and approval processes, a structure designed to defend the integrity of the organization. (Internet) communities, on the other hand, form around shared interests and needs, and have no more process than they require. The community exists for the project, not to support the company in which the project resides." [12]

Despite Anderson's philosophy of not hiring people based on their university degrees, Muñoz did not settle for a high school degree. At the age of 25, as CEO of 3D Robotics and despite the demands of running a major company and maintaining two families —he had separated

93

from Priscilla and was living in San Diego with a former girlfriend from Mexico, who had just given birth to another boy— Muñoz started online studies at DeVry University to get his engineering degree.

When I invited Muñoz to my program, *Oppenheimer Presenta,* on CNN en Español, for a 2013 program on drones, I asked several questions about his amazing career, which the young man responded with grace and modesty. But there was one question I did not ask during the program, but which I had thought about during our previous chats. Why was he continuing to study, if he was already the CEO of a major company?

His father, Dr. Muñoz Esteves had told me that from the time Jordi was a child, he had always insisted the boy get a university degree. "One time, when I scolded him for leaving his studies, he told me, 'Talent without a degree is worth more than a degree without talent,'" the father recalled. Despite this ingenious reply, however, Jordi had not abandoned the idea of finishing his studies. Was he doing it just to please his father? Why was he studying, in an online university that's not among the most prestigious in the United States, when he had enormous responsibilities at the head of a large company and with two families to maintain?

"I study for several reasons, among them because not having a career like my parents might make me feel inferior, and because a career gives you more peace of mind. You never know. 3D Robotics could go down the tubes, and a little piece of paper may give me slightly better opportunities to carry on," Muñoz told me. "But the most important thing is that if you want to go far, it's critical to have a solid foundation. When I started my company, I realized that some of the engineering problems took me three times longer than necessary to solve because I did not have the proper training. The university gives you knowledge already 'digested,' and that's a great help."[13]

WILL 3D ROBOTICS SURVIVE?

After hearing the history of 3D Robotics, I had to ask myself whether the company would be able to continue participating in the open-source community, and at the same time remain a profitable enterprise. Isn't it too romantic to believe that a company can prosper if it reveals all its secrets? Perhaps that kind of management philosophy is understandable in the case of chef Gastón Acurio, whose decision to share his recipes helped to promote Peruvian cuisine. But that's harder to accept in the field of technology.

If 3D Robotics continues to post on the Internet all its new technologies for unmanned aircraft, won't they be copied in China in a matter of hours and put on the market much faster and at much lower prices? Of course, Anderson notes. And that's already happening. But, loyal to his almost religious faith in the virtues of open-source innovation, he points out several factors which make him confident that his company can continue to benefit from the open-source community and at the same time remain profitable.

"A product that has been created in an open innovation environment does not have the same legal protections as a patented invention. But one can argue that it has a better chance of becoming a commercial success," Anderson argues. "Odds are that it was invented faster, better and more cheaply than it would have been if it had been created in secret."[14]

"WE HAVE FREE INNOVATION AND DEVELOPMENT"

By receiving contributions from volunteers around the world, instead of limiting itself to the engineer in the next cubicle, 3D Robotics saves hundreds of thousands of dollars per year in the research and development of new products, Anderson argues. While a traditional technology company spends a fortune in teams of engineers in their innovation departments, companies in open innovation communities get their ideas free of charge.

"By day our volunteers are leading professionals in their own fields —the sort that would have been impossible to hire away," Anderson says. "But by night they follow their passions and do great work for us as volunteers. They do it because we're collectively making something they both want for themselves and want to be a part of, and because it's open-source, they know that it will reach more people and attract more talent, creating a virtuous cycle that accelerates the innovation process."[15]

At the same time, the participants in the projects have become preachers for the cause. That means companies like 3D Robotics, aside from counting on engineers who collaborate as volunteers, also have free access to quality control and marketing "departments." "Any product that can build a community before launch has already proven itself in a way that few patents can match," Anderson noted.[16]

In some cases, like Jordi Muñoz when he began to collaborate with his blog, Anderson rewards the most valuable members of his community of volunteers with $500 checks. In other cases, 3D Robotics rewards its outstanding contributors with options to buy preferred shares in the company, Anderson said. In many other cases, the volunteers are successful professionals who do not want checks, believing that would only add to the costs of the product and run against the basic principle of the open-source community: to create products for the largest number of people possible and at the lowest prices.

HOW TO AVOID PIRACY

But if the process of innovation is shared on the Internet, how can one prevent the products from being immediately pirated? According to Anderson, he doesn't lose any sleep over that risk because 3D Robotics —and other companies that publish on the Internet how they make their products— generally have several advantages over the pirates.

First, it's difficult for someone in China or anywhere else to produce cheaper drones, Anderson argues. "If someone else decides to use our files, make no significant modifications or improvements and just manufacture them and compete with us, they'll have to do it much more cheaply than we can to get traction in the marketplace," Anderson wrote. "But the reality is that this is unlikely. Our products are already

JORDI MUÑOZ AND THE "MAKERS" MOVEMENT

very cheap, and the robots we use for manufacturing are the same ones they use in China, at the same price."[17]

Second, there's the issue of technical support. According to Anderson, "our community is our competitive advantage; they provide most of the customer support, in the form of discussion forums and blog tutorials... If you bought your board from a Chinese cloner on eBay, and it's not working, the community is unlikely to help —it's seen as not supporting the team that created the product in the first place."[18]

And third, there's a key element that 3D Robotics does not share with others: its protected trademark. "Clones can't use the same name. The only intellectual property that we protect is our trademarks, so if people want to make the same boards, they'll have to call them something else," Anderson noted.[16] It's true than an industrial pirate can manufacture the same platform for controlling drones and market it as being "compatible" with 3D Robotics products, but he cannot legally sell it as a 3D Robotics product or use the same logo. "It's a great way to maintain some commercial control while still being committed to the core principles of open source," he added.[19]

DRONES THAT DROP BEER WITH PARACHUTES

If 3D Robotics lacks anything, it's not competition. Not a week goes by without a competitor starting out somewhere in the world, in part due to the company's practice as an open-source innovation company that publishes its secrets on the Internet. While the United States, Israel and some European countries dominate the much larger industry for military drones, there are dozens of commercial drone factories in Latin America, Asia and Africa.

In Northam, South Africa, a drone company surprised the crowd at the Oppikoppi music festival in late 2013 by dropping plastic glasses of beer with parachutes from one of its unmanned aircraft. In Japan, Argentina, Peru, Chile and several other Latin American countries, companies are manufacturing drones to monitor farmlands, conduct archaeological surveys and preserve various species of jungle animals.

Other entrepreneurs have started to make drones for rescue operations in ski areas or natural disasters such as forest fires, where the use of manned helicopters to search for missing people would be impossible or dangerous and costly. In these cases, unmanned aircraft can fly over vast tracts of land and search for missing people with heat detectors, report their location and assist with their rescue.

At the end of 2013, the civilian drone industry went into a frenzy after the U.S. government issued the first two early approvals for commercial unmanned aircraft —the PUMA drone for monitoring oil spills and endangered species in Alaska, and the Scan Eagle X200 for use by the oil industry to monitor the movements of icebergs and whales in the Arctic— long before it was to publish the general regulations for the industry, scheduled for 2015.

Overnight, headlines proclaimed an imminent invasion by civilian-use drones. Virtually all the reports mentioned a popular YouTube video of a drone that delivered Domino's Pizza, the "Domi-Copter." Teal Group, an aerospace industry consulting company, forecast that annual sales of drones around the world would hit $11.4 billion in 2022. And the Association for Unmanned Vehicle Systems International (AUSI) predicted that drones could add $80 billion a year to the U.S. economy alone in the next decade, including the purchase of inputs and associated services.[20]

DRONES THAT DELIVER PACKAGES

Jeff Bezos, founder of Amazon.com, has announced that his new company, Amazon Prime Air, will be one of the first to use drones to regularly deliver packages to homes in just 30 minutes. "I know it sounds like science fiction, but it's not," Bezos told the CBS program *60 Minutes* in 2013.

Showing a video of a mini drone with eight electric motors and propellers that delivered a yellow box to a home, Bezos explained that his company could make deliveries from its warehouses to any home within 16 kilometers in just 30 minutes. "We will be able to deliver boxes of up to 5 pounds, which are 86 percent of the packages we transport. In urban areas, we will be able to cover a significant part of the population," he said. "It's good for the environment, better than trucks," he added, because the drones use electric motors. Amazon's package-delivering drones could begin flying in 2017 or 2018, he added. "This is going to work. It will become a reality, and it will be a lot of fun."

"IT'S A PROBLEM IF A DRONE HITS YOUR HEAD"

Technically, there's nothing to stop drones from starting to deliver pizzas, beer or medicines today, according to experts. The only obstacles blocking their even faster spread are legal, the fears about their safety and their possible use to violate the privacy of people.

"The principal problem with drones are the regulations, because there must be a guarantee that a robot that weighs three or four kilograms (6.6 to 8.8 pounds) does not crash into a house or a person," said Raúl Rojas González, a professor of computer and math sciences at the Freie Universität Berlin. He heads a team developing self-driving cars, drones and other experimental robots that have won several international prizes. "What we need, then, is the technology development to guarantee that the equipment is reliable," he told me."[21]

Rojas, whose team posted a YouTube video of a drone delivering a pizza long before the Domino's version became popular, added that authorizing drones to watch whale migrations in the Arctic or monitor farmlands is relatively simple because those tasks do not pose many safety problems. "But the issue of drones delivering pizzas or medicines is more complicated," he explained. Others are equally concerned about the threats to our privacy when the skies are full of drones. What husband is going to like it when a drone takes photos of his wife, sunbathing topless around their pool, the critics ask. Worse still, who's going to like it when drones with infrared cameras take photos of what's taking place *inside* our very homes, although that's already outlawed in many countries. Industry spokesmen answer that today, anyone can take a photo of a neighbor's pool by using a smartphone attached to a broomstick. The use of infrared photos is just around the corner. But privacy activists argue that unless the drones are properly regulated, not just governments but also our professional rivals and personal enemies will be able to sneak into our bedrooms.

"The stuff about drones that deliver pizza is marvelous, but that's the pretty side of the drones," I was told by John de Leon, a civil rights lawyer and former head of the Greater Miami American Civil Liberties Union. "There is a much uglier and much more dangerous face. We don't want to live in a country or a world where the police are monitoring us everywhere, 24 hours a day."[22]

THE CROWDFUNDING REVOLUTION

Anderson, the co-founder with Muñoz of 3D Robotics, is convinced there's a new world of possibilities for innovators because, aside from the open sources that allow everyone to know everything —or almost everything— new sources of financing for inventors are emerging. Until recently, you could be very innovative but it was difficult to access the financing required to turn a project into reality. But now, thanks to Kickstarter and other Internet sites dedicated to raising funds for new projects through contributions from large groups of small investors —popularly known as crowdfunding— the resources are within reach of everyone. Internet crowdfunding sites raised about $1.5 billion a year from small contributors in 2014 and were projected to raise $3 billion in 2014, according to a report by the Deloitte consulting company.

Kickstarter has revolutionized the world of innovation, Anderson argues. Through crowdfunding, or collective investments, small-time innovators who don't have access to big-time investors can publish their ideas on Kickstarter or other portals and sell their products before they actually hit the market. The investors are not buying part of the company, as traditional investors do. They are simply buying one or more copies of the final product. And if for any reason the project does not get off the ground, they get their money back. The concept is not much different from making reservations for a music concert or a hotel. You prepay with a credit card, but if the concert or the trip are canceled, you get your money back.

It's no accident that Kickstarter was born in 2009 as an Internet portal designed for the music and arts industry. One of its founders was Perry Chen, a young New York City musician and disk jockey. A few years before, Chen had tried to organize a big rock concert with some of the world's most famous DJs, but could not raise the $15,000 needed to launch the project. Chen canceled the concert, but started to think about how to overcome the lack of investors that was holding back musicians and concert organizers. Chen later moved to Brooklyn, New York, and was working as a waiter when he mentioned his idea about raising funds in advance to another young man who regularly had breakfast at his restaurant. The idea would have been difficult to execute in the past, but it was easy thanks to the Internet, Chen explained. The other young man, Yancey Stickler, liked the idea and shortly afterward the two launched Kickstarter.com.

Four years later, Kickstarter was promoting itself as "the world's largest platform for creative projects." It had already launched 108,000 inventions into the market and raised a total of $717 million, with a success rate of 44 percent for the projects listed, according to company reports. Among the successful Kickstarter projects were a new movie by Spike Lee, famed director of *Malcolm X,* who reached his goal of raising $1.3 million, and the Pebble Smart watch, which alerts us when we receive an e-mail, identifies the sender and displays the subject. We can then decide if the message is urgent or can wait, without having to constantly check our cell phones. The Pebble Smart watch hit the market at a lower price than a similar watch by Sony —and outsold it.

Pebble Smart was born with a promotional video that asked for $100,000 to start commercial production of the watch. To the surprise of its creators, the pitch reached its goal in just two hours. At the end of the first day, it had raised $1 million, and before the month was out it had received $10 million and pre-sold 85,000 watches.

"What was particularly interesting about the Pebble Kickstarter phenomenon was how the design team responded to the crowd of customers," Anderson noted in his book.[23] The contributors wanted the watch to be waterproof for swimming and to have a longer battery life. Those and other requested modifications were taken into consideration before the manufacturing started. The result was "a superior model: a small team using crowdfunding to move more quickly in all ways —R&D, finance and marketing— than a lumbering electronics giant," he added.[24]

CROWDFUNDING AND THE "MAKERS": GROWING PHENOMENONS

Dozens of other Internet sites dedicated to crowdfunding soon emerged for all types of projects, from high technology to real estate ventures. Other sites emerged around the same time, such as Quirky, which gathers opinions on how to create or improve a product, and Etsy, a site launched in 2005, before Kickstarter, to sell artisan products such as purses, jewelry and works of art. By 2012, Etsy already had 300 employees and was reporting sales of $65 million per month. Thanks to these and other sites, inventors today have many more opportunities for turning their ideas into reality.

Stories like the ones about the creators of the Pebble Smart watch or Muñoz, the unemployed young man who wound up heading 3D Robotics, are more common each day. In the era of innovation, thanks to open-source companies and financing through crowdfunding, the opportunities for launching new projects have grown more democratic. Growing numbers of people all over the world have the possibility of turning their creative projects into reality. And they are increasingly sharing, instead of competing with each other.

In 2014, Muñoz' drone company raised $35 million in venture capital, reported $20 million in income and predicted it would triple its revenues in 2015. Muñoz was already a young millionaire, at least on paper. When I last interviewed him, one year after our first meeting, his company already had manufacturing plants in San Diego and Tijuana, and he had just bought a smaller company in Austin, Texas. His company had launched a new civilian drone, the Iris, priced at $700 and aimed at photographers and reporters who want views from the sky, as well as architects and engineers who need airborne views of their projects. "We continue to be 'makers' and to publish all our software and diagrams for our unmanned helicopters. But our new business model will be to produce more sophisticated programs that will not be open-sourced," Muñoz told me.[25]

Muñoz also had finished his online engineering studies —he needed only to finish his thesis, and hoped to graduate in four months— and was already planning to retire as CEO and focus more on what always attracted him, innovation. "I want to be the company's chief of innovation, and have a little fun," he told me, adding that his job as CEO required him to spend almost all his time on administration and business matters.

As I said goodbye to Muñoz, I could not stop thinking about the large number of young innovators in Silicon Valley who "retire" before they hit 30, to have fun with new projects. Hopefully, his story can be another source of inspiration for the thousands of other "makers" helping each other across the world to turn their collaborative projects into reality.

4

Bre Pettis and the new Industrial Revolution

"3D printers will change everything"

The 3D printers that many predict will revolutionize the world are the perfect example of how the world's major innovations are usually the result of gradual, collaborative and often boring efforts and not —as many believe— the result of some "eureka" moment by a solitary genius. The 3D printers are nothing new, although President Obama put them in the spotlight when he started to talk about them in 2013. The printers, capable of reproducing three-dimensional objects, had been invented in 1986 by U.S. engineer Charles "Chuck" Hull and others working in parallel on similar technologies. Today, after many improvements, they are emerging as one of the innovations that will have the biggest impact on the global economy and our homes.

Many economists predict that 3D printers will spark an Industrial Revolution, much like the steam engine, which sparked the industrial production at the start of the 19th Century, and the personal computer, which transformed the world at the end of the 20th Century. 3D printers could soon eclipse mass production as we know it today and replace it with the customized production of items manufactured in our own homes. Many predict that the watchword for future companies will increasingly be "export the design, not the product," because we will download designs to our personal computers and produce our own goods —including shoes, clothes and dishes— in our homes, using whatever parts, colors and materials we desire.

And just as Steve Jobs made history as the pioneer of personal computers, it's likely that Bre Pettis will make history as the man who popularized the personal 3D printers. When Chuck Hull was starting out, 3D printers were huge things that sometimes filled entire rooms, like computers before the birth of personal computers. It was Pettis who started to produce smaller and cheaper 3D printers in a New York City workshop, with some friends who came out of the "makers" movement, and who later commercialized printers under the brand name MakerBot.

FROM SCHOOL TEACHER TO MOGUL

Pettis was a high school teacher who reinvented himself as a 3D printer entrepreneur. Barely six years after he quit his teacher's job and dedicated himself full time to his project, he sold his company for $604 million in 2013. His formula was to compete with companies that sold industrial 3D printers for more than $100,000 per unit, by producing personal, more rudimentary printers that sold for $1,500.

It took me six months to get an interview with Pettis. Only afterward did his media director explain the delay: the creator of MakerBot had been in secret negotiations that had just ended with the company's sale to Stratasys, one of the leading makers of industrial 3D printers. Stratasys at the same time had merged with the Israeli company Objet. The director told me Pettis had not wanted to give interviews until the negotiations were done and the sales contract was signed. But when I traveled to New York to interview Pettis, I figured out there was probably another reason for the delay. The new millionaire was an introvert, like many nerds, and froze in front of my video camera. Clearly, he did not much like to talk to journalists. He was visibly nervous when he welcomed me and my cameraman to his new office. And my interview could hardly have started on a worst note.

"I DON'T LIKE IT WHEN YOU CALL ME A MILLIONAIRE"

The new offices of MakerBot were in chaos. The company had just moved to new headquarters in Brooklyn, a few minutes from Manhattan by subway. The new offices were not finished, so dozens of young employees in jeans were working in hallways and even the lobby. In the few weeks since the company had been sold, its staff had tripled to about 320 people, but even then it was clear it needed more. Since President Barack Obama had mentioned 3D printers as the industry of the future in his State of the Union Address, and after the sale of MakerBot to Stratasys was announced, MakerBot and its personal 3D printers had become a focus of world attention. The media director told me she could not keep up with all the visitors who arrived from all over the world to see the industry of the future with their own eyes.

Aside from the general chaos in the offices, there were some interesting details. Pettis, a fan of science fiction TV programs, had put in the lobby a telephone cabin that I later learned was a replica of the time-travel machine in *Dr. Who*, a very popular BBC TV series. The idea was to signal that when you entered MakerBot's offices, you were entering a new dimension. Walking to Pettis' office, we passed several conference rooms with names taken from *Star Wars* movies, such as Millennium Falcon and Cloud City. At the end of the hallway, Pettis' office was a small room, the same size as the adjoining offices, with street views and full of objects produced by 3D printers.

Pettis was expecting us, and stood to greet us when I came in with a cameraman. He was tall, with a thick mane of unruly gray hair and triangular sideburns reminiscent of the 19th Century. He was dressed in black jeans, a black shirt and a black t-shirt under the shirt. He also wore thick black glasses, which added to his nerdy look. He looked like a teenage beanpole, with averted gazes and somewhat clumsy movements. After the introductions we sat down —he behind his desk— and I started out with a question that I thought —very wrongly, it turned out— would put him more at ease before the CNN en Español cameras.

106

"Let's start with your success story," I told him. "How does one go from school teacher to multimillionaire in just six years?"

To my surprise, he jumped back, visibly upset. He immediately asked the cameraman to stop and start again. Addressing me, and still clearly upset, he said, "I would not ask the question that way! I don't like it when you call me a multimillionaire! If you have to ask that question, ask me how I went from school teacher to CEO of MakerBot." When he saw that I was somewhere between stunned and amused, he continued his broadside. "How would you like it if someone called you a multimillionaire?" he asked. I shrugged my shoulders and smiled, sort of saying, "No danger of that, because I'm not one." Pettis went on: "Well, I don't like to be portrayed like that!" Pettis, like many other technology innovators, was very different from banking and industrial moguls like Donald Trump, who take offense if they are not described as billionaires. For Pettis, his main achievement was being an innovator, not a millionaire.

I decided it was a question worth pursuing, and asked it again in the words he preferred. How did he manage to go from school teacher to the head of MakerBot in just six years? Pettis took a deep breath and replied. "Well, I could not be a CEO if I had not been a school teacher. When you teach, you learn a lot about how to organize people and how to make things work. You have no budget. There are few resources, so you have to be super-ingenious. I was a middle-school teacher, with 11, 12 and 13 year old students, so there's a lot to be learned about management. That's how I learned a lot from teaching about being president of a company," he said.[1] Pettis then went on to tell me his story.

"AS A BOY I WANTED TO BE ABLE TO FIX ANYTHING"

From his childhood in Ithaca, in upstate New York, Pettis wanted to be a car mechanic. "I wanted to have all the tools, because I wanted to be able to fix anything," he said. "I had my first experience with innovation when I was seven or eight years old, when I fixed a broken bicycle. My uncle had shown me how a bike worked, and when it broke, I knew how to fix it. And that made me very happy. It was broken, and I was sad. I fixed it, and I was happy".[2]

"I was also a computer nerd," he added. "I was one of the first kids on the block to have a computer. My family had a software company in the early 1980, which gave me an advantage in many ways because I knew about computing at the start of the decade, when most people thought that having a computer was not a necessity."[3]

Pettis was a mediocre student in school. "I was not a good student. As a child, I wanted to learn things, but not necessarily the things taught in school. For a long time, I spent nights reading books and then fell asleep in class," he recalled. His family moved to Seattle when Pettis was a teenager. Pettis finished high school there, enrolled in Evergreen State College and studied psychology, mythology and scenic arts. "When I went to the university, I decided to study whatever I wanted. I followed my heart. I studied history, education, ethnomusicology, scenic arts, psychology, mythology, everything that was interesting to me," he said. He was not thinking much about job options when it came to his classes, Pettis added.

After graduating, Pettis got his first job as a production assistant in Jim Henson's Creature Shop, the puppet and visual effects company known around the world as the creators of Elmo and other characters in the *Sesame Street* television series and Miss Piggy in *The Muppets*. Pettis started out as an assistant in a company studio that made robots for movies. "I learned a lot there. One of the things you learn when you work on a film set is that you can work 16 to 18 hours a day, seven days a week, for a long time," he recalled. That pace of work produced adrenaline and a state of excitement that made him much more creative. There were no weekends, no work weeks. In the film industry, you have to meet your deadlines, and there's no time to relax. "The show must go on," he said, adding that he would later incorporate that manic pace of work into his own projects.

As an employee of the movie studios of Jim Henson's Creature Shop, Pettis was sent to work in a number of movies in London, Prague,

Los Angeles and other places around the world. "When I returned to my home in Seattle, I realized I missed it a lot," he recalled. At the age of 27, tired of so much travel, Pettis decided to get a teaching certificate and teach art at the high school level. He had always liked to work with young people, and his experience in the movie industry would make him an excellent hire for any school.

For the next few years, Pettis earned his living teaching in a Seattle public school. But he was restless, and soon began to produce videos for his students. "I realized that they paid more attention if they saw me on television than in person. So I started making videos and posting them on the Internet," he said. And after a while, his educational videos —showing how to make all sorts of things, from books with secret compartments to paper dolls and photographic cameras— were being watched by many more people than just his students.

Pettis became an active member of the "makers" movement, innovators who —like drone pioneers Chris Anderson and Jordi Muñoz and many others— created things collectively, sharing all their secrets on the Internet and nurturing each other with their respective discoveries. After a few years, Pettis was supplementing his teacher's salary by publishing his videos on the Web pages of one of the movement's main digital publications, *Make Magazine,* and eventually left his teacher's job to work full time on the Web videos.

FROM EDUCATIONAL VIDEOS TO 3D PRINTERS

In 2007, when he was 33 years old and living off the weekly Internet videos for *Make Magazine,* he visited New York City and decided to move there. "I came for a month. I figured, 'I am going to meet interesting people in New York and make videos with them.' I thought that I could go on later to Tokyo, Paris or Mexico City. But when I got to New York, I realized there was great energy here," he recalled. "People come here to do things. It's not an easy place, not a very relaxing place. But if you want to do something, it's an ideal place."

How did you go from making online educational videos to making 3D printers?, I asked him.

"When I moved to New York, I did not have a group of friends who owned tools and wanted to do things together. I needed a workshop, and I wanted to be able to do anything. So I recruited the smartest people I knew in New York and we started NYC Resistor, a kind of club for hardware nerds, or gadget nerds," he said. "I met all kinds of people there, including the people with whom I later founded MakerBot."

Where did you meet?

"We rented a place a few blocks from here. We shared the rent. Each of us put up $1,000, and that paid the rent for a couple of months. That's how we started out. In most countries, people have a garage or a basement, a workshop or some place to work. But there's not a lot of space in New York," Pettis said.

And what did you do there?

"We all brought our tools and our equipment, and we shared them. We could do anything, because we had the tools and the knowledge," he added.

But how did the idea of the personal 3D printers came up?, I asked. When you found the workshop, and put up $1,000 apiece to pay the rent, did you already have the idea of making 3D printers?

"No. The idea was to have a workshop."

Without knowing what you were going to do with it?

"We were all doing a lot of things, in our own sections."

So it was kind of a hobby, just getting together for fun?

"No. We were creating so much potential energy that something had to happen… The idea was to build the potential energy, so that something would emerge from it."

I confessed to Pettis that I was confused.

You met with your friends and told them, "Let's rent a space and do something," without any sort of specific goal?

"Yes," he replied, shrugging his shoulders as if that was the most natural thing in the world. "You get together with other people to develop ideas, to generate energy. And that's how, by swapping ideas and projects, we decided to make a device that could make anything —a 3D printer."

"3D PRINTERS WERE THE SIZE OF REFRIGERATORS"

Pettis told me that the idea of making a personal 3D printer came up in the workshop when he and other "makers" decided to buy one of the available printers to make their own objects, but realized they could not afford it. "At that time, 3D printers were industrial machines, the size of refrigerators or bigger. They cost $100,000. Obviously, we didn't have the money to buy one. But we wanted one. So, if you're a "maker" and you want something but you don't have the money to buy it, you make it yourself," he recalled. "We tried, tried and tried, doing and undoing" until —with the help of the Internet community active in the "makers" movement— they managed to produce the first low-cost 3D printer for personal use.

In 2009, four years after they opened the workshop, Pettis and his partners founded MakerBot with $75,000 invested by friends and relatives. In principle, the idea was to make printers so that everyone —and especially "makers" like themselves— could make anything they wanted. Along the way, they discovered that architects, engineers and designers also could use the small printers to make scale models much more quickly and for a lot less money.

Until then, an architect who wanted scale models of his or her project sent the plans to companies in Singapore, Taiwan or Japan, which had to make a mold, build the model and ship it back —a process that took weeks and could cost up to $5,000. With the new 3D printers, the same architects could make the model in their offices in a few hours. And if they did not like the results, they could change them many times in the same day for less than $10 per copy— the cost of the plastic used by the printers.

"We innovated so that other people can innovate," Pettis told me. "We make machines that motivate people to be creative. At the business level, that means that if you wanted to design something, if you wanted

111

to make something, if you wanted to create something, you needed a lot of capital and labor to make a prototype. It was very expensive. With a MakerBot, it's much more accessible. You can make a prototype, which used to take a month or more, in just a couple of hours. You don't have to send it by mail, wait for it to be returned, find out that it wasn't done right and send it back. Now you can make several copies each day. What's more, in the business world that means that products can be created much faster, that mistakes can be corrected much more quickly and therefore that better products can be developed."

REICHENTAL: "THIS IS AN INDUSTRIAL REVOLUTION THAT WILL CHANGE EVERYTHING"

Although Pettis and his MakerBot printers were generating headlines around the world because of their low cost and availability to millions of people, the companies making the most important 3D printers as I write these lines are the ones that make industrial versions for the aerospace, auto and manufacturing industries. And among them, the biggest is 3D Systems —no relation to 3D Robotics, the commercial drone company run by the young Mexican Jordi Muñoz. 3D Systems was founded three decades ago by Chuck Hull, the inventor of the 3D printing technology, and the company is currently headed by Abraham Reichental.

Reichental is an Israeli who served as a helicopter mechanic in the Israeli Defense Force before moving to the United States at the age of 24. Before he was recruited by 3D Systems, he was an executive in a leading packaged food company. When I interviewed him in mid-2013, 3D Systems was launching its own home 3D printer to compete with MakerBot. I interviewed him for CNN via satellite from Tel Aviv —he was on a business trip— and it was obvious to me from the start that he had a more global view than Pettis about the future of the 3D printer, because of his experience working for big multinational companies.

According to Reichental, 3D printers "will bring with them a new Industrial Revolution that will change everything".[4] Among other things, they will change the way we develop and manufacture goods, he explained. NASA is already using 3D printers in space to make replacements for broken spacecraft parts, and the aeronautical industry is using them to quickly replace broken parts instead of having to order them from a far-away manufacturer and wait weeks to receive them, he added.

Cargo and cruise ships, which today must carry all sorts of replacement parts and sometimes wind up stranded for months in port while waiting to receive the right spare parts, will be able to significantly cut their costs with 3D printers. Just put one aboard and they will reproduce the broken parts immediately. "We will increasingly see big companies, like General Electric and others, starting to use 3D printers to make replacement parts for airplane engines, power generators and medical equipment," Reichental predicted.

In the medical field, 3D printers are increasingly producing personalized titanium prosthesis for knee and hip replacements, and hearing aids made to the measure of each person's ear canals, he added. The prosthesis, which have been mostly produced in generic sizes that could lead to all sorts of problems and discomfort, can now be produced to the exact size required by each individual.

"And that's only the beginning of what's coming," Reichental added. "Clothes, shoes and jewelry are already being made with 3D printers. And within the next three to five years we will see food made in 3D printers, for its nutritional value as well as for special uses. I am a chocolate fanatic, for example, and I want to produce chocolates with 3D printers. I am also interested in developing 3D printers that can increase the nutritional value of the food produced —that can follow the list of the nutrients you want to put into your product. Printing in 3D will be not just creating food in a specific geometric form, but giving it a specific nutritional value. And the next step will be to produce smart and functional items."

Please forgive my ignorance, I told him, but I don't understand how it will be possible to print our clothes, our shoes, our jewelry in our homes. How will that work? How will we have access to the materials used by a 3D printer to make a shirt or a pair of shoes at home?

"Well, some of the materials will be bought together with the printers. We already offer a 3D printer at $1,300 that fits on your desk and comes with cartridges of materials very similar to the ink cartridges you now buy for your two-dimensional printers," he said. "We already have more than 100 materials available, including real nylon, adapted plastics, totally dense and chemically pure metals, materials similar to rubber and others similar to wax. Consumers will be able to buy the appropriate cartridge for their needs. You will opt to print some things in your home, and you also will be able to print others through our cloud printing service."

How does cloud printing work?

"Well, we already have 10 locales around the world where you can send the design of what you want to print. We immediately send you a price estimate and later deliver the product to your home. And that's the start of a constellation of Internet spots that will complement the possibility of producing things on our desktops or our neighborhoods. And I also believe this will be the start of new ecosystems and totally new business models. Because people for the first time will have the power to make millions of unique and customized items. And that's very transformative", Reichental added.

3D PRINTERS IN THE CORNER STORE

Reichental and other industry leaders say that we will soon begin to see 3D print stores in our shopping centers, where we will be able to print objects that we can't print at home. For example, if we want to print a shirt and our home 3D printer does not have cloth, we will have it printed in the nearest 3D store. "The local 3D print shop will one day be where you pick up your customized, locally manufactured products, just like you pick up your printed photos at the nearest Walmart today," according to a *Forbes* magazine report.[5]

The spread of these shops and home 3D printers also will spark a new worldwide battle over intellectual property, because many people will be copying trademarked products without paying the required royalties, *Forbes* added. Piracy of intellectual property will be one of the top issues in coming decades. In the same way the Internet at one time saw the spread of sites where people could download music without paying, there will be Internet sites for downloading designs and printing goods without paying royalties. This "will ignite a new wave of intellectual property issues," the magazine added.[6]

COUNTRIES WILL HAVE TO RETHINK THEIR ECONOMIC STRUCTURE

This "new Industrial Revolution" of 3D printers will not happen overnight, Reichental told me, but rather will be a gradual process that will take years. At the beginning, we will see a hybrid process, in which manufacturing companies will use 3D printers as a complement, to make their operations more efficient. And little by little, as the 3D printers improve and new materials are developed, the new technology will replace the old one.

"Clearly, this is a disruptive, high-impact and transformative technology. So first we will see a certain integration of this technology with traditional production methods. Something like what is being done already by companies like General Electric, which is integrating this technology into its manufacturing of airplane engines. And later we will see a hybrid process, a fusion of the traditional manufacturing industry with 3D printing," he said.

And still later? Do you believe that customized production in 3D printers will replace manufactured production?, I asked.

"I believe that although we will see a hybrid process at the start, this technology will surely disrupt the traditional manufacturing industry, in the sense that you will not have to go to another country to produce an item, because you will be able to make it somewhere much closer to the consumer," Reichental answered. "That means the supply chains will change, and the time of delivery to consumers will change. And that also means that the businesses that adopt this technology will have a comparative advantage, by being able to put their products on the market much faster than companies that depend on traditional supply chains."

How much time do you think that will take?

"This will happen at the same exponentially faster pace that other technologies have changed other things. That means that, for a long time, this process will seem like a lineal progression. And at some point we will see a shocking jump. And people will look at each other with amazement and ask, 'How did we not notice this was happening?'" he said. "I'll give you an example. In 2012, fully 72 percent of Apple's revenues came from products that did not even exist five years before. That's the impact of disruptive technologies and the same thing will happen with 3D printers."

What will happen in countries that depend on manufacturing, like China or Mexico. Will they collapse?

"I don't really believe that. I think the Chinese government and industry are very aware of the disruptive impact of 3D printers, and are up to date on what's being published on the issue. The Chinese government is closely following what the Obama administration is doing with its 3D manufacturing initiative. In my judgment, China is reacting even faster and putting more resources in that direction, because it knows the power of this technology and its possibilities for providing significant competitive advantages to the country or industry that adopts it," Reichental added. "So I don't believe that China or Mexico will go broke. What I do believe is that many leading countries will have to reinvent their business models and rethink their economic structure in order to have a hold on to a competitive advantage."

Specifically, Reichental recommended that Latin American countries should "launch a major initiative, at the national level, to move the manufacture of products" to new locales and "put all their energy into developing new business models that can take advantage of 3D printing." To start, he added, they will have to improve the training and education about the 3D printers, creating training centers in industrial regions and providing 3D printers to schools.

"What you will see then is the same phenomenon that we saw with fixed-line telephones and cellular phones: many countries that did not have a (good) fixed telephone infrastructure managed to jump directly to cell phones and assimilate the changes without any problems. They jumped over a technology they did not have, to adopt a new one. The same thing could happen in Mexico and other Latin American countries, if they make those small investments today," he added.

Of course, the simple purchase of 3D printers for schools, like the purchase of cell phones or school laptops, will not guarantee technological development. Although Reichental, Pettis and other industry leaders are anxious to sell thousands of 3D printers to schools throughout the world, independent experts agree that the countries that will benefit the most from the new technology are those that produce the best engineers, scientists, technicians and designers.

THE QUALITY OF EDUCATION: MORE IMPORTANT THAN EVER

Vivek Wadhwa, the innovation expert at Singularity University who served as my guide during one of my visits to Silicon Valley, summed it up this way: "The quality of education in Latin America will be more important than ever. It's not a matter of people knowing how to use a computer to send an e-mail, but knowing how to design or build products, which is much more difficult. That requires a knowledge of math, engineering and even English, to be able to interact with other parts of the world."[7]

The whole world, and not just Latin America, will be forced to change the content of their education systems, Wadhwa added. In the era of Google and free Internet encyclopedias, it no longer makes sense that schools grade students based on memorization or the accumulation of knowledge. Today, it is equally or more important that students learn how to think, to be creative, to solve problems and build on the knowledge of others. And, as we move deeper into the era of 3D printers, where "the design, more than the product" will be on sale, creative minds will be more and more in demand.

Asked about this, Reichental told me that manufacturing countries must provide a better education "and start to align the demand for qualified workers with the education programs. Because the majority of the world's countries today have a gap between those two things."

WILL GLOBAL UNEMPLOYMENT INCREASE?

As I listened to Reichental during our interview, I could not stop thinking about the social consequences of the new Industrial Revolution that the president of 3D Systems was describing with so much enthusiasm. If we're moving toward a world where home production with 3D printers largely replaces industrial production, what will happen to today's factory jobs? What will happen in the transportation industry? What will happen to the warehouses where companies now store their merchandise. Are we moving toward a future of higher unemployment?

"That's an excellent question," Reichental said. "I believe there's nothing that can revive the traditional manufacturing jobs in the United States. We all know that the traditional manufacturing jobs here and in other countries will not come back. We live in a time of ever-faster changes, in which the combination of robotics, sensors and mobile devices, as well as 3D printing and artificial intelligence, will generate production models that are very different. These new production environments will require different skill sets, different types of training and fewer workers. There will be less intensive labor and more intelligent automation."

Other admirers of the 3D printers' new Industrial Revolution, like Wadhwa, share the optimistic notion that in the future we will work increasingly fewer hours and yet earn increasingly higher salaries. "There will be a lot of new types of jobs, and people will work less and less, as has been happening for centuries," Wadhwa said. "For centuries, people worked 90 hours a week in farms. Now they work 40 hours a week in industry, and 20 years from now they will work 30 hours a week. And that will be good, because we will be working at quality, knowledge-based jobs instead of the tedious, boring and repetitive jobs in today's factories." As for the current factory jobs, Wadhwa said, "Those jobs are not worth protecting."

The forecasts by Reichental, Wadhwa and others that we will work less and less but in jobs more tied to the knowledge economy, while robots and 3D printers perform the repetitive tasks of the manufacturing industries, seemed logical but disturbing to me. For countries with good educational systems, which can create increasingly sophisticated products, it will be a better world where people will have more free time to achieve personal goals. But for the countries that fall behind in the race for education, the future might be much darker.

CHUCK HULL, INVENTOR OF 3D PRINTERS

When I asked Reichental to help me arrange an interview with Hull, the inventor of the 3D printer, he warned me that Hull was a shy engineer who did not like to speak in public or appear in the mass media too much. But I insisted, because my Google searches had found little about Hull, and after a few months I managed to get a phone interview with the inventor. Dealing with technology innovators was a new experience to me. While other entrepreneurs —let's not even talk about politicians— try everything to appear in the media, Hull, Pettis and other leaders of the technology world that I interviewed for this book live in a different world, and are interested more in being recognized by their peers than the public.

Hull, born in 1939, was still vice president and director of technology at 3D Systems, the company that he founded and was now headed by Reichental. During his long career, Hull had registered more than 60 patents, including the one for the 3D printer, which he patented under the complex name of "device for producing three-dimensional objects through stereolithography." The patent explained that this was a process for adding layer upon layer of materials until they formed the desired object.

Hull graduated with degrees in engineering and physics from the University of Colorado, and worked several years for the DuPont company and later for a smaller laboratory. That's where he started to think about a device to produce three-dimensional objects. Other engineers were already experimenting with the idea, but his boss was not very enthusiastic about the project.

"It was a small company, and the president had other jobs for me. But he agreed to let me work on my project, outside regular work hours, and use the company's laboratories. In the end, it worked out well for both of us," Hull recalled. When he patented the printer, Hull shared his invention with the company and both benefited, he explained.[8]

"MY PROJECT WAS REJECTED MORE THAN A DOZEN TIMES"

But after patenting the 3D printer, like so many other inventors, Hull failed several times to obtain the financing required to manufacture and market it. At first, no one wanted to put money in the project, and the early articles about the new technology published in the specialized media were skeptical, he recalled.

"My project was rejected many times. I don't remember how many, but it certainly was more than a dozen times," he said with a big laugh. "The people we asked to invest told us the technology was not good. Who would use this device? And for what?, they asked. To make matters worse, at that time everyone was predicting that all of the world's manufacturing would move to China, so there was even less incentive to invest in this. But that always happens with technologies that are going to change the world. At first, no one recognizes them."[9]

Finally, after many failed attempts, Hull found an investor in Vancouver, Canada, who put up the capital to launch the new company and manufacture the device. For the next couple of decades, the company worked to perfect the 3D printer, which was being used primarily to produce parts for the auto industry. It was, as Hull described it, a slow and gradual process. "You don't invent something and suddenly have a big impact in a lot of areas. That's not how things work," he said. On the contrary, after inventing something, you typically have to find a commercial application for your product, round up investments, hire people and establish a company. "And when you finish doing all of this, you realize that the original invention has many limitations and you need to reinvent it. So, this is a process that never ends."[10]

AFTER THE 3D PRINTERS, 4D PRINTERS

While many of us are still trying to digest the phenomenon of the new 3D printers, some innovators already are talking about 4D printers, which will produce objects that are not only customized but can transform and adapt themselves to different circumstances. Basically, these printers of the future will be like the 3D printers but will use smart, self-healing materials, like the ones that healed the synthetic skin of the robots in the *Terminator* movies after each battle.

Although the idea may seem too ambitious, the U.S. Department of Defense decided to invest in a feasibility study of the 4D printers in 2013 and commissioned three universities —Harvard, Illinois and Pittsburgh— to collaborate on it. "Rather than construct a static material or one that simply changes its shape, we're proposing the development of adaptive, biomimetic composites that reprogram their shape, properties and functionality on demand, based upon external stimuli," said Anna C. Balazs, a chemical engineering professor at the University of Pittsburgh and principal investigator in the project.[11] Skylar Tibbits, head of the self-assembly lab at the Massachusetts Institute of Technology, caught the world's attention when he demonstrated smart materials that shrink into the shape of cubes when they come in contact with water. "Imagine if water pipes could expand or contract to change capacity or change flow rate; or maybe undulate like peristalsis to move the water themselves", he declared.[12] By manipulating materials at the most basic level, he added, these kinds of ideas are not all that crazy.

MUCH ADO ABOUT NOTHING?

For some experts, all the hoopla about the Industrial Revolution of the 3D printers is much ado about nothing. Among them is Terry Gou, president of Foxconn, the world's largest company producing electronic devices for brands like Apple, Amazon, Cisco, Dell, Google, HP, Microsoft and Nokia. Gou told reporters in Taiwan that the 3D printers are a "gimmick" whose importance has been inflated by the media. Gou was so sure of this that he said that if he's wrong, and 3D printers revolutionize industry worldwide, he will change his surname and write it backward —Uog— according to the *South China Morning Post*.

Gou —or Uog, if the 3D printers succeed— is not the only skeptic on this technology. Many others argue that 3D printers cannot produce mass quantities of complex objects such as cell phones. Furthermore, even if 3D printers are perfected to produce cell phones that work well, they would be much more expensive than phones produced by mass manufacturing methods, they add. 3D printers also cannot use materials like leather, which limits what they can produce.

Gartner Inc. a well-known consultancy that studies the technology market, estimated that the sale of home 3D printers has been growing by 40 percent per year, but that the sales started from a level so low that in 2017 only 826,000 will be sold in the entire world. According to Peter Basiliere, Gartners' director of research, 3D printers will soon be "used by a majority of companies" to produce replacement parts or specific components, but are very unlikely to turn into a mass consumption item, like personal computers, in the near future.[13]

THE FUTURE IS ALREADY HERE

But there are already many signals that 3D printers will be used widely long before the predictions of some experts, and will transform a significant part of global industry. In 2014, some of the leading computer and office supply stores in the United States, like Staples and Office Depot, were already selling 3D printers to the general public at some of their locations, next to the shelves displaying traditional printers and personal computers.

The giant delivery company UPS already has announced it will start to offer 3D printing services in its branches, in the same way it has been offering by-the-hour computer access for those who don't have a computer at home or are traveling. That means UPS will soon turn into reality the prediction that consumers will be able to create a design on their home computers and —if they don't have a 3D printer or the materials required to produce the object at home— produce it in the nearest UPS store. UPS expects that the first adopters will be artists, designers and small companies that need scale models or prototypes for their new products, but that the use of 3D printers will gradually expand to everyday consumers, company spokespersons say.[14]

Microsoft, Intel and Apple, among others, are creating new operating systems that will allow us to use 3D printers from our personal computers. And in Europe, the European Space Agency (ESA) and more than 30 private companies are establishing five pilot factories in France, Germany, Italy, Norway and the United Kingdom to manufacture 3D printers that can produce metal objects before 2017. "Up to now, 3D printers could only work with plastics, which severely limited their industrial applications," said David Jarvis, ESA's director of new materials and energy. "We have finally entered the metal age, and now we can produce components with aluminum or titanium."[15] Hilde Loken, research director at Norsk Titanium in Norway, which specializes in the 3D production of titanium parts, agreed with her U.S. competitors that "we face a world of new possibilities, comparable to the start of mass production in the 20th Century. The 21st Century revolution will consist of massive, customized and localized production," she said.[16]

If Moore's law —which holds that computing capacity doubles every two years and prices fall accordingly— really works for 3D printing technology in the same way it worked for personal computers, the techno-utopians are closer to reality than the techno-skeptics. It is a gradual innovation, which evolved over three decades and jumped into the headlines when Bre Pettis decided to leave his job as a high school teacher and make personal 3D printers in his "makers" workshop in New York City. And everything seems to indicate that it's here to stay.

5

Rafael Yuste and the brain manipulators

Long live the cooperation! Down with competition!

Among all the innovations that I mention in this book, the one that I like the best —and which perhaps will have the most positive impact on humanity— is the brain research that Spanish scientist Rafael Yuste is doing at Columbia University in New York City. Yuste is co-director of the Brain Activity Map Project, which seeks to create the first map that will allow us to see —and perhaps control— the billions of neurons in the human brain.

The project, which President Barack Obama has promised to fund with $100 million per year, includes the participation of scientists from all over the world. By unraveling how neurons interact with each other, the research could help to diagnose diseases like depression, schizophrenia and epilepsy, and then find ways to treat them by manipulating the neurons. The ability to diagram and manipulate all the brain's activity will give rise to new diagnostic methods and new therapies, according to the project's supporters.

But manipulating the neurons also poses ethical problems never before faced by humanity, and seen only in science fiction movies. Could the U.S. or any other government control the neurons of citizens to make them think in a certain way, or not think at all? Will we reach the point where governments can manipulate the human brain to create smarter or dumber or more submissive people? Or will parents be able to reprogram the brains of their babies to make them better students?

WILL GOVERNMENTS BE ABLE TO READ OUR MINDS?

When I interviewed Yuste, he already had been featured in several articles in *The New York Times, El País* of Spain, the magazine *Science* and various other international publications. The magazine *Nature* also had selected him as one of the world's top five scientists working on the most revolutionary projects. I expected to meet a scientific celebrity, perhaps bloated by so much publicity and perhaps a little impatient with people —like me— who don't understand much about neurobiology. But I met a very different person.

Arriving at Yuste's laboratory at Columbia University on a quiet rainy morning, I was a bit worried that he would not react well to my questions on whether his project posed a danger to humanity. Yuste, who had just turned 50, greeted me with a broad smile, and a level of modesty and cordiality I did not expect. He was prematurely bald, had a mustache and a warm, almost permanent smile. His arm was in a cast strapped to his chest, the result of a soccer injury. "We were in Spain with our family, my nephews organized a game in a field and they said 'Join us, Uncle Rafa.' So I started to play with them, slipped on the grass, and here you have me," he told me, somewhere between amused and resigned.[1]

After inviting me into his laboratory, full of all kinds of microscopes and freezers, Yuste introduced me to the only two other scientists there at the time. The 16 researchers in his lab were almost like the United Nations, he joked. Four were from South Korea, three from the United States, two from Japan, two Germans, one Israeli, one Swiss, one from Finland of Hindu descent, one Canadian, one Czech and one Spaniard —himself. "It's very common," he said, shrugging his shoulders and explaining that all the top U.S. university labs have more foreign than U.S. scientists. After we sat down, I told Yuste, only half-jokingly, that many people believed his project was part of a U.S. government effort to manipulate the human brain.

"WE ARE VERY CONSCIOUS OF THE DANGERS"

If you're going to figure out how the human brain works so you can cure diseases —I asked— are you not in fact going to manipulate the human brain? And could this manipulation be used for other, less laudable ends?

"You are right," he replied. "But first, I can tell you that from the start, our group of scientists who proposed this project, and the U.S. government are very conscious of the possibilities for the misuse of the techniques we have been developing. The project is to develop techniques to map and manipulate brain activity. But the initial objective is to understand how the brain works and help patients. We owe that debt to millions of patients in the world. Surely you, like me, have close relatives who suffer from schizophrenia or epilepsy. We have to cure them."

How?, I asked him.

"For example, schizophrenia is a disease in which thoughts are disorganized. So we can try to develop techniques to connect one thought to another and fix the abnormal way in which schizophrenics think," Yuste said.

But you didn't answer my question, I said, gently. Isn't it dangerous to start manipulating the human brain?

"These techniques can also be used to achieve ends that are not so altruistic," he acknowledged. "But that's the same problem science faces when new techniques are developed. Think of nuclear power, or bacterias that can be used to achieve major advances for humanity or provoke devastating outbreaks. We have the responsibility, as citizens, to avoid that."

What are the dangers?, I insisted.

"I believe that one possibility would be, as you say, that we can read the minds of people, or interfere with their thoughts," Yuste said. "But, precisely because of that risk, we have proposed that the development of these techniques should be controlled and supervised by ethics committees made up of representatives of society as well as scientists and ethics experts. I can assure you that the scientists in our project, as well as the government, are watching this. President Obama himself mentioned it in his news conference. He said he would appoint an ethics committee to supervise the use of this kind of technology."

THE HUMAN BRAIN IS WHAT WE LEAST KNOW

When President Obama unveiled the Brain Activity Map Project on April 2, 2013, he described the effort as a historic step for humanity, saying that modern medicine knows how the body works but not the mind. "As humans, we can identify galaxies light years away, we can study particles smaller than an atom, but we still haven't unlocked the mystery of the three pounds of matter between our ears," Obama told the news conference announcing the initiative, drawing laughs from the usually dour journalists who cover the White House.[2]

Yuste told me that the plan to map the human brain is indeed making history, because that organ is the only part of the body that we don't know how it works. We know how the muscles, liver and heart work, at least well enough to try to fix them when they break down. But from the nose up we are in practically unknown territory, he explained.

That means we don't know the workings of our most important organ, because humans are cerebral animals, he added. The human mind is the product of the brain's activity. Everything that we are —our thoughts, our beliefs, our behavior, our movements, our perception—everything in our lives depends on the workings of the brain. So, if we manage to learn how it works, for the first time mankind will be able to understand itself from the inside. It will be like looking inside ourselves for the first time, Yuste explained.

"The first step will be to understand how the machine works," Yuste told me. "And when we understand how the brain works, we can then fix the problems created when the machine breaks down. It's like a car, which you can't fix unless you know how it works. It's that simple. Here we have a machine made up of 100 billion neurons which, when something goes wrong, generates different mental and neurological ailments. What we want, then, is to solve the problem of how to understand its workings, how the neurons connect to each other, how they communicate. And once we know that, I believe it will be much easier to attack and cure mental diseases."

"KNOWING THE BRAIN WILL MAKE US MORE FREE"

Fascinated by what I was hearing, but not satisfied with Yuste's explanation of how a "committee of experts" would be in charge of blocking the potential dangers of mapping and manipulating the human brain, I returned to my original question: How can you make sure that all this research is not used for evil? Yuste replied that the eventual benefits of brain research would far outweigh the negative effects, adding that if we had allowed our fears to paralyze scientific research we would still be in the Middle Ages.

"Honestly, I believe this can be one of the most important moments in the history of humanity. Because when humanity gets to know itself from the inside, how its mind works, it will become more free. We will understand the origins of many of our afflictions and will be able to fix not only medical problems but also behavioral problems," Yuste told me.

"I also believe this will allow us to develop a new type of technology that uses brain activity to directly control machines and optimize communication among people," he added. "This could be a big leap in human evolution, because it's something that philosophers, psychologists and physicians have been studying for thousands of years."

100 BILLION NEURONS

The human brain is extraordinarily complex, Yuste explained. It has 100 billion neurons, linked to each other in a way that has been described as impenetrable jungles. It may well be the most sophisticated chunk of matter in the universe, and we have it in our heads, every one of us. To study the brain is daunting, he confessed. In fact, there are many people who believe that the mystery of the human brain will never be solved.

Yuste believes the project is feasible, however. "We are meticulous scientists, and we say that studying the brain, like any other part of the body, is a matter of method and labor. Sooner or later, we will find the solution," he told me. When I asked him how they will do that, he replied that the secret is to study the movements and connections among the neurons, instead of studying the neurons themselves. "Look, I can explain this with a very simple analogy. Imagine you're home, watching a movie on the television. But you can only see one pixel on the screen. You don't know what the movie is all about. The brains of humans and other species have been studied with techniques that register the activity of just single neurons, and later that activity is compared to the activity of another neuron in another animal. That's like trying to watch the movie by looking at just one pixel," he said.

"No one has seen the brain's entire movie. I believe that when techniques are developed to register the activity of a large number of neurons, that's when we will start to see patterns of activity that could correspond to behavior, to thoughts, to motor activities, to speech," he added.

"WE SHOW VIDEOS TO MICE"

To unlock the mysteries of the human brain, Yuste and his team —and other research groups in other universities— are showing videos to mice and observing how their neurons react.

"Videos? Movies like Hollywood?," I asked. I had to laugh. Yuste also laughed, and nodded his head.

"Yes," he said, and went on to explain how the experiments work. The brains of humans and mammals, in general, are largely made up of what's called the cerebral cortex. In humans and primates this area is much more developed but very similar to the cerebral cortex of mice, Yuste told me. So mice are an obvious choice for research. If we can understand how the brain of a mouse works, we may begin to understand how the brain of a primate or a human being works. Because the only difference appears to be one of size, not quality.

Curious and amused, I asked for more details about the movie-watching mice. Yuste told me that indeed a big part of his research involves showing videos to mice, which have been anesthetized so they don't suffer. Using a special and very powerful infrared laser, researchers can then monitor the activity of a small group of neurons —about 4,000 out of the estimated 180,000 neurons that mice have— in a section of the visual cortex at the back of the brain that both mice and humans use for vision. When the mice watch the videos, researchers can then study the neurons' signals and how they connect with each other.

And what are you finding?, I asked.

"Some neurons fire this way, and others fire that way. But when we stop the video and we leave a blank screen, we see that the mice neurons continue to fire spontaneously," he said.

You stop the video?

"Exactly. And we have found that the spontaneous firings of these neurons look very similar to the firings of the neurons when the mice are using their eyes to see something. In other words, when we see the world, our brains are reactivating built-in patterns." Yuste added. "This is something, for example, like what the German philosopher Kant said in the 18th Century. He suggested that the world is really inside our minds, that when we see the world, we activate ideas that are already in our brains. In some ways, we are confirming one of the theories Kant suggested many centuries ago, in the sense that visual perception may well be something generated endogenously."

Isn't that what Plato also argued, I noted; that we live in a cave where we can only see reflections of things rather than the things themselves.

"Well, I think they were all going in that direction. We may believe in the simplistic idea that all the neurons in the brain are turned off until we open our eyes and see the world, and then they start to fire. But that couldn't be further from the truth. The brain is always active, whether or not we are looking at the world," he said.

Does that mean the brain works day and night, without stopping?

"Actually, it's a bit like when we dream. When we sleep, the dreams have no relationship to the world. And when we are awake, the dreams are related to what's happening around us, because if not, we would not have done too well in evolution," he joked. "It's possible, going back to the ideas of the philosophers Plato and Kant, that we have something internal, something that would be akin to the heart of our minds, and that is written in the language of neuron firings. Our challenge as scientists and physicians is to develop techniques to finally see the patterns of those neurons firing."

YUSTE'S START IN SPAIN

Yuste became one of the world's most innovative researchers almost by accident. When he was studying medicine at the Universidad Autónoma de Madrid, he was thinking of going into psychiatry, neurology or internal medicine. His parents were middle-class professionals —his father a lawyer and his mother a pharmacist— but there were no scientists in the family. As a child, he was always the best in his class, in science as well the liberal arts. He enrolled in one of the best public high schools in Madrid, the Ramiro de Maeztu, thanks to his high score in the entrance exam and graduated at the head of his class. Although he was always interested in science, it was his father's gift of a book by Spanish Nobel laureate and pathologist Santiago Ramón y Cajal that sparked his interest in research and made him study medicine.

Everything pointed in that direction until, just before graduating from medical school, he had a series of experiences that made him change course. To graduate, Yuste was required to spend three months in the psychiatry department, treating paranoid schizophrenic patients. They were the worst patients, the ones no doctors wanted to treat. They were violent people who usually spent their lives in and out of prison, and had to be constantly sedated to keep them from injuring themselves or others. To interview them, doctors and medical students were protected by security guards. More than once during his work, Yuste recalled, a patient told him, "I am going to follow you home and I am going to kill you." Yet, paradoxically, they were extraordinarily intelligent. "They were very brilliant. I was surprised by how smart they were," he said. They were people like Sherlock Holmes, because the minute you started to speak, from your accent they detected what city you were from, from what neighborhood, from what social class. So you realize that on one hand they have a brilliant mind, but on the other they have a broken part, a bad piece in the brain that's causing their disease."

It was there, during his work in the psychiatry department, that Yuste grew increasingly convinced that the treatment for paranoid schizophrenics was not really curing their ailments but only —if they were lucky— masking their symptoms.

FROM PSYCHIATRY TO RESEARCH

"At that point I realized that what psychiatry was doing with schizophrenics was using palliative treatments that do not cure the cause, just reduce the symptoms," Yuste said. "As doctors, we were treating schizophrenics with pills to reduce their attacks and keep them more or less under control. But we never solved the problem that they carry inside."

That's when Yuste decided to change course. "I decided that instead of dedicating myself to psychiatry, I would dedicate myself to basic research, in order to understand the workings of the cerebral cortex, which is where schizophrenics have the problem," he recalled. "It seemed much more interesting that someday, I or anyone who comes later would be able to cure these patients much more effectively by understanding how the cerebral cortex works."

The book by Ramón y Cajal that his father gave him when he was 14 years old and so impressed Yuste, published in English as *Advice for a Young Investigator,* seemed more on target than ever. First published in 1897 and a long-time best seller in Spain, the book offered advice to young scientists and described science as a solitary and heroic effort to save humanity. Yuste said he also recalled another classic book his mother gave him at about the same age, *Microbe Hunters* by U.S. microbiologist Paul de Kruif, as he was treating his schizophrenic patients. "I was captivated by those two books. And at the end of my medical studies I saw very clearly what I wanted to do with my life. I decided to be one of those silent heroes who work until midnight, isolated in their labs, and with their microscopes unlock secrets that help mankind," he told me.[3]

"I CAME TO THE UNITED STATES WITH TWO BAGS AND DIDN'T KNOW ANYONE"

After graduating from the Universidad Autónoma de Madrid in 1987, Yuste traveled to the United States to earn his doctorate at The Rockefeller University in New York City. "I came like many of the Spanish students in the United States, with two suitcases, not knowing anyone, to make my way in a new country," he told me.[4]

At Rockefeller, he worked on techniques for calcium imaging to measure the activity in neurons, under the supervision of Nobel laureate Torsten Wiesel. After earning his Ph.D in 1992, he went on to postgraduate work at the Biological Computation Research Department at Bell Laboratories in New Jersey, under the direction of the prominent neurobiologist Lawrence Katz. He was appointed an associate professor at Colombia University in 2001, and soon became a star researcher and professor.

THE MEETING THAT CHANGED HIS LIFE

In September of 2011, Yuste was invited to a meeting in Buckinghamshire, Great Britain, with 25 other scientists, most of them neurobiologists and physicists. The gathering was organized by four private foundations —two British and two from the United States— to exchange ideas on ambitious research projects that might be undertaken in the field of neuroscience. The idea was for each scientist to suggest what type of research should receive priority in the near future, and then discuss the proposals openly. It was an informal gathering without a set agenda, a true brainstorming session.

When Yuste's turn to speak came, he suggested the idea that would later attract the attention of the White House. He proposed developing techniques for mapping all the activity of the neural networks in animals and humans. He argued, as he would do many times later, that we cannot understand how the brain works today because we are only registering the activity of individual neurons and not a group of neurons. If we want to get to the bottom of psychiatric diseases, like the paranoid schizophrenia he treated as a student in Spain, we have to map all of the human brain, he argued.

As Yuste recalls it, the first reaction of his colleagues was not favorable. "When I suggested the idea, many of my colleagues started to say, 'That's impossible. It will cost a lot of money. And even if we get the money, we'd have to work with too much data. And even if we had the data, we wouldn't know what to do with it,'" he said. But as the discussion went on, it became increasingly evident that Yuste's idea was dominating the meeting. "With every criticism, the idea grew stronger," he recalled. "And after a while three or four key people endorsed me, including George Church, one of the promoters of the human genome project. Church got up and said, 'Your criticisms of Yuste are the same criticisms of our human genome project 15 years ago. And they were wrong.'"

Church and Yuste did not manage to persuade the majority, but they did persuade a small group with enough influence to get the ball rolling. "Out of that meeting came a very small group, five of us, excited with the idea of putting our project before the world and developing techniques for mapping brain activity," Yuste said. In the following months, the five scientists started to write scientific papers that were published in the most prestigious specialized magazines. And they sent a copy to the White House Office of Science and Technology Policy.

"I LEARNED IT WHEN I SAW OBAMA ON TELEVISION"

"They read it and loved it," Yuste said. The White House was looking for a high-impact project in science and technology that could astonish the world, just like NASA did when it put the first man on the moon in 1969. Like in the middle of the 20th Century, when the Soviet Union launched the first space satellite, the Sputnik, and the United States was afraid the Russians would win the technology race, in 2011 there was increasing concern in Washington that China would eclipse the United States. In fact, China was very far behind the United States in key science and technology indicators, but the U.S. perception was that Beijing was hot on its trail. Faced with a generalized paranoia that the United States was losing its place as a superpower, the White House invited the leading U.S. research centers to propose their most ambitious projects.

The Office of Science and Technology Policy at the White House received more than 200 proposals in 2012, and selected the one from Yuste's team. The Spanish scientist learned about the decision from television, like millions of others, as he listened to Obama's State of the Union address to Congress the night of Feb. 13, 2013.

Unveiling his plans for a new effort to boost innovation, science and technology, the president made a powerful pitch. "If we want to make the best products, we must invest in the best ideas. Every dollar we invested to map the human genome returned $140 to our economy —every dollar. Today, our scientists are mapping the human brain to unlock the answers to Alzheimer's. They're developing drugs to regenerate damaged organs; devising new material to make batteries 10 times more powerful. Now is not the time to gut these job-creating investments in science and innovation. Now is the time to reach a level of research and development not seen since the height of the Space Race. We need to make those investments," Obama declared. It was one of the rare times when both Democrats and Republicans in the chamber stood up to applaud the president. Yuste, sitting at home, jumped out of his seat. Obama had just talked about what he and his fellow scientists had proposed, even using the same language.

"I was watching television, like anyone else. When we heard Obama, we realized he was talking about us," Yuste told me months later. "It was an unforgettable moment. We started to call each other and say, 'We've been picked!' "

A short while later, *The New York Times* published a front-page story, and Yuste's photo, on the project to map the human brain mentioned by the president. In April of 2013, at a gathering of about 200 scientists in the East Wing of the White House, Obama, speaking before a blue sign that said, "BRAIN Initiative," announced an initial investment of $100 million for the launch in 2014 of the effort to map the human brain that Yuste had proposed.

WILL SIGMUND FREUD BE OVERTAKEN?

Mapping the human brain will likely bring about a total review of Sigmund Freud's theories, Yuste said when I asked him how the father of modern psychology would be regarded after the results of his research start to become public. "I believe this will have a major influence on changing Freudian theories. They could be updated to fall in line with the progress of the research," he said. "Humans, as smart as we think we are, move forward by trial and error. We gather facts, we test theories. Are they right or not? And thanks to this back and forth, with hits and misses, we move forward. Each one of us bases ourselves on the progress achieved by others before us. And because of this I would be very surprised if psychology, the Freudian theories, modern psychiatry and neurology are not changed in revolutionary ways by the development of techniques for directly observing brain activity."

How can you be so sure? I asked Yuste.

"Because we're talking about techniques we can use to see the activity of each and every one of the neurons in a brain circuit," he answered. "There are already techniques, for example magnetoencephalograms and nuclear magnetic resonance, which can be used to see what part of the brain lights up when a patient is thinking. But with these technique you can't see the neurons. You see the entire area of the brain that lights up. Each of these areas can have billions of neurons." Pointing with his index finger to the microscopes behind him in the lab, he added, "What we want to make is a kind of machine, a microscope like those, that we can use to detect the firings of the individual neurons —to see the pixels on the television set that I told you about, in order to understand how the image we see on the screen is created."

OTHER PROJECTS FOR CEREBRAL MANIPULATION

Although Yuste's project to map the human brain is the most ambitious in the field, there are others that appear to have been taken from science fiction movies, and that are attracting as much or more attention in the news media. One of them has allowed paralyzed patients to move robotic arms or legs with their brains, for example allowing someone with a robotic arm to pick up a cup of coffee.

Surprising results are also emerging from experiments on the connections between brain and robotics by John P. Donoghue, a neuroscientist at Brown University and Yuste's colleague in the human brain mapping project, and the work of Brazilian researcher Miguel Nicolelis at Duke University. Both scientists, working independently, inserted electrodes into the brains of paralyzed patients to register their brain activity and relay it to computers which in turn made a robot move. Within a few years, researchers hope to be able to allow paralyzed patients to drive cars or write texts using only their thoughts.

Other scientists, like Rajesh Rao, star researcher at the University of Washington and author of several books on the connections between brains and computers, managed to transmit thoughts from one person to another, and even showed that the thoughts of one person could trigger physical movements by others. Rao inserted electrodes into the brains of two people and directed one of them to look at a video game, without touching it, and think about the next move. The other person with electrodes in his brain, blocks away in another part of the university campus, then moved his index finger to carry out the motion the first person had thought about. The second subject felt something like a nervous tic that made him move the finger, according to a report in the *Washington Post*. The same thing happened throughout the course of the video game.

Scientists earlier had proven that thoughts can be transferred from humans to rats implanted with electrodes —for example, with a rat moving its tail when the human ordered it. But now Rao was proving that something similar could be done between human beings. The scientist acknowledged that the brain connections between two people with electrodes, or the connections to robots through computers, can transmit only very simple signals and not fully formed thoughts. And, for now, we have not reached the point where government can control thoughts, because the signal transmissions can only happen if people —or mice— have those electrodes implanted in their brains.

The future of this research is exciting and chilling at the same time. "We want to see if we can extract and transmit more complex forms of information from one brain to another," Rao said.[5] "Ideally, we can have a two-way form of communication instead of the one-way flow we have now, for more of a conversation between brains."

"WE ARE BUILDING ON THE SHOULDERS OF OTHERS"

By the year 2019, if not before, Yuste and his colleagues in the brain mapping project expect to be able to announce concrete results from their research and start on the road to repairing the flaws that cause schizophrenia, autism, some types of depression, the damages to the brain caused by heart attacks and several other ailments.

But when that time comes, it's likely that many scientists will be sharing the glory. Scientific research is probably the most collaborative of all innovation processes. After Yuste's project was approved, the U.S. government launched a competition among hundreds of universities and laboratories —Yuste's group at Columbia University was one of them— to work on the new map of the human brain. Dozens submitted projects to receive the funds promised by Obama. And in late 2013, Yuste and his lab received $2.5 million from the U.S. National Institute of Health to advance their research. He estimated the funds will allow the lab to operate for five years without having to seek other funding.

"All of humanity's progress is owed to scientists who are silent heroes, who go unnoticed, and who open the doors of progress, little by little, with their daily work," Yuste told me. "Some win Nobel prizes, but the largest part of science is done in teams... We have been working on this for more than 100 years. We work as if we are standing on the shoulders of those who came before us."[6]

What will happen in coming years?, I asked Yuste. Will the trend toward collaborative work grow? "Scientific collaboration is growing and will continue to grow, thanks to the Internet and because the barriers separating disciplines are falling," Yuste replied.

OTHER COUNTRIES' ADVANTAGES AND CHALLENGES

When I asked Yuste how all of this would affect Latin America and other developing regions around the world, the scientist pointed out that the Internet obviously allows Latin American universities to benefit from the ever-expanding access to information. But if emerging countries believe the Internet will allow them to really keep up with scientific research around the world, they are wrong, he added.

The Internet allows access to enormous amount of information, "but when push comes to shove, science is done by people in a traditional way, like apprentices in the Middle Ages," Yuste said. "Apprentices went to live with their masters in the Middle Ages, then left and opened their own shops. It's the same with science today. You go to a laboratory where there's someone doing science, you work with that person three or four years and you leave knowing how to do science. If you look at all the great discoveries, they are almost always the work of someone trained in the laboratory of someone else who also made great discoveries."[7]

That's why it's essential that Latin American universities send more graduates for doctoral and post-doctoral studies in the world's best universities, Yuste said. "That's a problem for Latin American universities. They have to send more people to train in those laboratories and then bring back the flames to light their own bonfires at home, to create their own schools. It's all about schools. I trained in a school, my mentor was successful in science, and his mentor as well. It's almost a matter of pedigree. The best advice I can give to Latin American countries is to select their best students, send them to the best laboratories in the world and then bring them back home to start their own schools. That's what China, South Korea and other Asian countries do."[8]

Yuste didn't have to remind me. It's increasingly clear that the old complaints about "brain drain" that some Latin American pseudo-intellectuals still cling to have been totally rebuffed. In the 21st century, the concept of the "brain drain" has been replaced by the concept of "brain circulation," in which university graduates from developing countries leave to study abroad but in one way or another always end up benefiting their birth countries. Some of them return home after spending years in the United States, Europe or China. Others, like Yuste, constantly visit their home countries to teach summer course or give lectures, sharing the latest advances in science with their local colleagues.

In a world that requires teamwork, the circulation of brains helps greatly to ease the isolation of academics and scientists. That has been acknowledged by China, South Korea and other Asian countries and more recently Chile and Brazil, which have started to send tens of thousands of their students to the best universities in the world in hope they will later return home —whether to visit or stay— and share the knowledge they acquired abroad.

HURRAH FOR COLLABORATION! DOWN WITH COMPETITION!

Yuste said that another reason for the growing collaboration in scientific research is that experts from different disciplines will be increasingly needed to work on joint projects. "It makes less sense every day for scientists to work in departments of physiology, pharmacology, neurology, etc., because those are all artificial barriers," he told me.

"And it's increasingly clear that the solution to a scientific problem often comes from mixing approaches from different fields. That's why scientific work requires more multidisciplinary cooperation every day. Because it makes no sense not to use all your resources when you're stuck on a problem, not to bring in experts from other areas who can help you. This is happening more and more. People are realizing that the old disciplines are artificial, accidents of history," he said.[9]

Even the borders between departments like physics, biochemistry, psychology and robotics are becoming increasingly blurry, he added. "I am in the biology department, but there are colleagues in the chemistry department working in my same area. That's why scientific collaboration is growing. Any rivalry, more than anything else, will be about who gets there first," he concluded.

After my interview with Yuste, as I walked nostalgically through the Columbia University campus —where I earned my masters' degree in journalism and had a wonderful time 30 years ago— I was still thinking about Yuste's comments on the growing collaboration among scientists. Obviously, this was not exclusive to science. It's also happening in the world of business innovators.

Is there really much difference between scientists who share their findings and chefs who share their recipes, like Gastón Acurio? Are there any real differences between Yuste's cooperation with his competitors, and between Jordi Muñoz, the young Mexican drone manufacturer, and the "makers" who believe in open-source innovation and publish all their secrets on the Internet?

Just like in science, the collaboration in entrepreneurial innovation is growing because the barriers between different disciplines are falling. The 3D printers will increasingly erase the differences between design, engineering and computing companies. Watches that perform electrocardiograms and computers that prescribe medicines will erase the borders between medicine, computing and robotics. Innovation will be a progressively more interdisciplinary and collaborative process. There will still be competition, of course. But the need for contributions from various disciplines will require more collaboration. Competition, as Yuste put it, will be a race not so much to see who can make something new, but who can make it first.

6

Pep Guardiola and the art of innovating while winning

FC Barcelona surprised its rivals constantly

The most interesting part of FC Barcelona coach Josep Pep Guardiola's winning streak when he led the team from 2008 to 2012 was not that he invented a new way of playing soccer —strictly speaking, he didn't invent it— but that he innovated while he was winning. We usually make drastic changes when we're down, but few of us have the wisdom and audacity to innovate when we're winning. Guardiola's great talent is that he perfected the art of incremental innovation, building on what he inherited and innovating every week —even after winning the previous week— and constantly surprising his rivals.

Many companies, and many people, should follow Guardiola's example of innovating while winning. If they had done that, large corporations like Kodak would not have filed for bankruptcy and others, like Compaq, Pan Am and Standard Oil, would still be alive. As it has often been cited, the Kodak case is one of the best examples of the dangers of failing to innovate. The company filed for bankruptcy in 2012, when it had 140,000 employees and an internationally recognized brand. That same year, Instagram, a digital photography company with barely 13 employees, was purchased by Facebook for $1 billion.

Guardiola, who won a record 14 national and international championships in his four years as Barcelona coach, is the first to acknowledge that the club's success did not start with him. Innovation in the team was a gradual, progressive process that started in the early 1970s —long before the birth of its star player, Lionel Messi, and Guardiola's start as its coach— when the club hired a string of coaches from the Netherlands to bring in their country's attacking style of play.

Barcelona hired Rinus Michels, former coach of the Dutch team Ajax, in 1971 and later hired Johan Cruyff and Frank Rijkaard, who brought to Spain the "total soccer" style of play — an attacking game, with quick passes and constant ball control— which earned the Dutch the world's admiration. Cruyff left an especially strong impression on Guardiola and Barcelona, first as a player on the team 1973–1978 and then as its coach, starting in 1988. Cruyff "started everything. He has been the most influential person in the club. I can't imagine Barcelona today without what he did 20 years ago. Those of us who came later added our touches, but I am eternally grateful to him," Guardiola said.[1]

Practically all FC Barcelona executives agree on the importance of the role Cruyff played. "This began 25 years ago, when Johan Cruyff took over. At the head of the team he won championships, and that's important. But what's really important is that he made a difference: he persuaded everyone in Catalonia how Barcelona should play. From then on, there's been no debate. Barça should play a certain way, and children should learn that way so that it's part of them when they grow up," said Manuel Estiarte, the club's director of external relations. Cruyff introduced a philosophy of the game that has guided Barcelona ever since. His successors, especially Guardiola, constantly changed tactics and style —like many successful companies— but never changed the central philosophy.

CRUYFF'S "TOTAL SOCCER"

What did Cruyff invent and Guardiola perfect? Contrary to what many believe, the Dutch model of fast, attacking soccer —in which all the players play all the positions, constantly moving through all the pitch and confusing their rivals— was not a Dutch invention, but rather was made popular by Hungary in the 1950s.

The Hungarians only half-jokingly called their style of play "socialist soccer," because all the players were equal and played all the positions. In "socialist soccer," everyone was a defender and everyone was an attacker. There were no distinctions. Michels imported that philosophy from the Netherlands to Barcelona, but after he left in 1975 the club experimented with various British and Spanish coaches, without major results. Cruyff's arrival as coach changed everything.

Cruyff reintroduced "total soccer," Xavier Sala i Martín, a star economist at Columbia University and Harvard Ph.D who had also served as Barcelona's treasurer and acting president, told me. Sala i Martín, who was always close to the club's administration, said that "unlike the traditional English style of play, which is a game of specialists, 'total soccer' is a game where everyone does everything. In English football, the center defender is a tall guy, very strong, very rough and very intimidating. He knows how to clear the ball with his head, but he doesn't know how to dribble or pass the ball. The other extreme is the little, skillful guy who runs a lot. The center forward is a tall guy who scores with his head. In 'total soccer,' unlike in the soccer of specialists, there are all kinds of players in all kinds of positions."

He acknowledged, however, that there's no hard proof that Cruyff's attacking brand of soccer is more effective. "There isn't one best way of playing soccer. Barça, the Netherlands and Hungary in the 1950s were attacking teams that won everything. But Italy won four World Cups with an ultra-defensive style of play. So we can't prove that the attacking game is better than the defensive game. There are different ways of playing, and at different times one or the other has been better," Sala i Martín added.

CRUYFF'S PHILOSOPHY

One part of the attacking game that Cruyff brought to Barcelona, after trying it with Ajax in the Netherlands, was to keep possession of the ball and pass it constantly. In Cruyff's famous words, "If you play on possession, you don't have to defend, because there's only one ball." He also put it this way: "Until the day comes when soccer is played with two balls, I always want to have the ball, because if I have it, you don't have it." Guardiola followed Cruyff's philosophy with absolute determination. "I am an egotist on that. I want the ball for myself," he said. "And if my opponent has it, I am going to take it away. I want him to know that I am going to take it, that I am coming after him."[2]

Sala i Martín said that for Cruyff, "the fundamental element of soccer is the pass, to pass the ball. That's different from the English philosophy, where the key is dribbling, which means you run down the sideline, dodging everyone, and at the end you center the ball so that a very tall guy waiting in front of the goal can head it into the net. Cruyff's philosophy, in contrast, was that you advance by making passes. And the pass doesn't have to be to the place where there's another player, but where he will be 30 seconds later."

"One of the marvelous things about Barcelona is how its players catch a pass, as if they have a glove on the foot. The tall, strong, rough players don't know how to do that. But if you have a field full of small and skillful players, you can do that all the time," Sala i Martín said.

Another Cruyff innovation, perfected later by Guardiola, was to always have a player free to receive the ball. "The entire team is designed to constantly pass and control the ball," Sala i Martín added. "And to be able to constantly pass the ball and always have someone free, you have to have control of the middle of the field. If the other team has two players in midfield, I need three. If they have three, I need four. If they put in four, I have to put in five." Once Barcelona establishes that control, the goalkeeper can start a play by passing the ball to the area where the team has superiority. While a goalkeeper in a traditional team usually sends the ball long into the middle of the field, hoping that one of his teammates gets it, Barcelona —in part because it does not have a lot of tall players— almost always starts off from the back. "The first one who has to figure out where there's a numerical advantage is the goalkeeper, who can then make a short pass to that area," Sala i Martín explained.

GUARDIOLA'S START

Guardiola was born in Santpedor, a small town in the center of Catalonia, and went to a Catholic school where he got hooked on soccer.
"There were almost no cars, the streets were full of mud. We played
all the time, like all the kids in small towns," the former Barcelona
coach recalled.[3] His fellow students in the Escola Llissach in Santpedor
remember him as a thin, shy kid who was always picked first when it
was time to play soccer —during lunch break or on the streets after
school. Toni Valverde, one of Guardiola's classmates, said the games
"started Monday and finished Friday, and the final score could be
something like 58 to 49. The objective every Monday was to get Pep
on your team. He was the most wanted."[4] At the age of nine, Pep's
father, a construction worker named Valentí, enrolled him in the La
Salle school in Manresa, a few miles from his home. Two scouts for
one of the best soccer schools in the area, the Gimnastic in Manresa, saw Guardiola play and invited him to train two or three times a
week in their school. Soon, Guardiola was playing for the Gimnastic team against other clubs in the region, including farm teams in
the FC Barcelona organization. He was the best player on the team.

When Guardiola was 11, his father saw a notice in a sports newspaper inviting young soccer players to tryouts for the lower divisions of
FC Barcelona and signed him up, without his knowledge. "The people
in Barcelona want to see you," Valentí told his son.[5] He didn't do well in
his first tryout, but he got a second chance and the boy was invited to
join the club. However, his parents decided to reject the offer. Barcelona
was too far away and their son was too young to go off on his own.
Josep played another two years for the Gimnastic team. Guardiola tried
out again for Barcelona when he was 13 and was again invited. This
time, the family accepted the offer to enroll him in La Masía, the youth
soccer academy in Barcelona that to this day remains the quarry that
produces some of the club's best players, including Messi.

La Masía is an old farmhouse, built in 1702, that was remodeled several times and in 1979 became the school and dormitory for teenagers

who came from other places to play for Barcelona's lower-division teams. It was not easy for Josep to move away from his parents and three brothers at such an early age, so he returned almost every weekend to his family and hometown. But for Guardiola, a diehard FC Barcelona fan, to be in that club was a dream come true. "In Catalonia, most kids are Barça fans from the time they are born. First, because the team wins, and kids love winners. When I was a kid, the Celtics were winning in the NBA, so I was a Celtics fan. Then came the Lakers and the Bulls. It's the same with kids. For me, Barcelona was part of my apprenticeship as a player and as a person. I lived almost all my life there," Guardiola said.[6]

"I got to the club when I was 13 years old. I studied and played soccer. I tried to get good grades, to make my parents happy, and trained in the afternoons. While that was going on, as I rose (in the Barcelona divisions), I would say, 'I am close.' But I never thought I would make the first team. I was simply having fun," Guardiola recalled.[7] That's where Cruyff, one of the founders of La Masía, first saw the future Barcelona player and coach and made him one of his favorite players.

GUARDIOLA THE PLAYER

Guardiola was spotted by Cruyff when he was 17 years old. As author Phil Ball tells it in his book *Morbo: The Story of Spanish Football*, in his first week in charge of the club, the coach "turned up unannounced at the 'Mini' stadium, a venue just down the road from the Camp Nou used by the youth and B teams. Just before half-time he wandered into the dugout and asked Charly Rexach, the youth team coach at the time, the name of the young skinny lad playing on the right side of midfield. 'Guardiola —good lad,' came the reply." Cruyff told Rexach to move him into the middle for the second half, to play *pivote*, a difficult position to adapt to and one not used by many teams in Spain. Pep Guardiola adjusted immediately to his new position. Two years later, at the age of 19, he began to play in the first division team and a year later became the star in Cruyff's Dream Team.

Years later, Cruyff said that the fact Guardiola was skinny, without a big body, had forced him to develop his brain more than other players. "Guardiola had to be smart. At that time, he had no other choice. He looked like me. If you don't have the physical power of the others, you need a lot of technique, move the ball quickly and avoid the collision. And to do that, you have to have good vision... You develop the ability to notice any detail, to fix in your retina the positions of your players. All of that helps you as a player, and as a coach," Cruyff added.[8]

Guardiola played for Barcelona for 11 years, until 2001. He won almost every trophy, including four consecutive championships of the Liga Española under Cruyff, from 1991 to 1994. He was a club hero, not only because he was a local player but because he always identified as a native of Catalonia. After Barcelona wins, Guardiola would kiss or wrap himself in the flag of the Catalan region, and often spoke in public in the Catalan language. His support for Catalan nationalism was no secret. (Later, as coach, he would be even less guarded in his political comments. In 2013, he publicly endorsed a referendum on independence proposed by Catalan nationalists for 2014.)

At the age of 30, Guardiola left Barcelona and went to play in Italy, for Brescia and then Roma, with only mediocre results and under the cloud of a scandal that complicated his life for years. While playing for Brescia, he was accused of doping, for a supposedly positive result for the steroid nandrolone following one game on Oct. 21, 2001, and another one two weeks later. Guardiola denied the allegation but was convicted in 2005 at the end of a trial that lasted a number of years and was given a suspended sentence of seven years in prison. Guardiola appealed and two years later was acquitted by an appeals court in Brescia.[9] Guardiola celebrated after the acquittal. "Finally, after two years, this book is closed. I could have taken advantage of the statute of limitations, but I wanted to appeal to prove my total innocence," he declared.[10] He had left Italy in 2003 to play in Qatar, where the Al Ahli club in Doha paid him a remarkable $4 million to play for two seasons. He wound up his playing career with the Dorados de Sinaloa club in Mexico, recruited by his old friend Juan Manuel Lillo, whom he would praise years later as one of his most important teachers.

RETURNING HOME

Guardiola returned to Spain in 2006 to launch his new career as coach. After obtaining his coach's license, he started talks with various teams —including Nastic in Tarragona, which was at the bottom of the first division— and finally accepted an offer to coach Barcelona's lower divisions in mid-2007. He went back home, seven years after he had left as a player, to coach the club's third-division team.

It was a turbulent time for the club. The new board of directors, led by FC Barcelona President Joan Laporta, had given the team a boost in 2003 with the hiring of Dutch coach Rijkaard and the Brazilian star Ronaldinho, who produced excellent results in the 2004 and 2005 seasons. But now the club was in decline. In 2007, Rijkaard's team was losing more and more often. A lack of discipline was rampant. Ronaldinho, the team's star, was a bit overweight and arrived late for training. There were even rumors that he sometimes came into the locker room wearing the same clothes from the previous day, after partying all night.

"The successes of the team and the self-censorship by the sports media did not allow a break in the normally healthy line that separates the private and public lives of soccer players. But Ronaldinho, who had his own table in a discotheque in Castelldefels, had stopped living for soccer," author Guillem Balagué wrote in a biography of Guardiola.[11] Samuel Eto'o, another Barcelona star, suffered a knee injury and was allowed by Rijkaard to rehabilitate far from the club, which increased his estrangement from the team. The American players Rafael Márquez and Deco took off a few extra days for Christmas and were not sanctioned. The players were demoralized, and the board of directors was increasingly worried about the future of the club. "To make things worse, Ronaldinho's relationship with one of Rijkaard's daughters became public," adding to the bad blood in the locker room, Balagué wrote. On May 8 of 2008, after Real Madrid thrashed Barcelona 4-1, Laporta, then president of FC Barcelona, announced that Rijkaard's contract would not be renewed after the end of the season.

GUARDIOLA WINS, BY DEFAULT

According to a number of team executives, Guardiola was not Laporta's first choice to replace Rijkaard. He was seen as too young and too inexperienced as a coach. Although he was a hometown hero, embodied the club's attacking style of soccer and was doing a good job with the Barcelona B team, he was practically a rookie at coaching. Laporta regarded him as a very risky option.

What FC Barcelona needed was a firm hand, someone to impose discipline on the team. For Laporta and many other members of the board of directors, that man was José Mourinho of Portugal, who had played for FC Barcelona and was then coaching Chelsea. Two Barcelona representatives went to Portugal to interview Mourinho, whose agent also had close ties to Barcelona because he also represented Rafael Márquez and Deco. According to some versions, Mourinho asked for a two-year contract at 9 million euros per year, plus one million euros per year for his top assistants.

According to other sources, Laporta —perhaps resentful that Guardiola had backed a rival in the 2003 elections for club president— also considered hiring Michael Laudrup, a Dane who had won several championships as a player with Ajax and Barcelona and was then coaching the Spanish club Getafe. A book about Laudrup quoted Ángel Torres, at the time executive director of Getafe, as saying that the Dane had already decided to resign and move to Barcelona, but the agreement fell through at the last minute, according to a report in Spain's *Mundo Deportivo*. Eventually, pushed by members of the board of directors, Laporta hired Guardiola, partly because Mourinho did not share Barcelona's offensive philosophy and partly because Guardiola had more ties to the club and would be cheaper to hire. On June 17, 2008, at the age of 37, Guardiola became the new coach of FC Barcelona.

GUARDIOLA FIRES RONALDINHO

Guardiola's first step after taking control of the first division team was to announce that he would fire Ronaldinho, the team's star, as well as Samuel and Deco. Guardiola wanted team players, a team with no room for loafers. He had to start with a dramatic move, because he was starting out with the wind against him: the general opinion in the sports media, and not a few members of the FC Barcelona club itself, was that he was not experienced enough to lead the first division team. His announcement that he would not renew the contracts of the three stars was a bombshell, designed to win the respect of fans and put pressure on the rest of the players.

Ronaldinho was quickly sent to AC Milan, Deco was transferred to Chelsea and Eto'o, seeing what was happening to the other stars or perhaps sensing that he could become the team's leader, got his act together and started to train seriously. At the same time, Guardiola began to encourage Messi to take on more responsibilities —he was then seen as still too young to be the team's captain— and recruited young players, like Gerard Piqué, who had come up through the club's own ranks.

At his first training session with the new team, in a field in St. Andrews, Scotland, Guardiola told his players about his philosophy. He would forgive errors, he said, but would not forgive giving less than a 100 percent effort. He would always be available to talk, about professional as well as personal issues. The new team would not tolerate cliques. Everyone had to understand that they would be better as a team than as individuals. And the team would continue the style that distinguished FC Barcelona: attacking soccer.

To reestablish discipline, Guardiola announced a system of penalties that he had imposed in the lower divisions, where he fined players 120 euros for arriving late for training, 1,500 euros for breaking the midnight curfew, and a suspension after the third curfew violation. To avoid nationality cliques that could erode team spirit, he ordered the players to speak only Spanish or Catalán and assigned them tables for team meals. Until that time, FC Barcelona players had chosen their own tables.

To make sure he had an effective organization, he also hired physical trainers, nutritionists, physical therapists, technical assistants and personal assistants for the players, as well as analysts to evaluate each game. The new Barcelona coach also installed a giant television set in his office, to study videos of recent games by his next opponents.

After a short while, and a start that scared many people —Guardiola's team lost its first game and tied the second— FC Barcelona started to win game after game, and then championships. The club hit its peak in 2009, when it won every tournament it entered: La Liga, the Supercopa de España, the UEFA Super Cup, the FIFA Club World Cup, the Copa del Rey and the UEFA Champion's League. Never before had a Spanish team won six titles in the same season.

FIRST, STUDY YOUR RIVAL

Guardiola is not the kind of coach who develops grand hypotheses to explain his success on the field. On the contrary, when asked for the secret of his success, he usually shrugs his shoulders, smiles and says modestly that the credit should go to his players. "More than a 'Guardiola era,' it was a 'Messi era,'" he declared more than once.[12] There's no secret formula for winning, he says. The only constant in his "method," if there is one, is to carefully study the opposing team, watching hours of videos of their last game to spot their weak points and try to exploit them.

According to Guardiola, his tactic is to figure out that his opponent "defends this way, so the open space (to attack) will be here. And this other team defends in this other way, so the space will be there. I may anticipate that we will have more space on the right, because their striker is a rocket but he can't run backwards. So we will have a lot of room to attack there. A tactic is just that. Figure out what they do, and then adapt the tasks of your own players."[13]

Guardiola's study of his opponents was one of the keys to his success as coach, according to Carlos Murillo Fort, a former top executive at the Barcelona club who has authored several books on the team and currently directs the masters' programs in international business and sports management at the Universidad Pompeu Fabra in Barcelona. "Guardiola is almost obsessive. He is more obsessive than obsessive people,"

Murillo told me. "His motto is perseverance. He is a student of the game, crazy about tactics, and he manages to win based on the many hours he spends watching and re-watching game videos."[14]

"THE KEY TO MY PROFESSION: FOLLOW THE PLAN"

Although all coaches plan their games —and sometimes the outcome is good and sometimes it's bad— Guardiola always drew lessons from his wins and loses. "With Guardiola you never heard the expression, 'That's soccer,' that so many other coaches use after a match. His style is educated, professional, analyzing everything and deriving lessons from everything," Murillo added. "After a loss, his first words in the press conference were to praise the adversary and acknowledge that 'today they were better than us.' Later he would try to explain some of the reasons for the loss, from the tactical and coaching point of view. And that had an educational effect on the players. He tried to give them the idea that errors can be fixed, that one can learn many things from a failure. They did not lose just because 'that's soccer.' They lost because they made mistakes or the other team played better."[15]

For Guardiola, and for any business, planning is fundamental. Nothing should be left to luck. Sports competition is a matter of strategies, where coaches plan how to use the weapons at their disposal in the most efficient manner. And Guardiola was happiest not just when he won, but when the match played out just as he had planned it. That confirmed to him that he was doing the right things, and helped him to continue winning.

"Planning how to do it before the game, and then conveying that to your people, that's what drives my profession," Guardiola said. "The key to everything is knowing your opponent, so you can do it better. It's not to defeat them or say 'I beat you.' No, I never see it as 'we beat them.' The nicest feeling is when what I planned, what I conveyed to my people, is coming true during the match. That's the most fulfilling moment. And when it's not happening, it's because we were wrong or because we expected something that didn't happen."[16]

Perhaps because of the importance he put on planning his matches, Guardiola did not celebrate his team's victories by running around crazily with his arms in the air or throwing himself to the ground, like Diego Armando Maradona and other players-turned-coaches. For Guardiola, a win was the coronation on a plan well executed, not a gift from the heavens. "His celebrations of victories were more natural," Murillo recalled. "When the team won, Guardiola took the entire squad to the center of the field, not just the players but also the trainers and assistants, the doctors and the 20 bench players. Messi was as important as the lowest physical therapist. And when his team lost, Guardiola took the responsibility. After a loss, his answer was to congratulate the opponent and say, 'Today they were better than us.' And then he tried to explain some of the reasons for the loss."

THE IMPORTANCE OF THE SURPRISE FACTOR

Guardiola always stayed within Cruyff's "total soccer" system, but he also introduced a number of changes in Barcelona's offensive style of play. One of the main changes was to strengthen the defense. While Cruyff focused all his energies on the attack —he was reported to have said, "I don't care if the other team scores three goals, as long as we score four"— Guardiola taught all the Barcelona players to back up to their own side and go after the ball when the other team was attacking. The idea was that if his team lost the ball, they should take it back immediately. Every time a rival player had the ball, the two closest Barcelona players had to try to get the ball back, blocking short passes, closing off spaces and boxing in their rival.

In Guardiola's Barcelona team, everyone attacked and everyone defended. And the defenders were not your usual defenders. While the center-backs in traditional teams were strong and tall, measuring nearly 6 feet, in Barcelona the center-back was Javier Mascherano, an Argentine who stood just 5 feet and 7 inches. The same went for Messi, who sometimes played center forward, sometimes midfielder and sometimes

156

defender, stealing balls on his own side of the field. "In Guardiola's brand of total soccer, the opponent doesn't know who plays in what position. It's a tactic for misleading the opponent... In other teams, you can tell your center defender, 'Follow that player everywhere and don't let him go.' But with Barça you can't do that, because everyone plays everywhere. And if you chase an opponent everywhere, you destroy your own lineup," said Sala i Martín. Guardiola himself put it this way: "Barcelona understands that it can win in a thousand ways. All are valid. All are useful."[17]

Guardiola also often threw in a surprise after the match had started. Sala i Martín recalled a classic between Barcelona and Real Madrid, in May of 2009, when Madrid was on a winning streak and Barcelona was far back in the standings. Guardiola ordered up video tapes of Madrid games taken from high above the field and spent hours watching them. After a lot of thinking, he got the idea to put Messi in the position known as a "False 9." Guardiola didn't tell anyone. He called Messi to his office, showed him the videos, explained where he should place himself and what he should do. They would start the match with the normal lineup, and 10 minutes into the game Messi would move into midfield to play as a "False 9." Messi's eyes lit up. Barcelona won 6-2.

"The innovation was not to put Messi in midfield, but the flexibility —to figure out how the opponent is playing and surprise him in the middle of the game. The winner is the more flexible team," Sala i Martín told me. Of course, Real Madrid figured out the trick and in their next match made sure to try to box in Messi if he played the "False 9" position. But Guardiola already had anticipated Madrid's change and put Messi in a different position. "Guardiola's way was to make changes continuously. His grand innovation was a system that was completely dynamic, but remained within the team's philosophy and DNA."

HOW TO MOTIVATE PLAYERS

Guardiola also decided that to motivate his team he had to treat each of his players in a different, individual way, because every person reacts in a different way to incentives as well as penalties. "Our job is to get the best out of the people we have. And that's the hardest thing to do, because everyone is different," Guardiola said. Quoting Julio Velasco, an Argentine who coached the Italian national volleyball team to several championships in the 1990s, Guardiola said that "the biggest lie in sports is that all players are equal."[18] There are players you can criticize in public, others who would be deeply offended and others who you have to invite to dinner and let them go by themselves where you want them to go, he said.

"They are not all the same, and they don't have to be treated the same. Yes, (they should be treated) with the same respect, but they are not all equal. You have to invite one to dinner, and take another one into your office. With another you don't have to talk about tactics, and with yet another you have to talk all day about what he does with his free time. You have to figure out what to say to someone, what to do to someone, how to trick someone, how to seduce him so that in the end you can bring him into your scheme and get the best out of him," Guardiola added.[19]

Mascherano, the Barcelona defender, is one of the many players who have praised Guardiola's treatment of each of his players. "He leads groups like no one else. I've seldom seen anyone lead group as well as he did in Barcelona when I had the pleasure of playing there. He is a soccer coach, but he is also a leader with whom you can talk about anything," the Argentine player said. "You are inspired by his way of living soccer. It makes you wake up every day and feel that what you do is worthy, that to train is the most important and normal thing, and that you need to do it for your own professional and personal fulfillment. Many times we're irritated by what's going on around us. Our environment can be tiresome. When we don't play, we complain, and those negative things stay with us. But he told us that we have to earn everything with effort and talent".[20]

At the same time he was demanding more discipline than his predecessor. Guardiola made changes that were welcomed by the players and improved team morale, such as abolishing the restrictions on players on the eve of matches. Under Rijkaard, when Barcelona played in another city, the players traveled the previous day and were restricted to hotels where they spent long and boring hours, frustrated by not being able to go out or see their families. Guardiola did away with that. When the team was playing away, it traveled the day of the match. And when it was playing at home, the players trained the morning of the game and went home for lunch. "I prefer that they be home, instead of locked up in a hotel with nothing to do," Guardiola would say. Eliminating the hotel isolation reduced their stress levels before the matches, he added. The players loved the changes.

But at the same time, Guardiola was unforgiving when players arrived late for training or did not follow his instructions. His style of leadership, in contrast to Rijkaard's, was managerial. Team strategy was not up for discussion. Guardiola dictated it. "The players you coach are not fools. If they see you doubt, they get it instantly, on the fly, in that very moment," Guardiola explained. "You talk to them when you're clear on what you're going to say. 'This is how we're going to do things.' Because soccer players are very intuitive. They smell even your blood. And when they see you weak, they stick it to you."[21]

MORE THAN A CLUB

It's no accident that Barcelona's motto is "More than a club" —*Més que un club*, in the Catalán language. Since its founding in 1899, but especially after the Spanish Civil War and the Franco dictatorship, the team was one of the most visible symbols of Catalan nationalism and opposition to Franco. When the club's president in 1968, Narcís de Carreras declared for the first time that FC Barcelona was "more than a club," the phrase quickly became its principal and distinguishing motto.

Club historians say that in 1925, during the dictatorship of Primo de Rivera, the government ordered the Barcelona stadium to close for six months because fans had booed the Royal March played at the start of a match. The club president at the time, Hans Gamper, had to resign and went into exile in Switzerland. When the civil war erupted in 1936, team president Josep Sunyol, who was a leader of the Esquerra Republicana de Catalunya, a left-wing party, was executed by a pro-Franco firing squad.

Shortly afterward, the club was practically taken over by the Franco dictatorship. Yet during the four decades of Franco rule, when authorities closed down all the political institutions that favored Catalan nationalism, the Barcelona team grew into one of the bastions of the struggle against Franco. Barcelona fans took advantage of home games to chant anti-Franco slogans, something that could not be done in any other public space. In part because of that political image, the classic Spanish soccer matches between Barcelona and Real Madrid took on the overtone of left vs. right, independence against central control, for many of their fans.

Today, long after the Franco era ended, the club continues to be one of the most visible emblems of Catalan nationalism. Jimmy Burns, author of the book *Barça: A people's passion*, has noted that, except for the harshest years of the Franco government takeover, the club always used the Catalan language for its official and internal documents; that its fans sing the club's song in Catalan; that team captains always displayed the Catalan flag on their armbands; and that in recent years all the players' uniforms have included a Catalan flag on the back of the shirts, just below the neck. In 1932, 1979 and 2006, the club signed declarations supporting Catalonian autonomy. According to Burns, "Barcelona is much more than a football club —it is a social and political phenomenon."[22]

UNICEF AND THE "GAMES FOR PEACE"

In recent years, beside its support for Catalan nationalism, Barcelona spread its "More than a club" mystique by supporting a number of humanitarian causes. In 1980 and 1990, the team played exhibitions against the best players in world to benefit UNICEF and the Foundation Against Drug Addiction, based in Spain. In 2005 it organized a friendly match against a first-ever selection of top Israeli and Palestinian players. And in 2013, in part to counter criticism of its agreement to wear jerseys advertising the Qatar Foundation —which news reports alleged was linked to Islamic fundamentalist groups— Barcelona offered to play another "game for peace" against an Israeli-Palestinian selection in Tel Aviv. The offer was canceled when the Palestinians refused to participate.

But Barcelona's most brilliant play to maintain its mystique as "more than a club" —and thereby increase its marketing of team jerseys, flags and other products that generate colossal profits around the world— was its 2006 offer to donate $2 million a year to UNICEF for poor children, in exchange for the right to display the U.N. agency's logo on the front of team jerseys.

"It was marketing in reverse. Instead of UNICEF paying Barcelona to put its logo on the jerseys, Barcelona paid UNICEF," said Murillo, the university professor and former team executive. "That really helped to reinforce the club's brand and portray the team as much more than a club."

When the five-year contract with UNICEF expired in 2011, the club's new president, Sandro Rosell, accepted a controversial $262 million, five year deal with the Qatar Foundation to put its logo on the front of the jersey. The UNICEF logo was moved to the back side. Laporta, the former club president who signed the deal with UNICEF, refused to participate in the club general assembly where the deal was approved, and later declared, "they have sold this jersey for a bowl of lentils," according to reports in Spain's www.antena3.com and www.MundoDeportivo.com.

The New York Times published a report on the new uniforms under the headline, "Barcelona Changes Jerseys and its Values." It noted that although in the past the club encouraged its stars, like Ronaldinho and Messi, to be seen helping poor children or the victims of natural disasters around the world, "the priorities of the 112-year-old club changed."[23] Criticisms over the Qatar Foundation deal only increased amid news reports that the foundation was one of the main donors to the terrorist Hamas group and Yusuf al Qaradawi, an extremist Egyptian scholar. It later became clear that the legitimate Qatar Foundation had been confused with a different organization, the Qatar Charitable Foundation, which had been outlawed in various countries for its alleged links to Islamic terrorism. Barcelona executives pointed out that there was no link between the Qatar Foundation and the violent organization, and replied to the underlying criticism by noting that the club was still paying UNICEF $2 million a year to put its logo on team jerseys —insisting that the team continued to be "more than a club."

THE "COLLAPSE" OF BARCELONA

After Guardiola left FC Barcelona and went to coach Bayern Munich in Germany in 2013, Barça suffered through a string of financial scandals and changes in its presidency and coaching staff that quickly translated into an alarming series of losses on the playing field. At the start of 2014, Rosell was forced to resign as president amid a scandal over the contract for the Brazilian starter Neymar. The club was alleged to have hidden from members an enormous payment for the player, which meant the club paid a total of 95 million euros instead of the 57.1 million euros it first reported. A short while later, the International Federation of Association Football (FIFA) penalized Barcelona for allegedly recruiting players younger than 18 years old. The new club president, Josep Maria Bartomeu, appealed the penalty as he sought to respond to FIFA requests for information on 33 minors allegedly contracted by the club. And Guardiola's successor as coach, Tito Vilanova, resigned after just one year on the job to start cancer treatments.

Shortly afterward, under Argentine coach Gerardo "Tata" Martino, Barcelona started to suffer what the Madrid newspaper *El País* described as "a monumental collapse." In 2014 the team not only lost to various lesser teams but was beaten by Real Madrid in the finals of the Copa del Rey, was eliminated early by Atlético de Madrid in the Champions League and failed to win the championship of La Liga de España. Even the Barcelona newspaper *La Vanguardia* began publishing reports about the "decay" of the Catalan squad.

Guardiola's Bayern Munich team meanwhile was winning match after match, locking in the 2014 championship of the German Bundesliga seven games before the end of the regular season. Using the same style of play he had installed in Barcelona, Guardiola blew away his German rivals so easily that the German newspaper *Bild* compared him to Albert Einstein. Cruyff, the pioneer of "total soccer," lamented the fall of Barcelona and said, "the best for Barça is the return of Pep Guardiola."[24]

YOU MUST INNOVATE WHILE YOU'RE WINNING

Jorge Valdano, a former Argentine player who coached a number of clubs, including Real Madrid, says Guardiola is "the Steve Jobs of soccer" because he introduced more innovations than any of his colleagues in recent years. "He is an innovator, a creator, a man of high emotions: courageous, a lover of the beauty of his work" who constantly surprises rivals with new ideas.[25]

"Barcelona transformed itself into a different team every six months," Valdano recalled. "Messi started out playing on a flank and wound up playing in midfield. Sometimes he played with four defenders, and later with three. There were matches where he played seven midfielders and no strikers. He surprised with profound innovations, things we had not seen in soccer for a long time." Perhaps more importantly, Guardiola "made the innovations while he was winning, which is when you have to do it. You have to be very, very sure of yourself to do that," Valdano concluded.

That should be the biggest lesson drawn from Guardiola's Barcelona for soccer teams, as well as companies and individuals. We have to innovate while we're winning. We have to study the competition and anticipate the future changes, even when we're winning. Many of the top companies that disappeared in recent years failed precisely because they did not invest enough time and money on reinventing themselves.

Would Kodak, the long-time world leader of the photo industry, have collapsed if it had reinvented itself when digital cameras first hit the market? Would companies like RCA, Compaq, General Foods, Standard Oil and Pan American have gone into bankruptcy if they had started to innovate during their peak years? Maybe companies, shops and professional people should hang a photo of Guardiola in their offices to remind them of the need to innovate constantly, especially when they are winning. Those who stick to the same thing will fall behind in the long run.

7

Branson, Musk, Kargieman and the art of reinventing oneself

"If we had not reinvented ourselves, we would not have survived"

I had a hard time taking Sir Richard Branson seriously after the British business mogul and adventurer, whose fortune has been estimated at $4.6 billion, told me that his Virgin Galactic company plans to "colonize" Mars in the next few years with human settlements and space hotels. We were filming a television show, and I tried to keep my bemused skepticism to myself. But privately, I thought that was the typical bluster of an eccentric millionaire used to making flamboyant declarations to publicize some of his new projects.

But as I spoke more with Branson and other space adventurers —many call them "space nuts"— I grew increasingly convinced that perhaps they were not so nutty. They are the most audacious innovators, the ones who defy many of the lessons taught in business schools about the secret of success. Branson is a man who, instead of sticking to fixed goals, reinvented himself a dozen times, jumping many times into areas that he knew little or nothing about such as civil aeronautics of space exploration. And while some societies still see people who reinvent themselves with something of disdain, Branson embraces his personal and business transformations as one of his key sources of pride. "If we had not reinvented ourselves, we would not have survived," he wrote with pride.[1] His hundreds of companies, of all types, are the result of entrepreneurial audacity, creativity and the art of reinventing himself constantly.

When I interviewed him, Branson already had more than 400 companies in his Virgin group and was a few months away from launching his *SpaceShipTwo* into space. He was running against the clock, trying to score a victory over his many rivals —including SpaceX, the company owned by the billionaire founder of PayPal, Elon Musk— in the new era of private space exploration and tourism. These "space nuts" were in a no-holds-barred race for something that most people saw as totally preposterous.

SPACE TRAVEL FOR $200,000

Branson turned up for our interview in jeans, a white shirt open at the neck, a black blazer, and long hair typical of the 1960s. He spoke with almost religious fervor about his new venture, which according to him was going to change the history of humanity. After building his Virgin Records music empire, his Virgin Atlantic airline and hundreds of other companies under the Virgin label, and after breaking navigational records by crossing the Atlantic and Pacific in the largest balloon ever built, Branson saw the conquest of space as the latest and most exciting challenge of his life.

Branson's space craft was a larger and improved version of *SpaceShip One*, which was launched in 2004 by the millionaire Paul Allen and won the AnsariX prize of $10 million. *SpaceShipOne* had made the first manned trip into space without government funds, but its key contribution was that it was reusable. In contrast to NASA rockets, which were lost in each launch, the spacecraft could go into space and return like an airplane. Branson had already invested $300 million in *SpaceShipTwo*, but he now gave it a much more ambitious goal: to launch the era of space tourism and colonization by private enterprise. It was nothing less than the galactic version of the conquest of the American west, like the new missions spearheaded by individuals later popularized by Hollywood as cowboys.

In contrast to Allen's *SpaceShipOne*, which was relatively small, Branson's *SpaceShipTwo* was twice the size —nearly 60 feet long— and could carry two pilots and six passengers. Branson started to sell trips at $200,000 per seat, and by 2013 about 600 people had signed up for the first trips, which include a flight of two to three hours and a brief weightless experience. Among the first to sign up was the *enfant terrible* of pop music, Justin Bieber. Branson's plan was to develop mass space tourism and use those revenues to explore space and colonize Mars.

Isn't it crazy to believe that after the novelty of the first space tourism trip is over, people are going to pay $200,000 to hang out in space for a few minutes? I asked Branson. The British mogul smiled and shook his head from side to side. "On the contrary. I believe that if they have the economic means to make a trip into space, and they can be guaranteed a safe return to Earth, the great majority of people would love to do it," he said. "It is the dream of many young people, and a dream that has not come through for many because they are only flown by governments and are very expensive. What Virgin wants to do in the next few years is to lower the costs of space travel so that many people can become astronauts someday. In the next 10 or 20 years, prices will become much more accessible, and instead of expensive space craft that will carry only the very rich, many, many more people will have the opportunity to go into space."[2]

ENTERTAINMENT FOR THE RICH?

I followed up quickly with another question. For the $200,000 cost of the ticket, what kind of perks will the passengers get? First class treatment, with special food? Branson replied that passengers "will get many amenities. Our spacecrafts are designed to be admired for their external and internal beauty. They have panoramic windows. The passengers will be floating in space, and they will have the biggest smiles of their lives. And when they are ready, they will buckle their seat belts and return to Earth."

But do these trips have any scientific value, or are they merely entertainment for the rich? I asked Branson. He reminded me, as I mentioned in the first chapter of this book, that many of mankind's biggest achievements, like the first transatlantic flights, were at first available only to rich people. In time, the prices dropped and everyone benefited. "You need the rich pioneers to start these flights," he said.[3]

It's true that most of the aviation pioneers, including the Wright brothers, financed their experimental flights with their own money. And the same could be said of other top inventors like Thomas Alva Edison, the inventor of the light bulb and holder of more than 1,000 other patents, who financed most of their experiments from their own pockets. Branson obviously saw himself as part of this tradition of millionaire innovators, and embraced it with pride.

"WE ARE GOING TO PUT SATELLITES IN SPACE"

But what scientific value can space tourism offer? I insisted. They will benefit humanity in a thousand ways, Branson answered. "Thanks to our space program, we will not only take people into space but we will carry out an enormous amount of scientific research. We will put satellites in space for a fraction of the cost today, which will significantly reduce the costs of your telephone calls, your Internet connection and your WI-FI. And that means that the 2 billion people who today have no access to those services will be able to get them at very cheap prices. That's why these trips will bring many, many benefits for everyone. That's the most fascinating part of the decision by commercial companies to get into this industry," he said.[4]

"WE NEED TO ESTABLISH COLONIES IN OTHER PLANETS"

Branson promotes his private flights into space not only as an alternative for scientific exploration, at a time when NASA and other government agencies around the world are suffering under budget cutbacks, but as a potential salvation for all humanity. He argues that we must colonize other planets as soon as possible because a giant meteorite could impact the Earth and destroy us at any moment. We saw a small hint of this in 2013, when a meteorite only about 18 meters wide hit the Urals region of Russia, injuring 1,500 people and damaging more than 7,000 buildings. How can we be sure that a much larger meteorite, capable of destroying the planet, will not destroy us in the future?

"We have to start to colonize other planets, because if a giant meteorite ever hits Earth, even Stephen Hawking has said it could wipe out the human race. That's why it's important, in order to preserve our species, to be able to establish colonies on other planets," Branson said. And the business mogul had already decided where to put the first colony: Mars. As he told me in our interview, he hoped to accomplish that in his lifetime.[5]

Branson seemed to have no doubt that there's life on other planets. The week that we spoke, the *Journal of Science* magazine had just reported that scientific evidence had confirmed the existence of a dry river in Mars, which could indicate that at some point there was, or maybe there still is, life on the Red Planet. "There's no doubt that there's life in thousands of other planets. Look, there are so many planets in the sky that there must be life on thousands and thousands of them," he said. The colonization of Mars will be possible very soon thanks to private enterprises like his own, Branson added.

Asked whether a manned mission to Mars is technically feasible in the next 15 years, Branson said he believed that is possible. "There's enough determination on the part of the private sector, probably working together with NASA," he said. "The private sector can do things at a much lower cost than government. We can do things for a fraction of the cost. If our space program goes as well as we expect, it will generate a lot of money and we will be able to reinvest those profits on programs like turning the colonization of Mars into a reality."[6]

"I WAS DYSLEXIC AND LEFT SCHOOL AT 15"

If innovative people tend to be extroverts, efficient, somewhat neurotic, open to experimentation and not too concerned about pleasing others, Branson meets the description because he has a good dose of all those traits. He made his fortune as a young man in the least traditional manner. Far from inheriting a fortune or a business, or graduating from a top university, he started out from zero. As he recalled in his books, as a child he was dyslexic, a bad student and probably suffered from attention deficit disorder, although that terminology was unknown at the time.

"I was dyslexic," he told me. "I left school when I was barely 15 years old to start a magazine against the Vietnam war, a very unjust war, and I wanted to provide a voice to young people. Throughout my life, I identified situations that I thought I could get into and start businesses that would have a positive impact on people's lives. Luckily, I come from a family with a lot of love, a tight family that always supported me in everything."

Like many British children, Branson —the son and grandson of middle-class attorneys — was sent to a boarding school at a very early age— in his case, eight. That was the traditional way in which English families tried to mold their kids and boost their independence and self-reliance. Branson recalls having a horrible time in boarding school. "I was dyslexic —and short sighted. Despite sitting at the front of the class, I couldn't read the blackboard. Only after a couple of terms did anyone think to have my eyes tested. Even when I could see, the letters and numbers made no sense at all," he wrote. "Since nobody had ever heard of dyslexia, being unable to read, write or spell just meant to the rest of the class and the teachers that you were either stupid or lazy. And at prep school, you were beaten for both."[7]

Luckily, Branson had one quality that helped him to overcome his academic deficiencies and survive his years in boarding school. He excelled at sports, and became captain of the school's soccer, rugby and cricket teams. "It is difficult to overestimate how important sport is at

170

English public schools. If you're good at sports, you are a school hero: the older boys won't bully you and the teachers won't mind you failing your exams."[8] But Branson was happiest when he returned to his parents' home in Shamley Green. His mother was always determined to keep him busy with tasks like cleaning the garden, and pushed him to take on jobs that earned him a little money, but always with a smile and a lot of love.

At the age of 13 he was switched to a private school with 800 boys in Buckinghamshire, where he found a new passion: although he was still battling dyslexia, he discovered that he liked to write. When a leg injury forced him to stop playing soccer for a lengthy period, he started an erotic novel. Two years later, amid the student revolts of the 1960s, he and a classmate named Jonny decided to publish a magazine that would reflect the complaints of their school's students. They considered various names like *Today, 1966, Focus, Modern Britain and Interview,* but settled on *Student.*

"YOU WILL WIND UP IN PRISON, OR A MILLIONAIRE"

Seeking advice and financial backing for the magazine, Branson wrote to 250 members of the British parliament, whose names he found in a *Who's Who,* and a number of companies he found in the phone book. Nobody replied, and Branson and his friend decided that in order to make it more attractive to advertisers, they had to broaden their coverage to a large number of schools. It was the Vietnam War era, and student protests and everything related to "student power" was in fashion, Branson recalled.

Branson's mother loaned the new publishers four pounds sterling to cover the costs of telephones and stamps, and his father ordered up stationery with the masthead "*Student.* The Magazine for Young Brits." As time went on, while his grades went from bad to worse, *Student* became the focus of his life.

"Had I been five or six years older, the sheer absurdity of the idea of trying to sell advertising to major companies in a magazine that did not yet exist, edited by two 15-year-old schoolboys, would have prevented me from picking up the phone at all. But I was too young to contemplate failure," Branson recalled.[9] But Branson had a stroke of luck after a few months. He managed to sell one ad for 250 pounds sterling and persuade the artist Gerald Scarfe to grant him an interview and donate one of his caricatures for the magazine. The first edition of *Student* was published in January of 1968.

By then, Branson had left school. As he recalled it, the last words he heard from one of his teachers were, "Congratulations Branson. My prediction is that you will either go to prison or become a millionaire." The magazine began to draw national attention after the two young editors, working out of Jonny's garage, managed to get an interview with the actress Vanessa Redgrave.

"We managed to persuade Vanessa Redgrave to change her mind from merely sending us best wishes for the success of *Student* to giving us an interview. That interview was a turning point for us," Branson recalled.[10] From that moment on, the two editors used Redgrave's name as proof of their legitimacy, which allowed them to attract other well-known figures like British painter David Hockney and French writer Jean-Paul Sartre. And, as the magazine published its increasingly heavyweight interviews, advertising started to increase and pay for the next edition.

"THE JOHN LENNON INTERVIEW ALMOST BANKRUPTED US"

The magazine's leap into the limelight, which ironically almost sent it into bankruptcy, came when John Lennon granted *Student* an interview. Lennon was a demi-god for young people at the time, and when his media chief promised the *Student* editors that he would donate a brand new song to the magazine, Branson and Jonny decided to print a special edition of 100,000 copies, with a floppy disk, and hired a leading designer to produce the front cover.

But what looked like a golden opportunity turned into a nightmare. According to Branson, weeks went by and Lennon's recording did not arrive. The young journalists were growing nervous: they had bet the future of the magazine on that issue, and every time they called Lennon's representatives they heard a new excuse. They eventually figured out what was happening: Lennon was in the middle of a grave personal crisis. His partner had just suffered a miscarriage and Lennon had been arrested for possession of marijuana. The couple were practically in hiding. "I was in trouble myself. Our plans for the special issue had put *Student* on the brink of bankruptcy. I was getting desperate," Branson recalled.

He was so desperate, in fact, that he hired a lawyer and threatened to sue Lennon for breach of a verbal contract. A few days later, Lennon's representatives called Branson and told him they had a recording for him. When he went to pick it up, all he could hear was the beating of a heart, Branson added. "It's the heartbeat of our baby," Lennon told him. The sound then stopped. "The baby died. That's the silence of our dead baby," Lennon added as Ono cried by his side. An aide to Lennon told Branson the recording was "conceptual art." The young editor decided to redesign the cover, accept the losses and move on."[11]

"I'VE HAD MANY FAILURES IN MY LIFE"

From that time on, Branson's career was a roller coaster of successes and failures —like the careers of almost all successful entrepreneurs. As he told me during our interview, "If you don't fail, you gain nothing. An entrepreneur should not fear failure. If you fail, try again. And if you fail again, you must try again, until you succeed… To be successful, you sometimes have to fail along the way. That makes the success all that more satisfactory."[12]

One of Branson's favorite anecdotes for illustrating his glorification of failure as one of the roads to success is the story of the Beatles. In the 1960s, the group was rejected by seven music labels before they were signed. No matter how good the idea, he said, it can always fall flat one or more times before it takes off.

What's the one failure that most affected you? I asked Branson after the on-camera interview. "I've had many failures in my life," he replied. "The two first businesses that I launched were small, and both failed. When I was in school, I wanted to make sure that I would have some money when I graduated, so I planted a bunch of Christmas trees. My idea was to sell the grown-up trees after I graduated. But rabbits came and ate them all. Then I tried to do the same with parakeets that people buy as pets, called budgerigars. I had heard that they reproduced very quickly. But rats came and killed all the parakeets. So at an early age, I learned the art of failure."[13]

For many years later, and even after he became a millionaire, Branson continued to score successes and suffer reverses. A few years after its launch, *Student* folded because of a lack of revenues. But by then Branson had started to diversify and was launching his Virgin record empire. His formula was to attack much more powerful companies —in the music, aviation or any other industry— with a mixture of irreverence and creativity, offering better prices, optimum service and the aura of solidarity with consumers against abuses by the companies that dominated the market. Trying to portray himself as a David fighting against the Goliaths of industry, he went so far as to deploy a battle tank in Times Square, in the heart of New York City, and aim its smoke-puffing cannon at a giant Coca-Cola sign as a publicity stunt for his Virgin Cola.

The recipe for attacking the big companies worked to an extent, although a number of his companies did not survive the battles. As he freely acknowledged to me, "we created companies that did not work out or were crushed by other, bigger, companies. We threw ourselves against Coca-Cola. We were winning in several countries but they sent in their tanks —you know, bags of cash— and our soft drink, Virgin Cola, disappeared from the shelves. The same thing happened later with his vodka company, his credit card company in Australia and several other companies in the Virgin family. Branson maintained that his strategy in the face of all those blows was to stand up again quickly and move on to the next business. "There's nothing wrong with making mistakes, as long as you don't make the same ones over and over.[14]

For Branson, one of the best pieces of advice he ever received came from a ski instructor who told him that if he wanted to learn how to ski well, he had to be willing to fall many times. The same goes for business, he told me. "We had had setbacks, but luckily we have had more wins than loses," he concluded.[15] What's important is the final result, not the failures along the way.

HOW VIRGIN RECORDS STARTED

While publishing *Student*, during the height of the student movement and the era of free love and hippies, Branson noticed that many of the students who wrote to or phoned the magazine wanted information on issues that no one was talking about openly, such as abortion. One of his own staffers, Debbie, had complained that after she became pregnant no one in the public health services or the churches had responded to her requests for information on how and where she could have an abortion, find guidance on venereal diseases and receive psychological counseling.

"We made a long list of typical problems faced by students, and resolved to do something about it," Branson recalled.[16] The magazine created a free telephone service called the Student Counseling Center and started to hand out fliers promoting it under the headline, "Give us Your Headaches." The idea was not to make money, but to promote the magazine, Branson said. But soon the center was receiving tons of calls, including some from doctors or clinics offering their services at moderate prices, and some from suicidal teenagers who needed to talk to someone —and sometimes showed up in person at the magazine's offices seeking help.

Soon, police also showed up, to let Branson know that he was breaking a law that banned the promotion of treatments for venereal diseases. Branson argued that he was only offering advice and agreed to change the way in which his magazine promoted the center. But police returned shortly afterward and arrested the publisher, then 19 years old, for continuing to break the law. It was only the first of several skirmishes with the law that never deterred him. "That court case taught me that although I was young, wore jeans and had very little money behind me, I need not be afraid of being bullied by the police or the establishment. Particularly if I had a good barrister," Branson recalled years later.[17]

Branson also noticed that all of the youths who accessed the center had something in common —they spent a large part of their time listening to music. All used what little money they had to buy the latest records by the Rolling Stones, Bob Dylan or Jefferson Airplane. It occurred to Branson that he could boost the magazine's finances— which were falling dangerously low —by offering mail-order discounted records. In the next edition of *Student,* he inserted an ad for the offer. Within hours, the magazine was flooded with orders "and more cash than we had ever seen before."[18] The Virgin Records Empire was being born, and the *Student* magazine soon passed into oblivion.

FROM MAILED RECORDS TO STORES AND THE LABEL

Neither Branson nor his colleagues knew anything about the music industry, but that did not stop him from quickly jumping into the business with the same audacity that always characterized the young entrepreneur. They adopted the name Virgin precisely because none of them had any experience in the record business: they were total virgins in the business. Their first company, Virgin Mail Order, quickly opened its first shop in London. In contrast to the leading record shops, where the staff didn't know much about music and sold the records like any other merchandise, Virgin's employees were young hippies who knew their music and treated potential buyers like friends. And the clients, who many times walked into the shop smiling after a hit of marijuana, could spend all the time they wanted in the shops, listening to music or lounging on sofas. In just a few months, Branson opened 14 Virgin record shops in Great Britain.

Branson didn't take long to understand that the real profits in the music industry were not in retail sales, but rather in the record producing companies. His businesses were growing, but his expenses kept rising. Faced with the choice of cutting costs or expanding his business, Branson opted for the latter. It was the kind of audacity that would characterize him in the future. "Only if you're bold can you get somewhere," he has said repeatedly. So the young Branson decided to buy a house and convert it into a recording studio, with money that his parents had set aside for when he turned 30 years old. Virgin started its own recordings of rock bands and created its own record label. By then, the *Student* magazine was requiring so much time and producing so many losses that Branson and his colleagues decided to close it down. The music business seemed much more exciting.

TO PRISON FOR TAX EVASION

In 1971, when Branson was just 20 years old, his record companies were still growing, and losing money. The problem was that Virgin offered such steep price discounts, and spent so much money on promotions, rents and the post office, that it could not turn a profit. To make things worse, a postal service strike had battered its mail-order sales. At one point the businesses owed 15,000 pounds sterling, plus a 20,000 pound mortgage on the recording studio.

Branson then had the bright idea of not paying customs tariffs on imported records. "I was breaking the law, but I had always got away with breaking rules before. In those days I felt I could do no wrong and that even if I did, I wouldn't be caught," he recalled years later.[19] After some successful smuggling runs, customs authorities caught up to him. Branson learned later that many other business people had been caught trying to use the same customs ruse. Customs agents raided Virgin and seized 10,000 records that had not paid import tariffs. He spent a night in prison, sleeping on a black plastic mattress and an old pillow. The first part of his teacher's prediction had come true: he was in prison.

Branson went free the next day after agreeing to pay 15,000 pounds immediately and another 45,000 in three installments over the next three years. If he failed to pay, he could be arrested again and put on trial. Branson was not yet 21, his companies were almost bankrupt and he had to come up with 45,000 pounds to avoid going to prison. He had learned his lesson, but now needed to make money urgently. "Avoiding prison was the most persuasive incentive I ever had," he joked in one of his books.[20]

However, Branson was lucky, and in 1973 one of the artists on his Virgin Music label launched an song that broke sales records in a matter of weeks. It saved the company from bankruptcy and began bringing in enormous profits. It was *Tubular Bells*, an instrumental by Mike Oldfield that went silver, gold and then platinum, selling more than 1 million copies. Overnight, Branson, then 22, pulled in the money he owed and established Virgin as a player in the music industry.

THE PURCHASE OF THE AIRLINE

Branson's music empire prospered with several other hits by the Sex Pistols, Boy George and other rock and punk bands. At the beginning of the 1980s, Virgin created a publishing house specializing in rock music and sports books. And in 1984 he received a call from a U.S. lawyer, Randolph Fields, asking if he might be interested in buying an airline. Fields was looking for investors to relaunch Laker Airways, the cheap ticket company founded by Sir Freddie Laker that had flown between New York and London and filed for bankruptcy two years before. "It was obvious that he had contacted lots of other investors before me —a record-label owner is hardly going to be his first call."[21] Branson started to like the idea because of his experience as a music industry executive. He traveled constantly and suffered the bad service offered by airlines. An airline with better service and lower prices might be able to carve out a niche for itself. But, much like his dive into the music business, he knew nothing about the airline business.

The only company offering cheap transatlantic flights at the time was People Express. Branson wanted to know how the company was doing, so he phoned to make a reservation. The number was busy. He kept calling all morning, and never got through. "I reasoned that either People Express was very poorly managed, in which case they would be an easy target for new competition, or that they were so much in demand that there was room for new competition. It was that continual engaged tone on my telephone throughout Saturday more than anything else which triggered my belief that we could set up and run an airline," Branson recalled.[22]

Virgin Atlantic's inaugural London-New York flight, on June 22, 1984, with 250 invited journalists on board, almost never happened because two days earlier the airplane had blown an engine during a test flight. An inspector from the British aeronautical agency sitting next to Branson put his hand on the owner's shoulder and told him, "Don't worry Richard. These things happen."[23] A flock of birds had been sucked into the engine. For the inspector, that was an everyday occurrence. But it was a potential catastrophe for Branson: the engine was not insured because Virgin Atlantic did not yet have its operating license. He was expecting it later that day or the next day. The replacement cost 600,000 pounds.

Virgin's bank did not want to issue the check, saying the company had maxed out its line of credit. Branson, afraid he would have to cancel the inaugural and that his financial tightrope would leak to the public, phoned Virgin's foreign subsidiaries and ordered them to transfer all the money they could to the main office as soon as possible. The bank agreed to issue the check, the motor was replaced and the maiden flight went off as planned. But Branson learned a lesson: his companies were living dangerously, and a single unfavorable decision by a bank at any time could endanger the entire Virgin empire, which already had 3,000 employees.

PROFESSIONAL MANAGERS AND WORLD RECORDS

Following the scare over Virgin Atlantic's inaugural flight, Branson expanded with picaresque and irreverent advertisements and by publicly challenging British Airways and other major airlines, which in his view offered awful service. Virgin Atlantic put video screens on it seats before any of its competitors, offered on-board massage services and provided door-to-door limousine service to business class passengers. Those were extremely effective publicity coups because services like the limousines could only be offered by a small airline like Virgin Atlantic, which flew only between London and New York, and not by leading airlines with hundreds of global routes.

The financial problems that threatened the entire Virgin group after the engine blew up during the Virgin Atlantic test flight persuaded Branson that he had to restructure the company, bring in professional managers and dedicate himself to what he did best —invent new things and have a good time. The Virgin group, aside from Virgin Records, Virgin Music and Virgin Atlantic, already had several other enterprises of all kinds including a clothing company, a chain of pubs and a real estate company. The new managers were horrified when they saw the improvisation that reigned in Virgin. They did not understand why the group did not use its total revenues to obtain better bank credits. And they could not believe that almost no one in the company used computers or had adequate inventory accounts. They immediately began to put things in order.

Branson was meanwhile launching into new adventures. He was just 33 years old and, following the tradition of British explorers, wanted to set new records in sailing and balloon navigation and parachuting. Besides, he needed to maintain a very visible presence in the media to compete with his much more powerful rivals. It was much cheaper for Branson to generate publicity with his adventures than to pay for costly TV advertising campaigns.

"I THOUGHT I HAD BRAIN DAMAGE"

His first attempt was to break the record for a transatlantic sail, aboard a boat emblazoned with the Virgin Atlantic logo. "A successful Atlantic crossing would attract publicity in both New York and London, our sole destinations," he recalled years later.[24] But the adventure ended badly. Just three days into the crossing, the boat, built small to maximize its speed, tipped over during a powerful storm off the coast of Ireland. Its crew, including Branson, had to jump into the water and get into an inflatable lifeboat. Rocked by the waves, they radioed for help and were rescued hours later by a passing ship. During the following weeks, Branson continued to hear the roar of the ocean. "I was beginning to think I had brain damage," he recalled.[25]

A year later, with a new boat and crew, Branson tried it again and succeeded. His sailboat, *Virgin Atlantic Challenger II,* crossed the Atlantic in three days, eight hours and 31 minutes, breaking the previous record by two hours and nine minutes. From there on, thrilled by the excitement and the publicity that his adventures generated, he set off to break other records. In 1987 he started to experiment with balloons, crossing the Atlantic aboard the *Virgin Atlantic Flyer.* In 1991 he set a speed record for crossing the Pacific. And over the next four years he made several attempts to go around the world in a balloon with Per Lindstrand, breaking a number of records. But none of those adventures could match his campaign to launch the first private spaceship for tourists and become its first passenger.

"BEING AN ADVENTURER AND A BUSINESSMAN IS NOT VERY DIFFERENT"

Intrigued by his adventures, I asked Branson during our interview what drew him to the expeditions. "My life's interest is to challenge myself with immensely unreachable goals and overcome them," he replied. But why does a multimillionaire businessman want to risk his life crossing the Atlantic aboard a small competition sailboat or the Pacific aboard a balloon? I insisted. What kind of satisfaction did he get from those adventures?

"Look, I believe that being an adventurer and a businessman is not all that different. "If someone tells me, 'No one has crossed the English

Channel, the Atlantic or the Pacific, or gone around the world aboard a balloon' and I can fly a balloon, then I am going to try to solve the technological problems, I am going to train physically to do it and in the end I am going to say, 'What the hell, let's try it!'" he replied. "I've had many marvelous adventures in my life. Now I experience them with my children, climbing mountains, trying to break transatlantic navigation records or kite surfing across the English Channel. And that's very satisfying. That's how I try to prove to myself, and prove to my children, that we can overcome any physical or technology challenge. It's not that different in business. You try to turn your dreams into reality."

"IF YOU'RE NOT INNOVATING, YOU GO BACKWARDS"

I also asked Branson about his next personal and business adventures. "Well, as far as space exploration, I am going into space with my children this year. And we will start to take passengers into space next year. Then we will put satellites in orbit, which will help many industries to make progress. And we hope that in the next few years we can start to think about orbital flights, space hotels and then the exploration of the universe. And finally, we want to make regular commercial flights much faster and cheaper —for example, Buenos Aires to London in two hours. Those are some of our dreams and challenges."[26]

Branson had never stopped coming up with new ideas, as bizarre as they seemed. He had started placing ads for his mail-order record business in his *Student* magazine, hired young rock music fans and put sofas in his music stores, and offered free limousine service to his airline passengers in business class. And now he was talking about space travel. His bet was on constant expansion, always looking ahead and never resting on his laurels.

"Innovation is what keeps successful companies alive," he has said repeatedly. "If you're not innovating, you go backwards." Almost all business administration schools teach that companies should focus on what they know, and the world's top companies do exactly that: Coca-Cola makes beverages, Microsoft makes computers and Nike make sports equipment. "But Virgin was the exception to the rule, even though all of the companies in the group had common characteristics, such as offering a fun experience and a low cost," Branson boasted. His philosophy is to constantly innovate in all areas, even though many times that is the most difficult road.

ELON MUSK AND HIS SPACEX PROJECT

Elon Musk, who made his fortune after founding PayPal, the Internet payment company, was Branson's main rival in the nascent industry of private space travel. And to many, the South Africa native who obtained a physics degree from the University of Pennsylvania and a master's in business administration from its Wharton School, is the far more serious of the two.

After selling PayPal for $1.5 billion in 2002, Musk, who owned nearly 12 percent of the company, could have easily retired to an island in the Pacific and lived a quiet life, investing in real estate or the stock market. He was just 30 years old and had a personal fortune of about $150 million. But within a short time he created three companies and invested all his fortune in them: SpaceX for space exploration, Tesla for manufacturing electric cars, and Solar City for making solar energy products.

Like Branson, or perhaps even more so, Musk was an idealist. He was more interested in making history as a benefactor of humanity than as a successful businessman. But Musk was much more serious than Branson in the way he managed his space company as a scientific project and a business. While Branson was making headlines recruiting Justin Bieber as a passenger in his first space tourism trips, Musk was quietly working with NASA on his long-term space projects.

And NASA was clearly taking Musk more seriously than Branson. In 2008 NASA gave him a $1.6 billion contract to make 12 deliveries of cargo, and eventually astronauts, to the International Space Station.

Starting in 2009, SpaceX would become the first private enterprise to regularly deliver space cargo for NASA.

When Musk was asked about his rivalry with Branson and the tourist space trips of Virgin Galactic, the South African-U.S. businessman would point out the differences. "I have nothing against tourism: Richard Branson is brilliant at creating a brand but he's not a technologist. What he's doing is fundamentally about entertainment, and I think it's cool, but it's not likely to affect humanity's future. That's what we're trying to do," he declared.[27]

Although his Tesla electric car company was attracting increasing attention in the media, Musk was obsessed with his space project. He has said that in all of history there was only half a dozen truly important events, such as the creation of life from a single cell, the start of multi cell organisms, the separation of plants and animals and the move of animals from water to land. "The next moment will be life becoming multi planetary, an unprecedented adventure that would dramatically enhance the richness and diversity of our collective consciousness," he has said.[28]

"It would also serve as a hedge against the myriad —and growing— threats to our survival. An asteroid or a super volcano could certainly destroy us, but we also face risks the dinosaurs never saw: an engineered virus, nuclear war, inadvertent creation of a micro black hole, or some some as-yet-unknown technology could spell the end of us. Sooner or later, we must expand life beyond our little blue mud ball —or go extinct," he added.[29] The principal obstacle to the discovery of new planets that can support life was the enormous costs of the single-use spacecraft, Musk said, and that's why he decided to solve that problem by building spacecraft that could be reused and were much cheaper than NASA's vehicles.

"I NEVER GIVE UP"

The first three attempts to launch SpaceX into orbital flights were spectacular failures and left the company on the edge of bankruptcy.

All three flights had technical problems and did not leave the Earth's orbit. In the first flight, one of the spacecraft's engines was damaged during takeoff. In the second, the vehicle could not reach orbiting altitude. The third flight, in 2008, was aborted after just two minutes. By then, Musk had burned through the $100 million he had committed to the space project.

To make things worse, his Tesla electric car company had run out of money. His dream of developing an electric vehicle that would help to cut gasoline consumption and environmental pollution around the world was crashing. Musk had to chose between keeping the last of the money he received from the sale of PayPal or invest his last dollar. Although scared, he did not hesitate. He invested his last $40 million in Tesla, bringing his personal investment in the electric car maker to $75 million.

At the time, Musk's personal life was in total chaos. He had just asked his wife, Justine, the mother of his five children, for a divorce. And six weeks later he sent her a text message announcing his engagement to a beautiful and much younger British actress, Justine wrote later in the women's magazine *Marie Claire*. Musk's divorce trial and his new love —they married in 2010 and divorced in 2012— became the talk of the gossip columns. "Elon was obsessed with his work. When he was home, his mind was elsewhere," Justine wrote. "We did what he said… 'I am your wife,' I told him repeatedly, 'not your employee. 'If you were my employee,' he said just as often, 'I would fire you.' "[30]

The lowest point of Musk's economic and personal crisis came at the end of 2008, shortly after the Tesla financial rescue and the third failed flight of *SpaceX*. After the U.S. financial crisis exploded that September, Wall Street was hit by the worst collapse since the Great Depression in 1929 and thousands of companies went broke. The collapse of the global economy came at a time when Musk had not only run out of money, but needed another $20 million to bankroll new *SpaceX* test flights.

At the end of 2008, when everything seemed to indicate that Musk's three companies were taking a dive, the businessman bet everything on the success of the fourth SpaceX test flight. Years later, when he was asked during a *60 Minutes* interview on CBS if he had ever thought about canceling that fourth flight, saving whatever money he could and retire to an easy life, Musk replied, "Never." Why not? "I don't ever give up. I'd have to be dead or completely incapacitated."[31]

Just eight weeks after the third failed test, Musk launched the fourth test, knowing full well that he did not have a single cent in the bank and that if he failed, he would be forced to close the company and fire all its employees. Luckily, the flight was successful. It was the first flight of a private spacecraft that carried out a mission. Until that time, only the U.S., Russian and Japanese governments and the European Space Agency had sent cargo capsules to the International Space Station. A few days later, on Dec. 25, 2008, NASA announced it was giving $1.6 billion to the young entrepreneur for cargo missions to the International Space Station. In just a few weeks, SpaceX had gone from being on the edge of bankruptcy to a key NASA partner.

A MARS COLONY WITH 80,000 PEOPLE?

With the crisis over and his companies on the mend, thanks in large part to NASA's decision to contract SpaceX and reduce its own budgets, Musk started to seriously plan the launch of manned flights to Mars. According to his calculations, that can become a reality in 2024. And he would like to be on the inaugural flight. "The first flight would be risky; if I felt comfortable that the company's mission will continue, that my kids have grown up, then I'd be on the first mission," he has said.[32]

Asked if it would not be better to leave space exploration up to governments, Musk said governments are much more effective supporting basic research than promoting the development of commercial ventures. "The government was very good about getting the basis of the Internet going, but it languished. Commercial companies took a hand around 1995, and then it accelerated. We need something like that in space," he said.[33]

During a conference at the Royal Aeronautical Society in London at the end of 2012, Musk proposed building a permanent colony in Mars with 80,000 people. He would first send 10 people to Mars —with one-way tickets— to start building the infrastructure for the future colony and increase the population gradually. Those pioneers would take with them construction machinery and the equipment needed to produce fertilizers, methane and oxygen from the nitrogen and carbon dioxide in Mars, he explained.

Science fiction? Not at all, Musk has argued. When Columbus sailed for the New World, the chances that he would return to Europe were minimal but that did not stop him. The same can be said about the pilgrims who founded the United States. A permanent colony in Mars is not only feasible, he argues, but necessary to guarantee the preservation of our species.

KARGIEMAN, THE ARGENTINE WHO LAUNCHES MINI SATELLITES

Musk and Branson are not the only ones revolutionizing the space industry. There are other less well-known "space nuts" around the world like Emiliano Kargieman, an Argentine who is hot on their heels with projects that are less flamboyant but equally transformative. To be honest, I had never heard of Kargieman until one of my visits to Silicon Valley, when I asked Salim Ismail, the entrepreneur-professor in charge of foreign relations at Singularity University, who he thought was the top innovator in Latin America. Without missing a beat, Ismail mentioned Kargieman. "He is going to revolutionize the global satellite industry," Ismael told me.

Kargieman is trying to democratize space, producing low-cost mini satellites to compete with the kinds of large satellites that only governments and international corporations can afford. While current satellites used to monitor borders and detect forest fires, among other tasks, are very costly and can take one photo every three days, Kargieman's idea is to launch a 15 mini satellite constellation that can snap a photo every five minutes. He was inspired by computers. At first, computers were so enormous and expensive that only governments and companies could acquire them. But then came personal computers, which were smaller and cheaper, and available to anyone.

In contrast to traditional satellites, which cost about $107 million, Kargieman is producing mini satellites that cost $100,000, weigh less than 4.5 pounds and already have been launched for tests from China and Russia. He plans to flood space with his mini satellites and allow anyone to create programs for them, in the same way anyone can create Internet applications.

"Obviously, the traditional satellites and ours are not the same," Kargieman told me during a lengthy interview. "Although they have the same capacity, ours are riskier because they are more likely to break down and malfunction, and they have a much shorter working life. But on the other hand, ours are so cheap that for the cost of putting one traditional satellite in space you can have 1,000 of ours. So if one fails, it's not that important because you will have the luxury of a constellation of small satellites and overall services will not be affected.

The Argentine entrepreneur —who studied math for five years but never completed his thesis and then returned to the university to study philosophy— argues that the aerospace industry, unlike computers, has remained frozen in time. Both industries started out as projects for armed forces. But while computers became an item of mass consumption, the aerospace industry remained in military hands and only now is the private sector trying to break into the business. The military agencies that launched satellites into space and then rented some of their capacity to telecommunications and television companies needed large and reliable satellites because they could not fail. The cost of sending up an astronaut to repair a satellite was unacceptable, he explained. Kargieman's satellites, however, are disposable and require a much lower investment.

Kargieman, like Branson, Musk and other new space adventurers, knew little about the aerospace industry before he jumped into the business. But during a trip to the NASA Space Center in 2010, he was struck by its technology gap: it was using obsolete technology because of a lack of funds, inertia and the loss of political support since the first U.S. astronaut stepped on the Moon. "What I saw was incredible. They were going into space with 1970s engineering," he told me. One night, sitting before his laptop at 2 am, Kargieman decided to transform the space industry.

"I COULD NOT CHOOSE BETWEEN TECHNOLOGY AND PHILOSOPHY"

In 2010, Kargieman was 35 years old and faced an existential crisis. He had studied math and philosophy at the Universidad de Buenos Aires and founded a number of relatively successful technology companies, but he did not see himself working in them for the rest of his life. Son of a psychiatrist and a psychoanalyst in Buenos Aires —said to have the highest number of psychologists per capita of any city in the world— he had been in love with computers since his parents gave him a Timex Sinclair when he was nine years old. "From childhood, I was fascinated by computers," he recalled. He started hacking as a teenager, in part because of *WarGames*, a 1983 movie about a young hacker who breaks into government computers, and in part because a cousin, Ivan, had a modem and was experimenting with it. The two youths started to hack public telephones and other people's computers, earning a certain fame among their peers and, like many other hackers, going on to advise companies on protecting their systems.

Kargieman was first hired by the Dirección General Impositiva, Argentina's tax collecting agency. Its director had contracted one of Kargieman's friends to put together a group of hackers and test the security of the agency's computers. From there on, the young hackers received more and more requests from companies and government agencies to test their computer security systems. They had so many jobs that at the age of 19 Kargieman and cousin Ivan founded a company, Core Security Technologies, and offered their services to clients abroad.

Their first foreign client was a Canadian company. "Once you start on this track, it's like a club. Everyone talks to everyone and when they know you and you do a good job, they call you," he recalled.

In 1998, when he was 23, he abandoned his diploma thesis in math and moved to California. His company was growing rapidly, and the founders saw greater opportunities in the U.S. and Brazilian markets. They were not wrong. Core Security Technologies, today based in Boston and with more than 100 employees in the United States and a similar number in Argentina, was soon hired by leading international companies, like Amazon.

Core Security continued to grow, but Kargieman left in 2006 to co-found Aconcagua Ventures, a venture capital company, with several partners. The company had an excellent goal, Kargieman said: to invest in the ideas of talented young Argentines like himself and turn them into global enterprises. But it did not turn out as he expected, in part because the global economic crisis in 2008 led the investors to be much more cautious in supporting the budding projects. "It was a very frustrating experience," Kargieman said. The young businessman wanted to invest in many projects, but Aconcagua Ventures wound up supporting only four. And only one was moving full steam ahead.

Disappointed, Kargieman started to look for something that would inspire him. He started to study philosophy. In 2009, married, with no children and some savings —"not a lot, because in Core we reinvested everything that came in," he said— he signed up for a six-month course at the Universidad de la Laguna in Spain's Canary Island. He returned to Buenos Aires and at the beginning of 2010 —still undecided on launching a new business or dedicating the rest of his life to teaching philosophy at a university— he saw a Singularity University announcement for a summer course on the latest developments in innovation. He signed up.

"I got there and sat at a table in front of a guy. When I asked him what he did, he said he was organizing a company to ship cargo to the Moon," Kargieman recalled. "I looked at him, to make sure he wasn't joking. It was Bob Richards, one of the founders of Singularity

University and Moon Express before that. When I asked him about his business model, he didn't want to say much. But that forced me to think a lot about the space industry. I realized there was a lot to do."[34]

THE NIGHT THAT CHANGED HIS LIFE

In the following day, Kargieman began to study the issue of satellites, taking advantage of the fact that Singularity University was on the campus of NASA's Ames Research Center. Although the campus is nothing special —it's on an old military base, in old buildings that have not been refurbished in years— many aerospace companies have laboratories there. Kargieman started to talk to as many people as he could about the satellite industry.

"One night, around two or three in the morning, I was in one of the Singularity University's study halls, analyzing the satellite market on my laptop, when I thought that something different was needed. I did some research and realized that, in principle, it seemed possible to manufacture smaller and cheaper satellites," he told me. "I was super-excited that night, and decided I was going to focus on that business. I saw the opportunity to implement an important change in an industry that had been stagnant for many years and had a great potential to improve our lives."

Kargieman started to put together a business plan, offering investors a network of cheap satellites that could be used for telephone and Internet communications, taking images of Earth for climate and agricultural monitoring and other custom projects designed by users. Anyone, for example, could use the small satellites to create a TV channel just for his neighborhood, or just for people interested in a specific topic, or perhaps a channel where surfers could monitor conditions at their nearest beaches. "This will open the doors to the world of special applications. Because in the long run, the applications will come from the users and not from our company, just like it happened with the Internet," Kargieman said.

He launched the new company, Satellogic, in 2010 with backing from private investors and INVAP, an Argentine company founded in the 1970s by the Argentine Atomic Energy Commission and the Province of Rio Negro. Although the Argentine government invested $1.6 million for the right to use the satellites for university research, Kargieman said the company is a private enterprise that he controls and has no national government participation.

Satellogic launched its first satellite in April of 2013, named *Cube-Bug-1* and nicknamed "Captain Beto" after a song by Argentine rocker Luis Alberto Spinetta, aboard a Chinese rocket that also delivered other satellites to space. A second satellite was deployed four months later, nicknamed "Manolito" after the character in the acclaimed Argentine comic strip *Mafalda*. And in mid-2014 Satellogic used a rocket launched from Yasny, Russia, to deploy the mini satellite *Tita*, named after the actress Tita Merello. It was the first launch without any government support at all, and was to be followed by 15 more over the next 12 months, Kargieman told journalists at the time.

By then, Kargieman was facing stiff competition from all sides, including NASA itself, Stanford University and companies like Planet Labs, which was planning to launch 28 mini satellites that would form a ring around Earth and transmit real-time information about traffic congestion and deforestation, among other issues. It remains to be seen whether Kargieman's Satellogic will establish itself as one of the leaders in the field of mini satellites. But it was off the ground and its three years of operations —a long time in the world of innovation— gave it a certain advantage in experience and knowledge of the market.

THE ART OF CONSTANT REINVENTION

It would be easy to see Musk or Branson as eccentric millionaires who promote space exploration in order to promote themselves or their companies, but that would be wrong. Both invested a good part of their fortunes on the effort, at times even risking their entire business empires. Instead of enjoying their fortunes, or accumulating more money and continuing to rise on the lists of the world's wealthiest people, they chose to risk much of what they had —in the case of Musk, everything— to push forward with their dream of saving humanity through space colonies.

They are businessmen who, like the Argentine Kargieman, reinvent themselves constantly, who are not afraid of change and who live their lives always looking ahead. In the case of Branson, his entire business history was one of persistent reinventions that again and again saved him from bankruptcy. He reinvented himself when the *Student* magazine went broke and he started his mail-order record business. He reinvented himself again after a postal strike, selling the records in shops, and then again as an airline executive and again as a galactic entrepreneur. And along the way he founded hundreds of other companies.

As I write this, Branson's companies have more than 40,000 employees and include private trains, jean stores, a chain of gyms, cosmetics, credit cards and insurance companies. Branson, like Musk and Guardiola, believes that it's not healthy for any company to always do the same thing. "That's not just a limitation. It's dangerous,"[35] he said, perhaps already thinking about his next business adventure.[35]

193

8

Salman Khan and the "flipped schools"

"We will never charge anything... It's a public charity"

Salman Khan, the man who is revolutionizing education around the world with his free online educational videos and practical exercises, is not earning a fortune like Bill Gates, Steven Jobs or Mark Zuckerberg. And perhaps he never will. Nevertheless, Khan radiates a much higher level of personal satisfaction than most other leading Internet innovators. Unlike many others, he is a "social innovator" whose mission as an entrepreneur is to help the world's poor.

He's been achieving that, and much more. It's no accident that *Time* magazine listed him as one of the 100 most influential people in the world, or that the *Forbes* magazine put him on its cover as a pioneer of 21st Century education. The Khan Academy's Web page (www. khanacademy.org) not only has 60 million visitors per year who receive free classes in math, algebra, history and other topics, but is turning upside down all of the traditional system of education in the United States and a growing number of other countries. Khan has become the most visible face of the new phenomenon of "flipped schools" in which students, instead of studying in school and doing homework at home, study at home with interactive videos and do the homework in school, with help from their teachers. That's exactly the opposite of what most of us did when we were in school.

194

Khan vows that he will never sell his enterprise, charge for its education videos or put advertising on the videos. What motivates him, he says, is to radically change the way in which children learn in school, in order to make the world a better place. "Our mission is to provide a free, top-tier education for everyone, anywhere. We will not only continue to offer our materials free of charge, but we will never become a commercial business or accept advertising," he said.[1]

When I interviewed him for more than an hour from his office in Mountain View, in the heart of Silicon Valley, Khan —a youthful 37-year-old raised in New Orleans, his parents had migrated from India and Bangladesh— already had about 50 employees in the Khan Academy, and his non-profit organization had an operating budget of $13 million a year.[2] Since founding the Web site for the Khan Academy from his home in 2008, he had helped tens of millions of students in 216 countries to improve their school performance.

Nevertheless, like many of you reading these lines, I found it difficult at first to believe that he was doing this for purely altruistic reasons. His biography was not one of an idealistic young man uninterested in material things, but rather the complete opposite. Khan's academic formation was typical of someone who wanted to become a top-notch executive or launch a company that would earn him millions and millions of dollars. Khan had degrees in four careers from the best universities in the world: bachelor's degrees in math, electronic engineering and computer sciences from the Massachusetts Institute of Technology, a master's in computer science from MIT and a master's in business administration from Harvard. And after graduating from Harvard, he went to work at an investment fund, Wohl Capital Management, analyzing investment projects. It looked like he was heading for a job where he would be making lots of money.

Was Khan's altruism sincere, or was it a strategy to gradually build an online educational empire and later sell it, I asked myself before the interview.

"WE WILL NEVER CHARGE ANYTHING"

Right at the start of our chat, I asked Khan about his personal and Khan Academy finances. I also wanted to know if he planned to sell the academy at some point and pocket millions of dollars, just as Zuckerberg did with Facebook after the company had racked up an extraordinary number of followers. Khan shook his head from side to side.

"You know, Khan Academy is an odd organization. In my previous life, I worked for a profit-making company, I now live in the middle of Silicon Valley, and in many ways we look like a traditional Silicon Valley company because we're on the Internet. But we're not," he told me. "In fact, we're not even a company. We are a non-profit organization, and our mission is to provide free education for the entire world. We will never charge, and you will never see advertising on our Web site. That's because of a fundamental belief. I got so much satisfaction when I started this, to help my nephews with math lessons, I got so much psychological gratification receiving letters from people who told me that I was helping them, that I felt this was all too important to turn it into just a company."

But how do you make a living?, I asked again.

"That's a normal question. How do we pay the bill. The answer is simple. We work thanks to philanthropy. We receive significant funds from the Gates Foundation, from Google, Ann and John Doerr, Reed Hastings of Netflix, the Carlos Slim foundation, the Jorge Lemann foundation in Brazil and many, many others. They see us as part of their philanthropic contribution to education. The number of people we help is so large that they see us as a good philanthropic investment," Khan explained.

Let's see if I understand this correctly, I insisted. The videos are free for everyone, and there's absolutely no advertising, of any type and in any place?

"Right. The Khan Academy is a non-profit. And I am not the owner of Khan Academy. No one owns Khan Academy. It is a charity," he said. "The videos are free. Not just the videos, but also the educational software, which is excellent —in my opinion, the most modern, better than anything else available on the commercial market. It's all paid for by foundations and philanthropic donations."

"I STARTED MAKING VIDEOS FOR MY COUSIN"

Khan told me that his giant Internet academy was born in 2004, when he was living in Boston and started to tutor by phone a 12-year-old cousin, Nadia, who lived in New Orleans. Nadia's family had visited Boston and the girl's mother told Khan that Nadia was having problems with her math class. "I was working as an analyst in an investment fund (Wohl Capital Management) and my cousin Nadia needed help with math, so I started to tutor her by phone," Khan told me. "That worked out well. She started to improve her performance in math classes, and I started to tutor her younger brothers, Ali and Arman. Then word started to get around the family that I was giving free private lessons. And of course more family members —and increasingly distant relatives— started to ask me to help their children."

"Two years later, in 2006, I was tutoring 10 to 15 cousins and family friends," he said. At that time, he was not yet making videos, but had started to develop software to help his cousins do practical exercises, correct them and grade their work. "Later, a friend suggested that I put my classes on video and post them on YouTube so all the cousins could see them. At first, I thought it was a dumb idea. I told him, 'YouTube is for videos of kittens playing piano, not for serious things like math.' I went home, got over the fact that it had not been my own idea and decided to try it," he recalled.

"The first two videos I posted on YouTube were on algebra and pre-algebra concepts. After a while, it became clear to me that many other people, besides my cousins, were watching them. The audience kept growing, and I was working on the software. In 2009, that's the only thing I was thinking about. I already had a little more than 100,000 people looking at the videos. I started the Khan Academy as a school with the mission of making free educational videos for anyone any-where in the world," he added. "It all started with my cousin Nadia."

A FAMILY CULTURE OF EDUCATION

Still somewhat skeptical about his tale, I asked Khan what had moti-vated him to provide free telephone tutoring to a dozen cousins. Although I knew that Indian students do very well in U.S. universi-ties, and I had seen during trips to India the importance that families put on education, I found it difficult to believe that a young man in the United States, instead of going to bars to have fun, would spend several nights each week giving free math lessons to cousins.

Why did you do it?, I asked him.

"Well, I am going to turn around your question. I don't understand why more people don't do that," Khan replied.

Perhaps because he was raised by a single mother and grew up without the presence of a father, his extended family has always been especially important for Khan. "I believe that connecting with family members is extremely gratifying. As we grow up and become indepen-dent, we start to live our own lives and we only see relatives at family gatherings or dinners. That's very superficial. And we all crave a connec-tion with the extended family. We all want to be able to connect with our parents. It wasn't only my cousins who benefited. I benefited as well. I could make a connection. In a more practical sense, when someone is 11 or 12 years old, that's the age when you can really help them, when their mind can be changed," he told me.

Curiously, Khan does not come from a wealthy family, like you might image for someone who puts aside earning a lot of money to dedicate himself to helping others. He was born in New Orleans and his father, a pediatrician born in Bangladesh, separated from his mother when he was very young. "I never got to know my father well before he died. I was raised by my mother, who was single," Khan said.

Khan said his family was poor when he was growing up. His mother worked in a supermarket and a hospital. "We had barely enough. My mother worked at a lot of things, but we had very limited resources," he told me. But, as in many Indian families in the United States whose children earn high grades in school, the top priority for his mother —who had a university degree— was always to provide a good education for her children. They had a family culture of education.

"My sister, who is three years older, was a good student. She was my tutor. And in our circle of friends I saw a lot of people, many of them the parents of my friends, who were doctors or engineers. I think that combination helped me to realize that education was very important," Khan added. "During most of my education, I was a good student, not an outstanding student. But I think around the 10th grade I started to realize the importance of education. I realized that if I really wanted to be successful in life, I had to take my education seriously. And that's when I started to work harder. I started to be more competitive, in a healthy way. And that helped me get into MIT, what pushed me forward."

After earning his degrees at MIT and Harvard, Khan went to work at Wohl Capital Management almost by chance. "It's funny, but I didn't even know what a hedge fund was when I went to the Harvard business school. But I had a class on capital markets, and loved it. I asked the professor what kind of job would have something to do with his class, and he told me I could work in a hedge fund. And I told him good, but what's a hedge fund?", Khan said. "I learned what a hedge fund was, and I found a job in a very small one, with an incredible mentor and supervisor. I really liked that job. It was fascinating. It was intellectually challenging and I learned how the investment world worked. It was place where I had a good career and was earning good money. If I was eventually promoted to my supervisor's job, as portfolio manager, I could have earned a really good salary. So it's not that I left that job because I didn't like it. What happened was that the Khan Academy was even more fascinating for me, gave me an even bigger psychological reward."

THE LETTER THAT CHANGED HIS LIFE

When I asked him about the precise moment when he decided to leave the hedge fund, and how difficult it was to do that, Khan told me that by 2008 he had been working on the educational videos and software for two or three years, and it was increasingly evident to him that what he was doing as a hobby had enormous potential. But he had recently married Umaima Marvi, an internal medicine physician, and the decision to dedicate all his time to doing something that brought in no income was very difficult. "My wife and I reviewed our finances, our student loans, and we said it was not the time to start a non-profit," he recalled.

But by the end of 2008, the volume of students watching the Khan Academy videos was so large that Khan could not handle the work alone. More than 100,000 students were accessing the Web site at the beginning of 2009, and students were increasingly asking for more materials, to be able to study other subject areas. "I started to receive many letters from people telling me how much I had helped them. There was one letter in particular, from an African-American student, who wrote that no one had ever taken him seriously, that he had been doing poorly in school, that he had not been heading to a university. And he found Khan Academy by luck, while trying to get some help with his studies during one summer. He wrote that when he took the university entrance exam, he had a perfect score in math, and that had never happened to him before. And so this student, who had never done well in math, was now at a university where everyone told him that he was a math genius and should specialize in mathematics. I particularly remember that letter," he added. "We received a lot of other letters, and we started to get some attention and recognition. My wife and I then said, well, we have some savings, which was in fact money we were going to use for a down payment on a house. But I said I would try to do it for one year, and maybe people would realize the many benefits of what we're doing. And then perhaps some philanthropist will decide to help us and pay me a reasonable salary so we could dedicate ourselves to this."

THE FIRST DONATION

Getting the first donation was not easy. The Khan Academy was continuing to grow, but no one was putting a dime into the project. Again and again, the business people Khan approached told him his work was very worthwhile, but they could not make any contributions at the time. In all, nine months passed before the first significant donation arrived —in the least expected way.

"When you start something like this, you're very naïve," Khan recalled. "You think that people will realize that you're doing something important, that it's a good cause that needs funds because it needs to hire a lot of people. But I spoke to a lot of people, and I was rejected by a lot of people. After nine months I grew more and more stressed. I started to dust off my resumé, thinking that I had no choice but to try to find a new job. My son had been born, and we were spending our savings." To top it all off, Khan and his wife had moved from Boston to Silicon Valley, one of the most expensive parts of the United States, because the fund where Khan worked had moved there.

The first important donation came from Ann Doerr, the wife of John Doerr, a Silicon Valley multimillionaire who made his fortune as a venture capital investor in technology companies. Khan received an e-mail from her with "I am a great admirer" on the subject line, and of course opened it immediately. He did not immediately recognize her as John Doerr's wife. She was asking for a street address where she could send him a donation. That was not unusual, because many people had sent him donations of $10, $20 and even $100 in that way. But a few weeks later he received a donation of $10,000 from Ann Doerr. Khan thanked her by e-mail, and she suggested they meet for lunch so he could tell her more about his online academy.

"We lived nearby, and we got together over lunch. She asked me about my mission, and I told her that I wanted to offer free education to anybody anywhere in the world. She told me that it seemed like an ambitious goal, but that she could not understand how I was making ends meet. I told her, 'The truth is, I am not making ends meet any more,' and that I was living off our savings. Ann was surprised. I drove home and I had barely parked the car when I got a text message from her saying, 'You have to be able to support yourself economically. I just sent you $100,000.'"

PRAISE FROM BILL GATES AND CARLOS SLIM

One month after the lunch with Ann Doerr, Khan received a message just as or even more gratifying. He was teaching a summer school class, which he had started for a close-up study of the "flipped schools," in which students go to school to do their homework. In the middle of a class, he received a text message from Ann and opened it immediately. "As you can imagine, I take her text messages very seriously," he told me with a smile.

His benefactor was telling him that at that very moment she was at a conference with 1,000 other people at the Aspen Ideas Festival, and that Bill Gates had just spent the last five minutes saying wonderful things about the Khan Academy. Khan could not believe it. He had never met Gates, or anyone even close to Gates. "I thought I was dreaming," he recalled. After the class, Khan ran to his computer and spent several days trying to find the video of Gates' presentation on YouTube. When he finally found it, he saw Gates on a stage, answering questions from an interviewer and saying that he had found an extraordinary site on the Web called khanacademy.org and that he was using it himself to help his 11-year-old Rory solve math and algebra problems. Gates said Rory was "devouring" Khan's short videos on all the subject areas. The Microsoft founder then recounted Khan's story, how he had quit his job to dedicate himself to improving the quality of education, and added that "it was really lucky his wife let him quit his banking job."

Khan recalled that when he saw Gates on YouTube, "I was very happy, but I was also very nervous, because those videos were made with my cousin Nadia in mind, not for Bill Gates." A short while later, Khan received a call from Gates' chief of staff, who said "Bill" wanted to meet him. Did he perhaps have an opening on his agenda to go up to Seattle and discuss how the Gates Foundation might help the Khan Academy. Khan said he looked at his agenda, which was blank, and replied, as seriously as he could, "Yes, of course, I can make some time for the visit."

He met with Gates in Seattle on Aug. 22, 2010. Khan was more than nervous. As he remembered it, he told Gates and his advisers what the Khan Academy was doing, but he was so anxious that 20 percent of his mind was focused on what he was saying and the other 80 percent was focused on just one thought: "Do you realize the guy in front of you, who is listening to you is BILL GATES?" After Khan finished his presentation, Gates asked some questions and at the end said, "This is fantastic," Khan recalled. A few weeks later, in September of 2010, the Gates Foundation announced its first donation to the Khan Academy, for $1.5 million.

Almost simultaneously, Google donated $2 million and the Khan Academy started to gather even more international attention. In October of the same year, Khan recruited Shantanu Sinha, a high school and MIT classmate then working for the McKinsey & Co. management consulting firm, as president of the Khan Academy. He also hired several software developers and moved the academy operations out of his home and to an office. His dream of creating a non-profit enterprise to revolutionize education around the world was starting to become a reality.

Khan later met with Mexican business mogul Carlos Slim, who was in California to visit his friend John Doerr. While chatting about how to improve the quality of education, Doerr had told Slim, "You have to meet Salman Khan." As Khan recalls it, "we met, and in that first meeting Carlos Slim proposed that we work together. Obviously, I felt honored."[3] Khan traveled to Mexico at the invitation of the Slim Foundation, and with its support the academy began to translate hundreds of videos on math into Spanish. At the end of 2013, the Khan Academy launched its Spanish-language Web site, es.khanacademy.org, with virtually all of its videos, practical exercises and progress charts translated into Spanish.

THE IDEA OF THE FLIPPED SCHOOLS

Khan told me from the start that the concept of "flipped schools" was not his invention. He had first heard the term in 2008, when he was starting to get e-mails from teachers saying that thanks to his videos they had "flipped" classes with excellent results. "What the teachers were telling me was that instead of teaching classes in school, they were telling students to watch my videos at home, each one at their own pace, and then were using the classroom time to do the exercises and solve problems," he recalled. "And that was a very simple change. What was done before in the classroom, the children could do on their own time and at their own pace. And what used to be homework, which the student had to do alone, could be done in the classroom, with other kids around them and the teacher nearby. The teacher could determine the level of each student and help them solve problems. And when all that is done, a lot of positive things begin to happen."

Like what?, I asked Khan.

"The lessons outside the classroom, at home, start to become more interactive because the students can watch them at their own pace, pause, rewind and watch them again. And there's no need to take notes about everything, because the video lessons are always available for consultation," Khan explained. "As soon as you take the lessons outside the school, you allow the students to study at their own pace. And if students can study at their own pace, then the more advanced students in the classroom can help the students moving at a slower pace. So 'flipping' the classes was not my idea, but the Khan Academy is a tool that helps to do it. It offers a personalized learning environment where students can learn concepts and advance, everyone at their own pace."

ELIMINATING CLASSROOM GAPS

According to Khan, the combination of educational videos and exercises customized for each student allow a fundamental change: they eliminate the gaps that students suffer when they miss a class because they were sick or did not understand the concept. In a traditional educational system, the time for learning something is fixed, while the students' ability to understand it varies. In other words, the class must keep moving at all costs to meet the requirement of teaching each concept within the established time period, independently of how much the students actually learn.

Student grades in the traditional educational system also reflect that model. Students receive a passing grade if they correctly answer 70, 80 or, in the toughest of cases, 90 percent of the questions in a test. But that also means they did not understand 30, 20 or 10 percent of the material, and are missing basic knowledge that they will need in the next classes. If a student does not understand math concepts, he or she will have difficulties following an algebra class, and so on down the road. With time, the gaps in knowledge accumulate and the students find it increasingly harder to continue. Many fall so far behind that they wind up repeating a year or even dropping out of school.

At the Khan Academy, however, no student can advance to the next lesson if they don't understand 100 percent of the previous lesson. This idea, known as "mastery learning," was popularized by Benjamin Bloom in 1968 but never managed to win broad acceptance in the United States. It was too difficult for the teachers to individually track the progress of each student, especially in large classes. Even if teachers managed to do it, there was the problem of how to give each student the exercises and explanations needed to cover their respective gaps. And teachers could never really do that because they had to stick to their time lines. The class must go on.

The difference today is that with online education, teachers can easily overcome these difficulties, Khan argues. If the student does not understand something on the video he's watching, he pushes the rewind button and watches it again. And if he still doesn't understand it, he can access an exercise specifically designed to help him solve the problem. Meanwhile, teachers can use their own computer to see exactly how each of their students are doing and which problems are most difficult, allowing them to focus on those issues. And if a student has problems understanding something because he forgot something he learned last year, that's not a problem. Unlike a blackboard, the videos are not erased. The lessons never disappear, because they are always available online. According to Khan, for the first time ever we can make sure that students no longer have gaps in their knowledge.

IS THIS THE END OF FLESH AND BLOOD TEACHERS?

Listening to Khan talk about the advantages of Internet-based interactive studies, I could not avoid asking him about the future of teaching, whether it was a profession destined to disappear. What do you think of critics, I asked, who say that videos cannot replace teachers, because there's no way that technology can educate as well as a flesh and blood teacher.

"I totally agree with that idea. I have small children and want them to go to a school, to a physical place, and I want them to have quality teachers and classmates in that school. When people talk about something virtual, they immediately begin to suspect that it will replace the physical part. Electronic commerce versus physical commerce. But for us, the Khan Academy is a tool to improve the performance of the physical school," Khan said.

A tool?

"Yes, a tool, because we can help to distribute the materials. We can help with the practice exercises, with the corrections of the exercises. We can give teachers charts to closely track the progress of each student, because we believe that teachers are the most important element in learning," he answered. "All this technology allows teachers to dedicate all their time to human interaction. The teacher can determine the level of each student, which students are doing well and which are having difficulties. And the teacher can sit down later with each student and make sure that child is not falling behind. That's why we believe the teacher is the most important element of all this process."

Is that what you mean, I asked Khan, when you talk about a "personalized education?"

"Absolutely. This idea of a personalized education is not new. If you go back 400 years and think about who had a good education, very few people had it. Only the nobility and princes were educated. They had personal tutors, and many times they had several personal tutors. And that personal tutor adapted the education to what the prince understood or did not understand. If you go back 200 years ago, when you start to see mass education, that's when they start to put 30 children in a classroom, moving all of them along at the same pace and giving them the same lessons, which some understand and some do not," Khan explained.

And then?

"Then you come to the point where the class splits. Some will continue studying in university and others will not. Today, with technology, we can personalize the lessons to free the teacher to work individually and at the level of each student, so that all students can go to university. And what we're seeing in the physical classrooms in public schools, in private schools, in rich neighborhoods and in poor neighborhoods, is that if you allow each student to work at his or her own pace, you start to see students you thought were not good in math, who were not interested, suddenly start to get interested because they can learn at their own pace.

THE PRUSSIAN MODEL OF EDUCATION

Almost all of us were educated under the system developed in the 18th Century by the King of Prussia, who established free and mandatory primary education with the goal, among others, of creating a docile working class, respectful of authority, and accustomed from childhood to following a schedule. The idea was for the children to learn to respect the authority of their parents, their teachers and their king, and wake up every day at the same time to go to work.

Johann Gottlieb Fichte, the philosopher who promoted this system of education, wrote that "if you want to influence a person... you must do more than merely talk to him; you must fashion him, and fashion him in such a way that he simply cannot will otherwise than what you wish him to will."[4] Although worthy of much praise for establishing free and mandatory primary education, the Prussian model did not exactly hide its role as mechanism for political control.

Long before Khan, many critics had pointed out that the Prussian model, by doing away with individualized and fragmented education, allowed the monarch to transmit his political ideas to children through the lesson plans fashioned by his government. But beyond the content, the model itself contained much more subtle ways of molding the minds of the students: students sat in rows to listen to their teacher, stood up every time their teacher entered the room, and the lessons were split into subject areas that had to be individually memorized, without any relationship to other areas in order to avoid stimulating critical thinking. The lessons also were delivered in successive 50-minute sessions that forced students to jump from one class to another —constant interruptions that did not allow the development of dangerous ideas. A bell rang at the end of the lesson, and class was over.

The Prussian model served the king's aims well, and helped to create a middle class of manual laborers who worked in factories during the Industrial Revolution, but who are no longer prepared for the innovation economy of the 21st Century, Khan argues. Today, a good education requires exactly the opposite: encouraging the students' creativity and capacity for problem-solving. A 2011 study by Cathy N. Davidson, a Duke University professor and co-director of the annual MacArthur Foundation's Digital Media and Learning Competitions, showed that 65 percent of the children then in grammar school could wind up working in jobs not yet invented.[5]

That's already happening. Millions of children who started school in 1960 never imagined they would be working with personal computers, which did not exist when they were born. Millions of others who started in 1970 never imaged they would be working for Internet companies, and still more millions who started school in 2000 never imagined that they might wind up working in the 3D printer, commercial drone or space tourism industries.

"Economic realities no longer favor a docile and disciplined working class with just the basic proficiencies in reading, math and the liberal arts. Today's world needs a workforce of creative, curious and self-directed lifelong learners who are capable of conceiving and implementing ideas," Khan argues. "Unfortunately, this is the type of student that the Prussian model actively suppresses."[6]

WHAT'S IMPORTANT IS NOT TEACHING, BUT LEARNING

Like most innovators in education, Khan is convinced that traditional schools put too much emphasis on teaching —the teachers' lectures, curriculum, etc.— and too little on learning. What is important is not the way in which children are taught, with either teachers or computers in front of them, but that they learn, and in the way that is easiest for them.

"We have to make an important distinction between giving a lesson and teaching," Khan told me. "Recently I had dinner with Wendy Kopp, founder of the Teach for America organization, and I asked her what is the most important thing a teacher can do to have an impact on students. In other words, who are the best teachers. And she told me I would be surprised by her answer: It's not a matter of who gives the best lessons, and it's not even who has a doctorate. She told me the best teacher is the teacher who can sit beside a student and change his or her thinking, who can mentor that student, who can encourage students to take control of their own learning. That is totally consistent with what we say."

"We all sat in high school classrooms, with someone up there giving us a lesson and reading to us from notes. And I don't think that any of us saw that as a fascinating experience," he told me. "On the other hand, we all had teachers who chatted with us, who gave us advice, who inspired us to do things. And, as time passed, we remember the teachers who talked to us and helped us improve our ability to learn. So what we are advocating—and this from someone who has done 3,000, nearly 4,000 videos for the Web—is that the videos and the lessons in classrooms are the least important part of the learning process. The most important part of leaning is to do things, solve problems and have your teacher and your classmates there to help you."

According to Khan, the practical exercises and the charts that teachers can use to track the progress of their students are also a fundamental technological advance, because they free teachers to dedicate more of their time to interacting with students and allow schools to focus more on the progress of each student.

RADIO AND TV ONLY "DISSEMINATED" INFORMATION

Aren't you exaggerating the benefits of the new educational technologies?, I asked Khan. After all, it's not the first time someone predicts that technology will revolutionize education. In the 1920s, when radio became popular, many people said radio would revolutionize education. The same thing happened with television in the 1950s, and with personal computers in the 1980s, I told him. And not much really changed. We still have the same Prussian system from 200 years ago —children sitting at their school desks, listening to their teacher. What makes you think that this time the technology will really revolutionize education, and we will not see a repetition of what happened with previous technologies?

"Excellent point," he answered. "When the personal computer was developed, Steve Jobs said it would be a revolution for the mind. And, like you said, when TV and radio came out people said they were going to broadcast quality education around the world. And the same thing happened with videocassettes recorders. But I think there are a couple of things that are different now. In the past, the technology was always something superficial, focused on disseminating information. And we also do some of that, with our videos. But what we consider to be the most important part of the new technology are not the videos, but the possibility of determining the level of each student so that we can provide him or her with exercises specific to their level of knowledge."

"The students have the videos there in case they need help, and we give the teachers charts to create a record of the progress of each student," he continued. "What we see is that the 30,000 classrooms that use Khan Academy don't just show a video and make students watch them. It is active learning, in which the students solve practical exercises. Many people think the Khan Academy is just videos, but for us that's the least important part of what we do. The most important part is working out the problems, the exercises, the charts, the tools for learning."

"WE DON'T GIVE YOU CERTIFICATES OR DEGREES"

Precisely because it is totally focused on learning, the Khan Academy does not issue certificates or diplomas, Khan told me. When students first access the academy's Web site, they take a brief test. Based on the score, the system adapts to what the student knows and doesn't know, and recommends specific problems and videos that will help him or her to improve on weak areas. Like a game where you earn points as you advance, the student feels motivated to learn more, he explained.

It's a proactive system that can be used by one student at the individual level or, better yet, by a student and a mentor. Students can name one of their parents or teachers, or both, as mentors and bring them into the learning process. "And if I put you down as a 'mentor' in the system, the mentor can see how I am advancing and make recommendations. And the mentor can manage an entire classroom that way," he added.

According to Khan, the system generated excellent results when it was adopted by the Los Altos school district in Silicon Valley. Students were rewarded with electronic "prizes" as they increased their scores in the interactive exercises, and that turned them into even more active participants in the educational process. And the great fear of many teachers —that the "flipped"classrooms would lead to lower scores in standardized tests— turned out to be unfounded. Contrary to what many believed —that the Khan method would help students improve their conceptual understanding of math and other subjects but would not improve their test scores— 96 percent of the 5th grade students passed their final exams, compared to 91 percent before their schools "flipped" the classrooms, Khan said.

The same improvement was seen when the program was put in place in poor neighborhoods, he added. At the Unity High School in Oakland, Ca., where 95 percent of the students are African-Americans or Hispanics and 85 percent receive subsidized lunch, the students improved their algebra scores by 10 to 40 percent. School Principal David Castillo described the results as "stunning" because the videos, exercises and "flipped" classes helped many students to become more interested in learning, "with responsibility replacing apathy and effort replacing laziness."[7]

A FORMULA FOR RICH COUNTRIES?

The system seems ideal when Khan describes it, but I could not stop wondering if it was not designed for wealthy countries where the children —even those from poor homes— are usually moderately well fed and have computers at home. Is your educational model, I asked Khan, applicable to a child who lives in a shack in Honduras, who eats only one meal each day, and who doesn't have a computer at home?

"That's really a major problem, that shack in Honduras. But even in the United States 30 percent of the people do not have home access to a high-speed Internet connection," he answered. "Nevertheless, there are a couple of hopeful trends. Things will not be fixed overnight, but within five to 10 years even students in rural India and Honduras will have access to computers that will cost less than $100, probably less than $50. And if there's not a computer for each student, perhaps there will be a local center where children can share computers. And if you do it that way, the cost of a computer drops to pennies per student per day."[8]

Khan added that Internet costs are also falling dramatically. In the next five or 10 years, the Internet and computers will spread even more rapidly than previous technologies like the telephone, refrigerators, microwave ovens and the automobile. Perhaps the Khan Academy formula many not work today in the poorest areas of Honduras, he said, but it will in a very short time.

"HOMEWORK PROMOTES INEQUALITY"

The Prussian educational system that prevails in much of the world also generates significant social inequality because it requires students to do some of their school work at home, instead of at their schools. In the traditional system, most students from middle or upper class families have someone at home who can help with their homework —a mother, a father, an older sibling or a tutor. "But what happens with students from poor families?" Khan asked me. "Who is going to help the students do their homework when their parents are not educated, or they get home from work too tired to help their children? And when are the children supposed to do their homework if they have to work after school to help their parents?"[9]

Homework contributes to creating an unjust society, Khan argued, in which the educationally rich gets richer and the educationally poor gets poorer. That's why the "flipped schools", in which the children do their "homework" in classrooms with the help of their teachers, are a tremendous factor in social leveling, he added.

"SUMMER VACATIONS ARE A DUMB IDEA"

One of the ideas that I heard Khan mention in some of his Internet presentations was that summer school vacations should be abolished. Intrigued, I asked him what was so bad about giving kids a break from school.

"I probably don't have a lot of fans among the little kids," Khan joked. "It's true, I have said that summer vacations seem to be a dumb idea. They seem dumb to me because the only reason they exist is that when public schools and schools in general were created, most of the students lived in agricultural areas and had to help their parents with the farm during the summers. This still happens in some places, but today the great majority of people around the world live in cities and don't have to work on the farm."[10]

When I pointed out that he had not answered the question —what's so bad about giving kids a break— Khan referred to various studies indicating that summer vacations not only interrupt the learning process and allow children to forget many things but also tend to increase social and economic gaps. Many middle and upper class students take supplementary courses or undertake intellectually stimulating activities during their summers, which allow them to advance more quickly when the new school year starts, while the children of poor families fall increasingly behind, according to those studies.

"With the students resting during summer vacations, both schools and students are idle and unproductive. In fact, sometimes poor children cannot go to summer school. They are bored, and can get into trouble with the law during the summer. And you have teachers who are idle during the summer. In my opinion, we have to take advantage of that," he told me.[11]

"People have told me that summer vacations were the best times of their lives, because they could use their creativity and do interesting things. I say the entire school year should be that way," Khan added. "All learning should be personalized. So I would say that the entire year should be like the best of summer camp, but you would be learning throughout the year."[12]

"MULTI AGE AND MULTI GRADE SCHOOLS"

According to Khan, it also doesn't make much sense to group students by age, and fill a class with students of the same age. That's another dumb legacy from the past, he says. "It's not that there's something terrible about children of the same age going into the same classroom. We all did that. But the idea of grouping children by age is 200 years old. The famous one-room rural schools had children of many ages. And if you go back thousands of years, the learning environment was the tribe and the extended family. You learned from your cousins, you learned from your siblings. That was a natural process," he explained.

But there's more to learn today, I said.

"But anyone with young children can see that smaller kids learn from the older kids, and the older kids practice their leadership as they help the little ones. We have lost that with the current system of traditional schools," he replied. "I believe this is a good opportunity to bring back the concept of multi age learning communities."[13]

How would that work?

"When I say multi age, I can even imagine elderly people as part of the process. I want my mother to be part of the education of my children. I want my mother to be part of the education of other children. That's also an underused capital. There are a lot of elderly, experienced people who would love to work with these kids. Another underused capital is teenagers who don't participate in the process of teaching younger kids," Khan noted.[14]

Isn't it a bit utopian to believe that teenagers will want to teach the younger kids?, I asked Khan.

"When people talk about teen angst and rebelliousness, that teenagers want to be independent, much of that comes from the fact that traditional schools lead them to think only of themselves," he said. "I believe that when they are 13 or 14, they are ready to take on some responsibilities. Many of them need to have responsibilities. It's a perfect opportunity for the 13 and 14 year old adolescents to start mentoring the younger students, to help them learn. And at the same time to develop their own leadership skills.[15]

SCHOOLS IN 2025

Jumping ahead, I asked Khan how he imagined the school system would look like in 2020 or 2025.

"I imagine the classroom in 2020 or 2025 —and I hope this happens earlier because I have two children, four and two years old— definitely will still be a physical classroom. That space will be the axis of learning. I hope the classroom itself will be different from what we had, which was like a museum. Instead of having 30 kids in a class with one teacher, and another 30 kids with another teacher in the classroom next door, I hope we will break down the walls," the educator said. "The only reason those walls were needed was because the school was based on lessons, on classes. All the desks faced the front, and the students had to watch and take notes. Now we will have an interactive school environment. You will be having conversations, you will be learning at your own pace, you will be doing practical exercises. So now we can break down those walls, and we will have a common, ample and vibrant space, a big, quiet work space, an inspiring place, like a library. And the children will learn at their own pace."

And what will teachers do?

"The students will have mentors. Some of their mentors may be older students, who will monitor the younger ones. And there will also be regular teachers who will guide the students and help them achieve their goals," Khan replied.[16]

I wanted to know if students would be getting report cards.

"Students will be evaluated not just on their exam scores." Khan explained. "Exams will continue to be important, but students will also be evaluated in two other ways that to my mind are even more important. The first is how their peers regard them. If I am hiring someone, that's what is important to me: how good are you at teaching, how good are you at communicating. And the second is your creativity, the portfolio of things you have created. It's good that you received an excellent score in algebra, but can you apply that knowledge. Can you

216

do something with it? For me, the school will be a place where children learn more, create more and are evaluated based on these criteria."[17]

THE BOOM IN ONLINE EDUCATION

Since Khan began to post his educational videos for his cousins on YouTube in 2007 and 2008, online education in the United States has boomed. K12, a for-profit site for primary school students that was launched before the Khan Academy, has grown tremendously thanks to Khan's educational revolution. And starting in 2012, online education expanded massively to universities with the launch of Internet sites like Coursera.org, edX.org and Udacity.com, which offer free university classes to millions of students.

Several star professors at Harvard, Columbia and other prestigious U.S. universities started to offer free Internet courses and soon discovered —like Khan— that thousands of people were watching them. A short while later, the professors decided to offer their own free online courses known as MOOCs —massive open online courses. Leading universities, facing the choice of joining the MOOCs or running the risk of being left behind, eventually opted to join the movement. As I write these lines, Coursera.org was offering more than 400 courses— with videos and interactive exams —which had been taken by 5.5 million people in just two years. In Latin America, Khan Academy and portals with similar concepts, like Educabilia.com, Educatina.com and Kuepa.com, were growing at a dizzying pace. The education revolution was a fact.

CAN SILICON VALLEY BE COPIED?

As we wound up our interview, I had to ask Khan about the secret of Silicon Valley, and whether it's possible to duplicate it in another part of the world. Khan reminded me that he moved to Mountain View in Silicon Valley not on his own, but because Wohl Capital Management had moved there. But he would have been highly unlikely to meet people like Ann Doerr, his first big donor, in any other city in the United States or the world, he added.

"It's a place where people are used to taking risks and making big bets, even philanthropic bets like this one. People like Ann Doerr, people like Bill Gates, Google, are used to constantly considering new ideas and deciding which ones deserve an opportunity. They obviously have the resources to do that. In Silicon Valley we have a culture of taking risks. Risks for profit, or risks for non-profits. We are surrounded by people who are deep into technology. All those are positive things," he told me.

"On the other hand, there is a negative, that this is a very expensive place to live. I have been tempted many times to move somewhere else," he said. "At Khan Academy, we try to pay good salaries, and we can do it, but it's difficult to compete on salary with Google or Facebook. I think the people who work in Khan Academy need good salaries, need to support their families. But they are also here because they believe they have a mission in life and can make a difference."[18]

Asked if the Silicon Valley phenomenon could be duplicated in Mexico City, Buenos Aires, or some other city in Latin America or Asia, Khan said yes. "In this era of the Internet and connectivity, which allows any person to connect to any other, there's no reason why this cannot happen anywhere else," he said. The key is to have a "culture" like the one in Silicon Valley, he added, which covers several factors: the willingness of wealthy innovators to invest in new projects; quality education thanks to a prestigious university like Stanford; and the societal acceptance of failure as a natural part of any innovation project.

"The first positive aspect is that the people who became rich in Silicon Valley, the previous generation of entrepreneurs, are mostly not people who think a lot about how big their homes are or how elegant are their cars. Obviously, there are people with big homes and elegant cars. But the culture in general is to use your capital to do something interesting, to develop the next innovation. People in Silicon Valley, at parties, don't boast about their homes or their cars. Rather, they boast about their next project, their next team of young people working on an ambitious project. Those are the things that make them proud," Khan told me.

Silicon Valley also has a great inventory of very skilled people, those people attract others and they all respect those who try and fail again and again. "Silicon Valley is a place where people with a quality education, people with great knowledge and capacity, are willing to take risks and are willing to accept failure. I think that in many parts of the world, people with a good education and people with skills are afraid to take risks. Because they think, 'I've done a lot so far, and if I start a business now and I fail, my family will be ashamed of me, will think that I threw away my achievements'," Khan continued.

"In many parts of the world, that is seen as something negative. In Silicon Valley, to take risks and fail is seen as something positive. You keep trying, again and again," he added. "So I do believe that any place in the world that has access to capital and talent, and a culture that allows people to take risks and fail, can generate a very positive environment."[19]

9

Zolezzi, Von Ahn and the social innovators

"Technology must reach those most in need"

Most people have never heard of Alfredo Zolezzi, but they probably will, and soon. Zolezzi is a Chilean industrial designer who invented a purification system that promises to provide drinking water to the 780 million people around the world who have access only to contaminated water. Only 2.5 billion people around the world have full-time access to clean water. Vivek Wadhwa, vice president for innovation at Singularity University and a professor at Duke and Emory universities, described Zolezzi to me —perhaps with an excess of enthusiasm but with evident sincerity— as "the Thomas Alva Edison of Latin America," putting him on the same level as the inventor of the light bulb.

More compellingly, however, Zolezzi is one of the several Latin American social innovators who could have sold his invention for millions of dollars, yet is creating a non-profit organization to ensure his water purification system reaches the poorest of the poor all over the world.

Zolezzi started to experiment with water purification in 2010, with the help of several scientists in the small laboratory at his company, Advanced Innovation Center (AIC) in the Chilean city of Viña del Mar. He had already been working for years in cutting-edge projects in the oil and mining industries, some of them with relative success and enormous potential. But he was not satisfied with his life. He was 55 years old and faced serious problems over one of his top inventions —a system to turn solid oil into liquid oil, developed with technical assistance from the U.S. Department of Energy, that allowed the reactivation of abandoned oil wells.

According to what Zolezzi told me, some of his partners in the project started to fight among themselves for control of the company after a New York bank valued the global impact of the oil technology at $15 billion. The company they created became paralyzed amid an arbitration process that had lasted for many years.

Zolezzi already had been fantasizing for a long time about dedicating himself to innovation with a social purpose, to give his life more meaning. "One day, I figured out I was spending 80 percent of my time just surviving. I was spending little time with my family or creative activities. That's when I started to look around," he told me in an interview.[1]

In 2010, while experimenting with a way to convert petroleum into plasma and thereby improve the refining process, Zolezzi started to think about using a similar method on water. "I told myself, 'the search for liquid petroleum so far has brought us only problems. We have to invent something else. What would happen if instead of using plasma on low-quality crude, we use it on bad-quality water? Can we turn dirty water into potable water? A child dies every 21 seconds in the world because of contaminated water. Can we invent a technology that ends that tragedy?' "[2]

THE LAUNCH OF THE PROJECT

With the help of several scientists and cooperation agreements between his laboratory in Viña del Mar and NASA, Zolezzi developed his water purification device, the Plasma Water Sanitation System. It's a relatively simple device that uses a glass tube with an internal chamber and an electrical charge to turn dirty water into a plasma state, which then becomes potable water. The advantage of Zolezzi's device was its simplicity —it kills all virus and bacteria— and a cost much lower than other water purification technologies. But Zolezzi did not have the backing of any well-known institution. How could he save the world with a company in Viña del Mar that no one had ever heard of?

Zolezzi decided that before he could put his product on the market, he needed to test it in a poor area that did not have potable water, so that he could announce his results later. His first step was to hire a laboratory in Chile to test the water produced by his device and certify that it met Chile's sanitary requirements. Next, with that certificate in hand, the Chilean innovator approached the non-profit *Un Techo Para Mi País* (TECHNO) —A Roof for My Country— for help finding a poor and relatively small neighborhood, well organized and with a desire to improve itself, where he could test his device.

TECHNO knew Chile's poorest shantytowns better than anyone because it had worked for many years recruiting young volunteers, most of them university students, to build prefabricated housing in just two days for poor families. In August of 2011, TECHNO officials told Zolezzi they had found an ideal community for his experiment, a shantytown known as Campamento San José de Cerrillos in Santiago de Chile. "They told me it was a small community and well organized. Instead of going to the health authorities to ask for a permit that would have taken who knows how long, we and the residents installed the equipment," Zolezzi recalled.

Was that legal?, I asked.

"I have no idea," Zolezzi answered with a laugh. "But we went and we did it together with the people. The solution was co-managed with the residents."

Zolezzi's device started out making potable water for 19 families, producing 50 liters of potable water per day per family. Before the system was put in place, the people of San José, especially the children and the elderly, had suffered all sorts of diseases linked to contaminated waters. But afterward the health of the residents improved substantially. People stopped getting sick and spent less money on doctors, and they no longer had to buy bottled water or boil their water. "The results were immediate. We were starting to connect science with the fight against poverty," Zolezzi recalled.[3]

The experiment in San José had been a success, but now Zolezzi had a serious problem: he had run out of money. Between the salaries of the engineers and scientists who worked in his company and the costs of developing the water purification system and installing the device in San José, he had spent $5 million from his own savings — money that had come from the sale of a small part of the technology for turning solid oil into liquid.

"I didn't have a nickel. I had put 100 percent of my savings, and a little bit more, into the project," Zolezzi told me. "But I did not want to go to the banks or venture capital investors. I did not want to follow the standard route, selling the technology to a big corporation that would use it for products designed for wealthy people, people with the means to pay for it. I wanted to make sure this technology would first reach those who need it the most."

Zolezzi wanted not just to develop the new technology, but to create a new business model with a social purpose. "I did not want to give up doing business or making money. On the contrary, I wanted to make money. But I wanted to make sure this new technology would reach the poor people," the inventor explained. He was looking for a new business model that would allow him to profit from the sale of his technology for industrial use —for example, in the beverage industry— while at the same time allowing him to provide it, at no profit, to anyone who lacks potable water anywhere on the planet.

Zolezzi was well aware that 90 percent of the water consumed in the world is used in industry and agriculture, and only the remaining 10 percent goes to domestic use. He also knew that a good part of that 10 percent went to the middle and upper classes, and never reached the poor. He feared that if he sold his technology to industrial or agricultural companies, they would not be really interested in producing clean water for the poorest people in Africa, Asia and Latin America. At best, they would use the technology to help the poor only marginally, perhaps undertaking a few activities through their departments of corporate responsibility. Zolezzi had a bigger goal. He wanted his project to save hundreds of millions of lives —on a world scale.

Practically broke and seeking outside help to continue with his humanitarian project, Zolezzi was helped by friends in TECHNO to arrange a meeting with the Avina Foundation, a group dedicated to promoting sustainable development in Latin America. He knew the foundation had the money and the contacts to help him. At the foundation's offices in Santiago, he met with Guillermo Scallan, director of social innovation projects.

SCALLAN: "AT FIRST, I THOUGHT HE WAS CRAZY"

After listening to Zolezzi's story, Scallan's first reaction was one of skepticism and mistrust. Zolezzi's tale of his ups and downs with the invention to turn solid petroleum into liquid, and his claim that he had discovered a cheap solution for the world's potable water problem, seemed too fantastic to be true. Scallan had to ask himself if Zolezzi was a world-class innovator who had invented a $15 billion technology for the oil industry, a madman or a liar.

If Zolezzi had really invented the technology for the oil industry, why had he not sold it, Scallan thought as he listened to his visitor. And if it was true, as Zolezzi claimed, that a disagreement with partners had blocked an offer of $800 million for the technology, with a down payment of $80 million, why had the case never appeared on the front pages of Chilean newspapers? Scallan listened to his visitor with patience, but with enormous doubts.

"At first, I thought he was crazy, like many of the crazy people who come to my office," Scallan recalled with a smile, adding that it was not the first time he had met with an inventor who claimed to have worked for NASA and to have made an extraordinary scientific discovery that had gone unnoticed because of legal problems. "When he told me the story of how he had lost the opportunity to sell his patent on oil technology, I did not believe him. I told him, 'Look, forgive me for telling you this, but I don't believe you. Could you bring me the documents on the case, the arbitration you say is going on, so that an attorney we trust can see them?' "[4]

A few days later, Zolezzi started to send documents to the Avina Foundation, and Scallan started to take him seriously. Scallan asked the well-known Chilean lawyer Juan Pablo Hermosilla to review the arbitration documents Zolezzi had sent him, and the attorney concluded that his story was not a fabrication. Scallan also confirmed Zolezzi's oil technology had been successfully tested in seven oil fields in Utah.

At the same time, Scallan learned that the directors board of Zolezzi's company, Advanced Innovation Center (AIC), included a number of world-class scientists. One of them, Dr. Rainer Meinke, a German-born world authority on magnetos and superconductivity with more than 100 articles published in leading scientific magazines, had just arrived in Chile for a conference.

"When I met Meinke and asked him why he was in Chile, and why he was on Zolezzi's directors board, he told me that he had worked a long time with NASA, developing magnetic shields and trying to figure out how man would move in space in the future, but that Zolezzi had given new meaning to his life by asking him to help save lives all over the world," Scallan recalled. "I overcame my initial doubts very quickly."[5]

THE FIRST INTERNATIONAL VALIDATION

Scallan started to seriously consider the possibility that Avina would fund Zolezzi's water project. "Alfredo came to Avina practically broke. He did not have one nickel to go forward, and could not continue to pay salaries. We decided to support him, but to make sure the project was serious we agreed on a series of steps, and the money would be transferred after each step was completed," Scallan said. The Avina Foundation decided to contribute $600,000, from its own funds as well as from other foundations, for the first stage of the joint collaboration.

The first and most important step was to obtain an international validation of the water project. What Zolezzi had achieved in San José was nice and good publicity, but without an international verification the project would not be taken very seriously by international investors. The Avina Foundation therefore provided the resources to start the process of verifying Zolezzi's water purification system with the National Sanitation Foundation (NSF) in the United States and registering the patents with the U.S. Patent and Trademark Office. If the NSF certified that the water produced by Zolezzi's device was potable, the Avina Foundation would finance the next steps of the project.

Soon afterward, at the end of 2013, the NSF issued its ruling. The organization confirmed that Zolezzi's technology changed dirty water into potable water. The NSF report noted that no living virus or bacteria was found in the water produced by the new purification system. That was the validation that Zolezzi and the Avina Foundation needed to move forward.

THE NEW MODEL OF SOCIAL INNOVATION

Zolezzi recalled that in his first talks with the Avina Foundation, what truly fueled his enthusiasm were the suggestions he received for achieving his humanitarian objectives. "When I told Scallan that I was out of money, and that I had no choice but to start negotiations with venture capital funds, he told me that Avina could support me with money to pay for patents, salaries and travel so that I could avoid falling into the hands of the venture capital investors until I had a validated product that would allow me to enter into a negotiation without having to betray my principles," Zolezzi said. "I loved his answer."[6]

With the help of Avina, Zolezzi created a novel formula for social innovation: On one side, Zolezzi would sell his water purification technology for industrial use. On the other, he would create a humanitarian organization that would donate his potable water systems to the poor.

"All the marvelous technologies that we use are made for people who can afford them," Zolezzi told me. "If I sell mine to a corporation, it will develop products for the high-end sectors, like equipment for kitchens, restaurants, offices, etc. There are 2.5 billion people who drive cars, yet when they get home they have to drink bottled water. Imagine developing a little device that people can put in their kitchen and turn dirty water into potable water. That is a billion-dollar market. But I want to do something more than just take my check and go home. What good is technology if a child still dies every 21 second because of a lack of clean water? I am determined to prove that it's also possible to innovate in the business model, to bring together social innovation and technological innovation."[7]

"I WAS NEVER A GENIUS, NOT EVEN GIFTED"

One of the things that most surprised me about Zolezzi is that even though Wadhwa and other innovation gurus in the United States had described him to me as a genius, he does not have a science background or post-graduate diplomas. Zolezzi studied in the private Mackay School in Viña del Mar and graduated from the School of Architecture and Design at the Universidad Católica de Valparaíso with a degree in industrial design. During his school years he participated in many sports, playing rugby, earning a black belt in Taekwondo and later running marathons. But he was never the best student in his class.

"I was always very creative, since childhood, but I was never a genius or gifted or anything like that," he told me. "I went to a good school, a good university, but I was never the best or even the second-best student in my class. I had good grades, but I was not brilliant."[8]

While studying at the Universidad Católica, he started to invent things, like a new traffic light, a machine for painting objects and a variation of an airbag. Still later, he studied the use of ultrasound to improve the productivity of copper, which took him to Russia to work in cooperation with Russian scientists for several years. He went on to work on several other projects, including one that used ultrasound to liquify petroleum. In all the projects, he told me, his role was to develop an idea and then bring together scientists to turn it into reality.

"I am not a scientist. I don't do the equations. If I need that, I find a scientist to do it," Zolezzi declared. "I have a model, and I make things work. What impresses people is when they realize I am not a genius, that I don't have doctoral degrees, that I am not an expert on anything."[9]

THE PROJECT TAKES OFF

Zolezzi's project started to take shape on a global scale in 2014, when his company and the Avina Foundation, with the assistance of the Inter American Development Bank and other international organizations and corporations, launched a pilot plan to test the water purification system in Ghana, India, Kenya, Bolivia, Brazil, Paraguay, Chile and Haiti. Why so many countries?, I asked him. Because it's not the same to install the purification equipment in the Bolivian Altiplano, where it's very cold, and in a tropical country where it's very hot, he told me. Before investing millions of dollars on the project, they had to be absolutely sure it was going to work.

"Once the pilot program ends, we will make the final decision on which version of the equipment will be produced," Zolezzi said. His company is already in advanced negotiations with two giant multinationals: Pentair, a world leader on water filters and industrial pumps, and Jarden, a top company in kitchen goods and appliances. "We wanted two manufacturers because it's risky to have just one."[10] If everything goes well, by 2016 Zolezzi's device could be providing potable water to tens of millions of people around the world.

But what Zolezzi was most enthusiastic about was his project to create a humanitarian organization aimed at channeling the new technology to the poorest of the poor. It was not a new idea. Nobel prize winner Mohammad Yunus, among others, had long been promoting the idea of non-profit "social businesses," which were being tested in several countries. But Zolezzi was convinced his formula for cooperation between for-profit and non-profit companies would be much more effective.

Under the plan worked out with the Avina Foundation, Zolezzi was to establish a for-profit multinational corporation, based in the United States, that would sell his technology to appliance makers or carbonated beverage bottlers —who now use more than 80 liters of water to produce just one liter of beverage and could achieve enormous savings of water. Zolezzi's for-profit corporation then would hand over the technology free of charge to Alianza Para el Agua —Alliance for Water— established by a number of non-government organizations. Alianza in turn would own 10 percent of Zolezzi's for-profit corporation, guaranteeing it a constant revenue stream so it would not have to depend on donations. It would be an integrated model for social innovation, mixing for-profit companies with humanitarian organizations.

"Our technology could be overtaken very quickly, and probably will be, because that's what happens with any new technology. The important thing is the survival of this new model for social innovation, that it serve as a channel to distribute the new technologies to the poor," Zolezzi told me.[11] His heart, obviously, was not on the scientific side of his invention, but on the social side.

ASHOKA AND THE SOCIAL ENTREPRENEURS

Like Salman Khan, the creator of the Khan Academy that is revolutionizing education all over the world, Zolezzi is part of the spreading movement of social entrepreneurs. The heroes of these business people are not Bill Gates, Steve Jobs or other innovators who made billions of dollars, but rather other, less well-known entrepreneurs who are trying to improve the world. Their heroes are people like Nicholas Negroponte, director of the One Laptop per Child program at the Media Laboratory at the Massachusetts Institute of Technology (MIT). The program already has distributed laptop computers, manufactured for less than $150, to nearly two million children. They also admire the founders of Soccket, a $99 soccer ball that stores enough electrical power during a game to light up a hut for several hours, and many other innovators more interested in saving the world than in becoming billionaires.

Many of these innovators are receiving help from foundations focused on stimulating social enterprises, such as Ashoka. Founded in 1980, Ashoka has branches in 70 countries and has provided financial and technical assistance to about 3,000 social entrepreneurs. How does it work? Ashoka selects innovators with good ideas for improving the lives of poor people, and pays their salaries for three years so they can devote all their time to developing the projects. It also provides them with legal and strategic advice.

"We look for entrepreneurs who are in the early stages of their projects, with powerful ideas for solving a social problem, and we try to help them turn the ideas into reality," Armando Laborde, Ashoka director for Mexico and Central America, told me in an interview. "After passing through a very rigorous selection process, which includes a series of interviews, Ashoka offers to cover their personal expenses and assistance contacting foundations, business people and the media, so that they can develop the business."

Paula Cardenau, a former Ashoka director for Argentina and Latin America, is one of the many social entrepreneurs trying to help the 31 million young Latin Americans from the poorest sectors who are neither working nor studying —the so-called "ni-nis." Cardenau noticed that corporations are increasingly hiring out their digital services, contracting other companies to handle their marketing campaigns on Facebook, Twitter and other social networks, to digitize their archives and transcribe audio recordings into texts. Why not create a social business, Cardenau asked herself, that provides those services by hiring young ni-nis, who in many cases spend their days on the social networks and know perfectly well how to use them.

In 2013 she created Arbusta, a social business that offers precisely those services to companies of all types. "The women could not believe that they could earn money playing on Facebook," Cardenau recalled. "Arbusta also has been slowly generating a change within the corporate world, proving that young men and women from poor backgrounds can provide quality services."[12]

In 2014, Arbusta's young ni-nis were already working for a number of major companies, including Mercado Libre and Grupo RHUO, and the business was creating an Internet platform to offer micro-services such as transcriptions of conference or interview recordings.

But aren't the companies exploiting those young people, paying them less than other employees?, I asked Cardenau. If they are not paying less, why would the companies contract the services of Arbusta? On the contrary, Cardenau told me. Arbusta pays its young people higher salaries than normal. And the companies hire Arbusta because they know they are providing opportunities to young people who have few options for getting regular jobs —some of them because they have criminal records. "Many companies say it's part of their social responsibility, but that's not what it is, because they are not making a donation. They are paying for a service," Cardenau said.

At first, Arbusta looks like just another philanthropic organization. But it is a social company: it has a business plan and seeks to make a profit and sustain itself, rather than live off donations. "I don't know if Arbusta will one day pay dividends, but none of us here are thinking about that. We're thinking about how to help more and more people," Cardenau concluded.

PELLIZARI, THE ARGENTINE WHO MAKES CLOTHES FOR THE HANDICAPPED

Beatriz Pellizari, another of the people assisted by Ashoka in Argentina, created a social company named Amagi that makes and sells fashionable clothes for the physically handicapped. Pellizari told me she was injured in a car crash when she was 18 years old and could not walk for 18 months. Since then, she has been thinking hard about what she could do to improve the self-esteem and social integration of disabled people. One of her key memories from the time she was incapacitated was being unable to dress herself, which took away her privacy as well as her fashionable clothes. So in 2011 she started to work on the idea of making elegant clothes for the disabled and created Amagi, which means freedom in the Sumerian language.

"We want people with disabilities to be able to dress themselves, without help from anyone, and to feel comfortable, pretty, fashionable," Pellizari told me. "In Latin America, there were no companies doing that. There are foreign companies that do that, but they are not social businesses, and so their prices are very high… These kinds of clothes were not accessible to the middle class. We started to think about this, with a big emphasis on aesthetics because clothes help a lot with the self-esteem."[13]

Amagi's market is potentially huge. An estimated 15 percent of the world's population has some disability. According to the International Labor Organization, Argentina alone has 5.1 million disabled people and 21 percent of its homes have at least one disabled person. After developing the idea, Pellizari took her business plan to a contest in Netherlands and won first prize among social companies.

With that award under her arm, and help from colleagues in Ashoka and another social business incubator called Enjambre, Pellizari received her first investment of $10,000 from a Brazilian fund. From then on, Amagi started to design its own clothes collection, made by another social business called La Costurera, or the seamstress in Spanish. More investments arrived, and Amagi was on a roll.

"This is a social business. It seeks profits, but does not share the profits like a traditional company," Pellizari told me. "Profits are reinvested in the business to make it grow, generate more business and create a value chain with other social businesses. We pay salaries, but we don't distribute profits. And we're pretty far from the traditional philanthropy, because we want to be able to sustain ourselves."

Pellizari confessed to me that her great inspiration was Muhammad Yunus, the Bangladeshi winner of the Nobel peace prize, and his ideas on social businesses. Yunus is best known around the world as the father of micro credits for the poor: his Grameen Bank showed the world how the poor can receive loans and pay them back more punctually than the rich. And that's precisely why he was awarded the Nobel. But his principal crusade for the past several decades has been the promotion of social businesses around the world.

YUNUS: CAPITALISM TOOK THE WRONG ROAD

I had the opportunity to interview Yunus twice, in 2007 and 2013, and his proposal on social businesses fascinated me. I expected to meet an idealist and a dreamer, largely unconnected to reality. Yet I found a pragmatic idealist, with an excellent knowledge of the business world. Yunus studied economy at Vanderbilt University in the United States and after graduating returned to Bangladesh to teach. But after a while he grew bored with teaching economic theories, he told me. In 1974, he heard that some very poor women in a nearby village were being extorted by loan-sharks and decided to lend $27 out of his own pocket to 42 of the women, with no collateral.

He quickly learned the women always paid their debts on time. Their motive was very simple: they did not want to fall again into the claws of the loan-sharks. In the next few years, Yunus created his now famous Grameen Bank for the poor, which has loaned more than $6 billion and reported a repayment rate of 99 percent. After winning the Nobel prize in 2007, Yunus and his Yunus Foundation focused their work on repeating that experience with similar enterprises, preaching a type of "social capitalism" that co-exists with the kind of capitalism focused exclusively on profits.

When I first interviewed him, during one of his visits to Miami, Yunus told me that "capitalism took the wrong road" when it moved away from a social function. Instead of making donations, he argued, business people should create social companies —in addition to their for-profit companies— that can be self-sufficient and much more sustainable than non-government or philanthropic organizations that depend on charity. The social businesses proposed by Yunus operate like any business, but profits are reinvested in the business or other social enterprises and shareholders can only hope to recover their initial investment, not to earn dividends.

"While the goal of a traditional company is to make money, the goal of a social business is to fix a social problem," Yunus told me.[14] "With social businesses, we're not going to make money for ourselves. We will not make any personal gains from this company. We can recover the money we invested, but no more than that because we created this company to fix human problems, and that remains our intention."

Intrigued, I asked Yunus if it wasn't a little unrealistic to think that business people will create companies to solve social problems. Aren't business people in business exclusively to make money?

"I tell business people that instead of donating their money, they should invest it in a social business so that the money can carry out the same work as the money they donate, but it is recycled. Instead of giving to charity, I ask them to invest in a business that does exactly the same thing, a business that creates jobs, a business that provides health services, a business that builds housing, whatever they want to do. But it should be done in the form of a business, so that the money they invest returns to them and they can invest it again. Then the money will be working for them over and over, fixing a problem," he answered. "And that's a much better way of using the money than giving it to charity. In charity projects, the money goes out and does great work but never returns. If you do the same thing with a social business, the money goes out, does the same work but then returns to your hands, and you can reinvest it."[15]

CORPORATE SOCIAL RESPONSIBILITY IS OUTDATED

Yunus told me about several social businesses operating with great success all over the world. In Bangladesh, for example, there is an ophthalmological hospital that is a social business, performing about 10,000 cataract surgeries each year. "In our country we have many patients with cataracts, but we don't have the infrastructure to do cataract surgeries. So we created a hospital dedicated especially to cataract surgeries. We made the investment. We have a very pretty hospital building, all the equipment, the surgeons and the people needed for this. And we do the surgeries. What we do is we charge market prices in (big) cities, and from there we get the money to do the surgeries almost free of charge for people in other parts of the country who don't have the money. Because we charge fees to the people on top, we can offer our services practically free to those on the bottom. Overall, the hospital has enough money to cover all its costs, and we don't have to look for donors to stay afloat."[16]

The Nobel laureate added that the hospital does not turn anyone away. Because it is managed like a business, he said, "the hospital has enough money to cover all the costs of the building, the equipment, the surgeons, nurses and everything else. And because the money invested returns to us, we can build a new hospital each year. In that way, we are creating a chain of hospitals all over the country."

What incentives would you offer business people to start social businesses?, I asked Yunus.

"The incentive is your achievement, that you did something the world applauds," he answered. "If you fix a social problem, the whole world will applaud you, no matter who you are, because you have done something for humanity. If you help to solve a small problem, you will receive admiration, you will receive gratitude. If you help to fix a big problem, then the whole world will be at your feet, because you have done something for the world that was not done before. That's the important part, that if you do something, as a person or as a company, people will not forget."

And is that enough to persuade business people?, I insisted.

"Yes. If you keep just making money, people will not remember you, because you're not being useful to them, you're only doing it for yourself. So, if you're an egotist, you can continue to be an egotist and no one is going to care about you because everything you have done is for yourself. But if you're generous and have done something for others, then the whole world will remember you," Yunus said. "After all, we're on this planet for a very short time. We arrive, we stay awhile, say good-bye and leave. And while we're here, if we want to contribute a grain of sand to this planet, we have to do something that will make people remember us. That's what social businesses are about."

"People always ask, 'what's the incentive for a social business, if there are no dividends for the investors?, I say that I agree that making a profit is a big incentive, but I disagree that making a profit is the only incentive. There are many other incentives. Making money brings happiness, I agree, but making others happy brings super-happiness. That's what we see. Through the social businesses, we bring super-happiness. And once you start getting involved in the social businesses, you start enjoying that super-happiness," Yunus added.

But Professor Yunus, I said, when you propose that companies start social businesses instead of funding charity projects, are you saying that the entire notion of corporate social responsibility is outdated?

"The idea of corporate social responsibility came out of a good cause, because corporations started to feel that in their day-to-day operations they did not have the time to do something good for society, that they were only looking to make money. That's when the idea of corporate social responsibility emerged. At the end of the year you would count your money, figure out your profits and donate part of the profits to help people in need. That's how corporate social responsibility started. But with time, even that started to become commercialized. People started to ask, why should I give my money to other people instead of using that money to improve the image of my company? And then social responsibility very often became just money to build up the company's image. And that's going in the wrong direction. What I say is that social businesses are something much bigger than social responsibility."

How do those two things go together?, I asked.

"You can start with the money for corporate social responsibility, money that you have at the end of the year. Instead of donating that

236

money, why not invest it in a social business? In that way, the money will be recycled again and again. That's a simple solution: don't give your corporate social responsibility money to a charity, but create a company, a social business," Yunus explained. "And that company will grow each year because it will have more money to invest, or you can start a different social business, and you can turn this flow of money into something permanent instead of seeing it disappear at the end of each year. So even as a part of the idea of corporate social responsibility, the concept of a social business is more attractive."

Many people believe that governments and not businesses are responsible for solving the problem of poverty, I told Yunus. What do you think of the idea that big corporations are the problem, not the solution to social problems?

"Well, we can leave everything up to government and go to sleep, or spend all our time making money. Those scenarios don't look good to me," he answered. "Human beings are here to fix our problems. Yes, the government has a responsibility for solving our problems, but that doesn't mean that citizens have no responsibility at all for solving our problems. When someone's house is on fire, we don't wait for the firemen to arrive and fight the fire. We just go ahead and fight it. We deal with the fire, we don't sit back and wait for the firemen to arrive. It's the same with social problems. We can't cross our arms and wait."

ENDEAVOR: FOR-PROFIT SOCIAL BUSINESSES

While the Yunus Foundation, Ashoka and other international organizations focus on promoting non-profit social businesses that do not distribute profits to investors, there are other organizations that assist social innovators who create companies that are for-profit yet have social goals. Fernando Fabre, president of Endeavor, a non-profit based in New York City, told me that its founders worked in Ashoka but realized one day that there was a need for a non-profit that helps innovators launch for-profit companies.

Peter Kellner and Linda Rottenberg decided to start the organization in 1977, shortly after graduating from Harvard University. Rottenberg had just been in Argentina, and a conversation with a Buenos Aires taxi drive led her to conceive the idea of Endeavor. The taxi driver told her that he had just graduated from university with an engineering degree. And when the surprised Rottenberg asked why he had not started some sort of business, the driver responded with a hint of revulsion. "A businessman?" he asked.

That's when the light went on in her head, Rottenberg said. She concluded that in many Latin American countries, the role of business men and women is not only held in low esteem, but that there was not even a Spanish word for entrepreneur at the time. Rottenberg and Kellner decided to create a non-profit to encourage entrepreneurship, create jobs and promote a new societal attitude toward entrepreneurs and innovators in Latin America.

With the help of a number of U.S. and Latin American business leaders, Endeavor began to sponsor young innovators who had good business ideas. Today, Endeavor has offices in 20 countries, including Mexico, Brazil, Argentina, Chile, Colombia, Peru and Uruguay. Fabre, the Mexican who heads Endeavor, told me that in each city where the organization has an office there is a group of successful business leaders who help the organization identify the best business proposals. "We look for innovation, ambition and good business models," Fabre told me. "And once we pick them, we offer them mentoring so they can make better decisions and grow faster."[17]

Since its foundation, Endeavor has sponsored about 500 companies, including about 300 that were successful and 200 that were either sold or failed, Fabre said.

When I asked Fabre if Endeavor or the business people who support it earn a commission from the companies they help to grow, Fabre said no. "The business people help as philanthropy. They believe their country needs high-impact entrepreneurs to generate economic development and jobs," he said. In most cases, Endeavor selects an innovator and offers him or her free mentoring as well as access to a network of about 60 investment funds that support the organization. More recently, Endeavor started to participate in some entrepreneurial activities with its own finances. "We participate as co-investors." Fabre said. "So if an entrepreneur receives $10 million from the investment funds, we can co-invest $1 million of our own money."

GÓMEZ JUNCO, THE MEXICAN WHO GIVES AWAY ENERGY

Enrique Gómez Junco, founder of Optima Energía, based in the Mexican city of Monterrey, is an Endeavor-backed innovator developing one of the most interesting business models: his for-profit company provides cities with efficient street lighting free of charge, in exchange for a percentage of its savings in electricity. When I first heard about him, I was skeptical. But after speaking with Gómez Junco and Endeavor officials, it became clear to me that his business model has a high social and environmental potential and can help to reduce the opportunities for official corruption.

The Gómez Junco company approaches municipal governments in Mexico and offers to install, free of charge, a much more modern and durable public lighting system that generates savings of 60 percent in electricity, in exchange for a payment based on what the municipality would save on its electricity bill. The arrangement works from the first month, so that if the municipality's electricity bill drops from 100 to 40 pesos, for example, the town must pay Gómez Junco's company about 45 pesos but keeps the other 15 pesos to build bridges, schools or hospitals. The cities don't just save money. They receive free public lightning equipment, with LED technology that is brighter, lasts 18 years longer than the current lights and is better for the environment, Gómez Junco says.

"The LED lamps are much more eco-friendly than the old ones because they don't have mercury and last 20 years. Many Mexican municipalities still use the old yellow lamps that have mercury and barely last two years. They are thrown away every two years, and that contaminates the soil," the Mexican businessman told me. "Besides, the system of lighting with white lights and LED technology provides much better light than the old yellow lamps. And that is a tremendous help to reducing crime because the white lights make it easier to record street videos, the identification of license plates and faces."[18]

Another advantage of Gómez Junco's "gift" to municipalities is that his system of "performance contracting" guarantees the services are really delivered and reduces the possibility of corruption. "The great advantage of this model is that we're the ones who make the investment and provide the service, so there's no room for politicians to overpay in exchange for bribes," Gómez Junco told me. When I asked him, only half-joking, if that might be an obstacle when it came to deals with municipal officials, he said, "Of course. We have lost many contracts because of corruption."

GÓMEZ JUNCO'S START

How did he get the idea, I asked. As Gómez Junco explained it to me, the model of performance contracting has been around for many years in the United States, Germany and other developed countries, where big multinational companies advance the money for infrastructure projects and are later reimbursed by the cities. The model has not been widely used in Latin America, in part because it involves large sums of money and the banks have been afraid to lend money without sufficient guarantees to the private companies that carry out these types of projects.

The idea of starting to apply this business model in Mexico emerged from a coincidence, and a need. Gómez Junco, a graduate in chemical engineering from the Instituto Tecnológico de Monterrey, owned a company that installed solar energy and other electricity-saving equipment in hotels since 1988. His clients included a number of hotel chains, among them some large ones. One day, when Gómez Junco was trying to sell his systems to a hotel operator in Cancún, the man told him, "If you're so sure this is going to save so much electricity, why don't you pay for it, and I will pay you from what I save?" Gómez Junco accepted the challenge, and from there on started to apply that model to a growing number of hotels.

The world crisis in 2008 hit the Mexican hotel sector hard, however, and two years later Gómez Junco began trying to expand his model to municipal public lighting. But he ran into a problem: while energy conversion projects for a hotel costs an average of $100,000, the conversion of a municipality costs an average of $20 million. Where was he going to find the capital to install lights in municipalities? With the help of Endeavor, which had been advising him since 2005 and had already urged him to hire a financial director, establish a management council with outside members and seek external credits, Gómez Junco changed the direction of Optima Energía.

The company became less of a family affair and more professional, and started to seek loans from the World Bank and other development lending institutions to undertake more ambitious projects. By 2014, Optima Energía already had signed agreements with six Mexican cities —including Acapulco, Cajeme and Linares— and was expecting to do more than $100 million in business. Toward the end of our conversation, I asked Gómez Junco why his model is not being applied elsewhere in Latin America. If it works so well, and generates so many savings and ecological benefits, one would think there would be many more companies investing in public works and service projects in exchange for part of the savings, I noted.

"In Mexico, and in Latin America in general, there have been very significant efforts, especially by the international development banks, to establish this type of model. The greatest limitation has been the capacity of our companies to obtain credits," he answered. "The capacity of Optima Energía to seek $20 million in financing did not emerge overnight. It took us 10 years to create a framework for making this possible, because commercial banks are afraid to lend to small companies that don't have enough collateral. But that should start to change as the results come in. I don't have any doubt that this will become the norm for all municipalities all over the world, not only because it's profitable but because of its social and security benefits, and especially its impact on the environment."

LUIS VON AHN, THE GUATEMALAN WHO INVENTED DUOLINGO

Guatemala-born Luis Von Ahn, 34, one of the most successful Latin American innovators in the world, is another entrepreneur who has started for-profit social companies that offer their products free of charge. Von Ahn, who studied in Guatemala until the age of 17 and then moved to the United States to earn his bachelor's degree in math at Duke University, is the inventor of those pesky little boxes with distorted letters and numbers that appear on our computer screens when we try to buy a ticket to a music concert, or we try to enter any Web site that wants to make sure we are real people and not a computer. The CAPTCHA verification system, which Von Ahn developed originally for Yahoo when he was 22 years old, requires that we type the correct letters and numbers into a box. It is used by about 180 million people every day around the world.

But that was only the first of Von Ahn's big inventions. In 2003, when he was 23 years old and was about to earn his doctorate in computer sciences at Carnegie Mellon University, he sold Google a game he had developed and called ESP Game for "between $1 million and $10 million" —he would not give me the exact price, saying he had signed a confidentiality agreement. Google later renamed it Image Labeler and uses it to label and find images.

"I had patented it," Von Ahn told me in an interview. "The game was written up in the news media, a lot of people were using it, and the people at Google called me and told me, 'We like it. Can you come and explain it?' I went to explain to them how it works, and in the same meeting they told me, 'We want to buy it' "[19] Three years later, in 2006, by then teaching at Carnegie Mellon, Von Ahn and one of his students invented a variant of the CAPTCHA authentication system, which they called RECAPTCHA and sold to Google "for between $10 million and $100 million," Von Ahn told me.

242

It's a verification system similar to the first, but it takes advantage of the words typed by the users to help to correct errors in digitized books. As the young entrepreneur explained to me, the average person takes about 10 seconds to transcribe the distorted letters in his verification tests, which means that all over the world, CAPTCHA users spend roughly 500,000 hours per day on that task. "I felt bad that so many people were wasting so much time, and I started to think about how those 10 seconds could be used for something more beneficial to society," he said. "And it occurred to me that when people were typing the CAPTCHAS, they could not only be identifying themselves as human beings but also could be helping us to put on the Internet digitized books that contained illegible words or letters."[20] In other words, Von Ahn created a system for selecting illegible letters and words from digitized books and replacing them with the correct letters and words provided by the massive numbers of CAPTCHA users.

In 2012, already a millionaire at the age of 32, Von Ahn created his first social company: Duolingo, a for-profit Web site that offers free language courses. Eighteen months after its creation, it already had 25 million users. The formula created by Von Ahn to be able to offer his online course free of charge is one of most innovative ideas that I ran across during my research for this book.

VON AHN'S SECRET FOR GIVING AWAY LANGUAGE LESSONS

"I wanted to do something different, something for education. I had just sold my second company to Google. I had enough money to retire, but I wanted to do something for education," Von Ahn told me. "And I had an idea, because I grew up in Guatemala and saw many people who wanted to learn English but did not have the money. I started to look at the language learning market, and it turned out that there were 1.2 billion people learning languages, of which 800 million were low-income people learning English. But the problem is that the courses are very expensive. There are computer courses that cost $1,000."[21]

Von Ahn set out to offer free language courses on the Internet, but first needed to figure out some way of making money from the project. If the students were not going to pay, then who would pay for the costs of building and maintaining the Web site and administering the courses. That's when he thought to use the production of his users, in a way similar to RECAPTCHA.

"Our Web site tells the students, 'If you want to practice, help us to translate this document from English to Spanish,'" Von Ahn told me. "After the document has been translated, and there's a final version that is collaboratively agreed to be the best, then we sell that version to the company that sent it to us. For example, CNN is one of our clients. They send us a story in English, we give it to our students to translate it into Spanish and we send the translation back to CNN for use in its Spanish-language Web site."[22]

It's a good business for everyone, Von Ahn added. The students pay nothing. Duolingo pays its 35 employees from the revenues it receives from clients like CNN, and the clients save money by reducing their translation costs. While a professional translator in the United States charges 10 cents per word, Duolingo, depending on the volume, charges about three cents per word, he added.

And how do you know that the documents has been translated correctly?, I asked him, somewhere between surprised and amused. "A number of people translate the same document. Each person can see the other translations. They vote on which is the best translation, and at the end there's a single version, produced by a number of the students. And the quality is high enough for CNN to be satisfied," Von Ahn told me.

After it was recognized by Apple as the best iPhone application of 2013, Duolingo started to break into the Asian market in 2014, which sparked a dramatic increase in the volume of its users. Duolingo indeed now competes with several much bigger companies that offer language courses, including Open English, established in Miami by Andrés Moreno, a young Venezuelan who collected investments in his company totaling $120 million. Other companies competing in the same sector are Voxy and the big traditional companies like Pearson and Rosetta

Stone. But Duolingo is one of the few that offers totally free courses and is considered primarily as a social company, according to Von Ahn, who remains a professor at Carnegie Mellon.

IN INDIA, AMBULANCES FOR PEOPLE WHO CAN'T PAY

During the 2008 terrorist attack on the Taj Hotel in Mumbai, India, one of the first ambulances that arrived to pick up the wounded was from ZHL, a social company that offers free ambulance service to those who can't afford to pay, and charges a fee to those who can. The company had been created three years earlier by Shaffi Mather, a successful real estate businessman from the state of Kerala who became a social innovator after concluding that the ambulance services in India had enormous problems. Several of his employees, friends and relatives involved in accidents had been forced to wait hours for the arrival of an ambulance. Clearly, it was a problem that was costing many lives and required an urgent solution.

Mather and three friends created the company now known as ZHL, a for-profit company whose mission is to provide top-notch ambulance service, 24 hours per day, to anyone who needs it. It seemed like a mission impossible, but as it turned out, it was not. ZHL, in association with the Ambulance Access for All Foundation, subsidizes services for the poor with the money it charges to the rich and still makes a profit —much like the social hospital that performs cataract surgeries in Bangladesh. In 2007, ZHL received an investment of more than $1 million to buy more ambulances. By 2013, it had 2,700 employees and about 1,000 ambulances, operating in six Indian states, that had transported more than 16 million patients to public hospitals.

IN THE UNITED STATES, PROGRAMS TO SHARE CAR RIDES

Although the social innovators who draw the most attention are those who want to provide potable water or ambulances for hundreds of millions of poor people, many others are dedicated to fixing the problems of the middle classes in large cities. In the United States and Europe, for example, there's been an increase in the use of smartphone applications that bring together people who want to share car rides, such as Avego.com, RewardRide.com, Carpooling.com or Zimride.com. In all these companies, social innovators have set out to make commuting to work more pleasant, cut gasoline costs, ease traffic congestion and reduce environmental pollution.

An estimated 77 percent of U.S. residents drive alone to their jobs, 10 percent have one or more passengers and only 5 percent use public transportation. This is congesting traffic in cities and generating increasingly severe traffic jams, to the point where the average U.S. resident loses 34 hours per year stuck in traffic.[23] The problem is even worse in Mexico City, Bogotá or Buenos Aires, where many drivers probably lose 10 or 20 times more hours in traffic jams. And as the number of vehicles on the streets grow, governments must spend increasing amounts of money widening avenues and building new roads, which in turn aggravates pollution.

Facing these challenges, for-profit companies like RewardRide.com and Avego.com have set out to attack all these problems at the same time, while saving money in gasoline and parking, by putting drivers in touch with passengers. Avego.com, which also operates under the name of Carma, became popular in 2013 when a train strike in San Francisco left about 400,000 people without a way of getting to work. The number of people who started to use the Carma Web site on their smartphones spiked by 500 percent in a single day.

The company, which was started in 2007 in Cork, Ireland, began operating in 2011 in several U.S. states, including California and Washington, and focused mostly on company workers and university students. The payment system varies according to the city. In the state of Washington, for example, the state government pays $30 per month to each user in order to ease traffic congestion and save millions in public transportation projects. In other cities, Carma charges each passenger 20 U.S. cents per mile, passes 17 to the drivers and keeps three as its commission. By 2014, it had about 10,000 users.

How does the company keep thieves and other dangerous persons from signing up? The same way that credit cards and other companies check out their clients: gathering information from each user. In the city of Baltimore, which uses the Carma services, the municipal Department of Transportation asks each person who wants to join for their name, address, telephone, the phone number of their work supervisor and how long they have been employed in the same job. It's easy to check out the answers, and anyone who provides false information is not added to the program's database.

"We are making the private car part of the public transit network," said Sean O'Sullivan, the founder of Avego.[24] Drivers are helping to ease traffic congestion in cities by making available their extra seats, and earning money to pay for their gasoline and parking. And the passengers, who in many cases don't have cars or simply don't want to drive, save money because they don't have to pay for a car, gasoline or parking. In other words, this is a great business for everyone, and one that helps to ease an enormous problem in modern life.

CORPORATE SOCIAL RESPONSIBLITY VS. SOCIAL COMPANIES

The proliferation of social innovators around the world is very good news, especially because they offer a good alternative to philanthropy and corporate social responsibility. Most experts agree that Latin America needs a new model for social assistance, because the region's corporations and wealthy people rank very low on the world scale of contributions to philanthropic works. The reasons for the low rankings are many, including the fact that most countries in the region do not offer tax incentives to donors, and the generalized belief that governments should be responsible for taking care of the poor. What's more, in several Latin American countries, companies and wealthy people account for almost all taxes collected, leading many of them to believe that they are already doing enough for their countries.

According to the World Giving Index, a ranking of philanthropy in 135 countries prepared by the London-based Charities Aid Foundation, most Latin American countries rank in the lower half of the list. The study, based on Gallup polls, lists Great Britain, Netherlands, Canada, Australia and the United States among the countries where people donate the most money. With few exceptions —like Chile in 18th place, Paraguay in 25th, Haiti in 30th and Uruguay in 35th— the majority of Latin American countries rank far down. Brazil is in 72nd place, Peru and Ecuador are tied for 80th, Argentina is in 84th place, Venezuela in 100th and El Salvador in 110th. While 76 percent of the people in Great Britain and 62 percent of the people in the United States said they made cash donations in the previous year, only 23 percent said the same in Brazil, 22 percent in Mexico, 21 percent in Peru, 20 percent in Argentina and 14 percent in Venezuela, according to the Index.[25]

Social innovators and companies are starting to fill a void in addressing the needs of the poor, and very often can do it much more effectively than philanthropy or corporate social responsibility. As Yunus told me, philanthropy is money that cannot be recycled, while social enterprises can be self-sustainable and generate income that can be used to create other social companies. In many cases, corporate social responsibility also has become little more than an extension of the public relations departments of large corporations, interested more in positive publicity than in helping to fix social problems.

Social innovators are the heroes of the new world economy. Some have non-profit companies like the Khan Academy, which offers free online educational videos. Others have for-profit companies like Gómez Junco's public lighting company. And still others have mixed business models, like Zolezzi's water purification company. But all are helping to improve the world, and to create a more humane form of capitalism. When Zolezzi asked me what good was technology when a child died every 21 seconds for a lack of potable water, and told me that it was time to turn technological innovation into social innovation, he hit the nail on the head. Innovation will continue to emerge from the leading companies and most prestigious universities. But if part of the new technologies are developed through social companies, we will live in a better world.

10

The five secrets of innovation

"You snooze, you lose"

In the middle of the second decade of the 21st Century, what we predicted in our books *Cuentos Chinos* (which was published in English under the title *Saving the Americas*) and *Basta de Historias* became a reality: the boom in raw materials that was so beneficial to many Latin American countries in the earlier decade had ended, and the countries that had stuck to their exports of raw materials —without investing in quality education, science, technology and innovation— were starting to suffer the consequences. The party was over. Economic growth, which hit a regional average of nearly 6 percent a year around 2005 —and in some countries, like Argentina, even hit 9 percent and generated a triumphant posturing that led President Cristina Fernández de Kirchner to boast her country was growing "at Chinese rates"— fell to a regional average of 2.5 percent in 2014, and even lower in Argentina and Venezuela.

Even Mexico, Colombia, Peru and other countries that were growing at more than the regional average did not grow enough to provide jobs for the millions of people who were joining the labor force each year. The region's great challenge, more than ever, was to dramatically improve the quality of the education, promote innovation and export products with more added value in order to avoid falling increasingly behind the rest of the world

How to regain the time lost? Can we compete with South Korea, Singapore, Israel and other countries that have turned into technology powers in recent years? Of course we can. But we have to do much more than just trying to produce computer geniuses. Although the media usually identifies innovation with the Internet and geniuses like Bill Gates and Steve Jobs, innovation is much more than that. Our countries must innovate, whether by inventing new products of any type (commonly known as "product innovation") or discovering more efficient ways to produce existing products ("process innovation"). The important thing is to innovate, create new products or processes of all kinds, with increasing value-added, that can be sold on the global market, and not stay stuck in the same place. You snooze, you lose.

PEOPLE ALSO MUST REINVENT THEMSELVES

People, as well as countries, must reinvent themselves constantly to achieve more in the new creative economy of the 21st Century. As we explained in the previous pages, more and more people will be working in jobs that did not exist when they started elementary school. The Industrial Revolution that will be fueled by 3D printers, robots and "the Internet of things" will eliminate many jobs and create many others. Cars that drive themselves will displace taxi drivers, commercial drones will replace FedEx and UPS delivery trucks and robots will take on a growing share of manufacturing jobs —something already happening, especially since the recent increase in labor costs in China. But new types of jobs will also emerge, like remote operators for self-driving taxis, drone pilots and consultants who can advise us on what type of robots we should buy for specific tasks at home and in the office. There will be less and less demand for the industrial, repetitive jobs of the 20th Century, and more and more openings for intellectual and creative work. This is the age of creativity.

"My generation had it easy. We had to 'find' a job. But, more than ever, our kids will have to 'invent' a job," wrote *The New York Times* columnist Thomas Friedman. "Sure, the lucky ones will find their first jobs, but given the pace of change today, even they will have to reinvent, re-engineer and re-imagine that job much more than their parents."[1]

Everything indicates that we will increasingly work for shorter periods per company but for more companies, or for ourselves. That's already happening. According to U.S. Department of Labor statistics, the average time that salaried U.S. workers have at their current jobs is barely four years and seven months. The time is even shorter among young workers: salaried workers aged 25 to 34 averaged barely three years and two months on the same job.[2] The days when many people spent all or a big part of their working lives with the same company are history. For an increasing number of people in the United States and elsewhere, reinventing themselves will be a constant imperative of their working lives.

Luckily, perhaps this will not be as tragic as it seems, because today it is already easier to invent a job than it was a decade ago, at least for those who received a quality education. Thanks to the democratization of technology, each day there are more young people who create their own jobs, such as Web designers and Internet providers of all kinds of products and services. The framework for self-employment also has expanded enormously: increasingly, the Internet allows us to sell our products or access jobs in any part of the world. And thanks to new sources of financing, like crowdfunding —the system of raising funds for products under development— we will have increasing opportunities to find funding for our projects. Today, young people have access to a world of opportunities their parents did not have. But to take advantage of these opportunities, we have to offer them not only a better education —as measured by the PISA and other standard international exams— but a creative education and an environment conducive to entrepreneurship.

FAR BEHIND ON INNOVATION

An extensive World Bank study on innovation in Latin America, published in 2014 under the title, "Many Firms but Little Innovation," offered a somber picture of productive creativity in the region. The study concluded that "Latin America and the Caribbean suffer from an innovation gap. On average, its entrepreneurs introduce new products less frequently, invest less in research and development, and hold fewer patents than entrepreneurs in other regions."[3]

The statistics speak for themselves. As we pointed out in the first chapter, all the Latin American and Caribbean countries combined submit barely 1,200 patent applications per year to the World Intellectual Property Organization —about 10 percent of the South Korean applications to the United Nations organization. Israel, with only 8 million people, also submits more patent applications for new inventions than all Latin American and Caribbean countries together, with 600 million people.

Part of the problem is the lack of innovation among Latin American companies, which many observers blame on the lack of vision among the region's business people. The business sector, for its part, blames anachronistic legal frameworks that penalize creativity. Whatever the reason, it's clear that Latin American companies on average launch 20 percent fewer products than their peers in the developing world. The World Bank study showed that while 95 percent of companies in Lithuania and 90 percent of companies in Poland reported launching a new product in the previous year, less than 40 percent of Mexican and Venezuelan companies reported the same numbers.

Perhaps the most alarming statistic is one we highlighted at the beginning of this book, showing that barely 2.4 percent of the world's total investment in research and development takes place in Latin America and the Caribbean. While 37.5 percent of the world investment in research and development takes place in the United States and Canada, and 25.4 percent takes place in Asia, Latin America accounts for an insignificant share.[4] What's more, the largest share of the miniscule 2.4 percent invested in Latin America took place in just three countries —Brazil with 66 percent of the region's total, Mexico with 12 percent and Argentina with 7 percent.[5] Facing such bleak numbers, countries that are lagging behind must, more than ever, take steps essential to entering the first world of innovation.

FIRST SECRET: CREATE A CULTURE OF INNOVATION

As we have shown, there is a growing consensus that in order to generate more innovation, countries must take several steps: improve the quality of education, promote science and engineering studies, increase investment in research and development, offer fiscal breaks to companies that develop new products, abolish bureaucratic regulations that hinder the creation of new companies, offer credits to entrepreneurs and protect intellectual property. All these steps are undoubtedly important. But my conclusion, after speaking with dozens of leading innovators and the gurus of innovation in Silicon Valley, is that these measures are useless unless they take place in a culture that encourages and glorifies innovation.

Most great innovations come from the bottom up, thanks to a culture of entrepreneurship and collective admiration for those who take risks. They are not the result of government plans. Gastón Acurio did not spark a boom in Peruvian food as the result of a government project, Jordi Muñoz did not become a pioneer in the commercial drone industry with the assistance of any government, and Richard Branson did not build his music store empire or his space tourism company thanks to some government program. Neither did Salman Khan, the man who's revolutionizing education all over the world, or the Chilean Alfredo Zolezzi or the Guatemalan Luis Von Ahn or other leading innovators. In the majority of cases, innovations are the product of a culture that venerates innovators and allows them to realize their potential.

What is a culture of innovation? It's an environment that produces a collective enthusiasm for creativity, that glorifies productive innovators just like great artists and great sports figures, and that challenges people to take risks without fear of being stigmatized by failure. Without a culture of innovation, it's useless to offer government incentives, to produce large numbers of engineers and least of all to establish the science and technology parks that a number of presidents are promoting —in most cases to promote themselves.

To create a culture of innovation that encourages creativity from the bottom up is not as difficult as it looks. Today, with mass media and social networks, it is much easier to generate a collective enthusiasm for creativity and innovation. Public opinion campaigns are effective, as proven by the success of mass media anti-smoking campaigns long before social networks came into being. If the United States, Europe and several Latin American countries managed to dramatically reduce their number of smokers with TV campaigns warning of the dangers of cigarettes —a chemical addiction— how can we not combat problems not linked to a physical dependence, like the lack of tolerance for failure? Changing a culture and turning innovators into popular heroes is a matter of political will, which can be fostered by politicians, business people, academics and the media.

For many, that should be the most important function of any government. Andy Freire, an Argentine who was one of the founders of Officenet —which raised $50 million from Goldman Sachs investors and was later sold to the U.S. giant Staples— and is now investing in startups and promoting a culture of entrepreneurship in Argentina, said that Latin America "must generate a counterculture that encourages taking risks, something that must come from above." Freire, a magna cum laude graduate in economy from the Universidad de San Andrés in Argentina with postgraduate studies in Harvard, told me that the key to entrepreneurship is to make it "a national policy, instead of just the policy of the Deputy Secretary for Economic Development." Noticing that his answer made me laugh, he added, "Seriously. Today, all the initiatives to spur innovation that I know of rank 35th on the list of government priorities."[6]

Freire is probably right, but there are other ways to generate innovation that produce concrete results and help change cultures hostile to entrepreneurship. Some of the most effective include media campaigns by civil society to foster a national and family culture of admiration for scientists and technicians, which pushes children to follow the examples of successful scientists. Another way to generate innovation is through awards. Economic prizes have long been a great support for specific innovations as well as to foster general creativity.

WE NEED A MESSI IN SCIENCE, A NEYMAR IN TECHNOLOGY

Shortly before the end of the 2014 World Cup, when Argentina and Brazil were qualifying for the semifinals and many of us believed one of them would be crowned champion, I published a column in *The Miami Herald*, titled "Latin America needs a Messi in Science," asking why we Latin Americans could not produce a Messi, a Neymar or a James in science or technology. The question already had been asked by the president of the InterAmerican Development Bank (IDB), Luis Alberto Moreno, during a conference in Brazil. In the same way that Latin America turns out some of the best soccer players in the world, Moreno said, the region should also produce the next "Neymar of software" or the next "Messi of robotics."

He proposed that our countries should treat science with the same passion and discipline we dedicate to sports, and establish new systems for turning out technology talent. The IDB president was right. Like soccer, played by millions of children every day, countries need a huge pool of scientists to increase their chances of producing one or more geniuses. A new Messi or a new Neymar always comes along because there is a huge pool of children trying to imitate them, and because soccer clubs have farm teams to develop players with great potential.

Regrettably, however, Latin America has a relatively small pool of scientists per capita, compared to the United States, Europe or Asia. While Latin America has 560 researchers per million people, South Korea has 5,451, according to World Bank figures. It's no coincidence that South Korea registers so many more patents. Not only does it have more scientists per capita but it has a culture and news media that constantly celebrate those who succeed in science and technology, turning them into instant heroes for thousands of young people. In my travels to China, India, Singapore and other Asian countries, I was always impressed by the big headlines the news media gave to the winners of the math or science Olympics, as though they were sports heroes. Latin America must create a culture of admiration for scientists. Much like it admires its soccer players, it must admire its scientists.

THE AWARDS THAT CHANGED THE WORLD

Although many people don't know this, many of the biggest inventions in history came as the result of economic prizes offered to the winners of technology challenges. The first transatlantic flight, by Charles A. Lindbergh in 1927, was the result of a contest for the $25,000 prize to the first pilot to fly non-stop between Paris and New York. The prize was offered in 1919 by Raymond Orteig, a French hotelier living in the United States, for a period of five years. Until 1927, the 5,800 kilometers between New York and Paris was nearly twice the distance of the longest airplane flight in history. It was a colossal challenge, so difficult that very few tried it and a number of pilots turned around soon after taking off. When the deadline for the prize expired, Orteig extended it for another five years. In 1926 and 1927, several pilots were killed trying to beat the new record.

According to historians, Lindbergh, then a 25-year-old U.S. pilot, was the least likely to win the prize. Unlike other pilots who tried, he was unknown and no aeronautical company wanted to sell him a motor for his airplane, fearing his death would give the company a bad name. Nevertheless, Lindbergh surprised the world and landed safely at Le Bourget on the outskirts of Paris after a flight of 33½ hours.

"This is an aspect of incentive competitions: they're open to all comers —and all comers often show up, including the underdog. Sometimes the underdog wins," Peter H. Diamandis and Steven Kotler wrote in their book, *Abundance. The future is better than you think*. Diamandis, one of the founders of Singularity University, told me during an interview that he had read Lindbergh's autobiography and was impressed by the story of the Orteig Prize.

The prize had been front-page news around the world and sparked a new era in the history of aviation. After Lindbergh, other pilots crossed the Atlantic and commercial aviation turned into a global industry. In barely 18 months, the number of airplane passengers in the United States soared from 6,000 to 180,000, and the number of aircraft grew fourfold. The Orteig Prize had been an impressive accelerant for innovation.

Nine teams of aviators had invested a total of $400,000 to win the prize, even though the losers received no reward at all, Diamandis noted.

Inspired by the Lindbergh example, and frustrated by NASA's failure to launch a similar prize at a time that it was cutting its budget for space travel, Diamandis decided to create his own prize—the X Prize, later renamed the Ansari X Prize, of $10 million for the first company to build a suborbital and reusable spacecraft. Millionaire Paul Allen won the prize in 2004 with a manned space craft, built without government funds, that was the forerunner of the private space vehicles built later by Sir Richard Branson and Elon Musk. The U.S. Government, for its part, created its own digital platform in 2010, Challenge.gov, to allow all its branches to offer awards. In its first two years, the platform launched more than 200 competitions with prizes totaling more than $34 million. As I read about Challenge.gov, I had to wonder why more prizes like those are not offered in Latin America.

"EVERY GREAT INVENTION STARTED AS A CRAZY IDEA"

Long before Lindbergh crossed the Atlantic and won the Orteig Prize, the British parliament had offered a prize of 20,000 pounds in 1714 to the first person who discovered how to measure longitude at sea, critical to navigation. The success of the British prize led other European countries to offer their own awards for solutions to specific problems. In 1795, Napoleon I offered a prize of 12,000 francs for a method of preserving food that would help feed his army on its march into Russia. After experimenting for 15 years, Paris candy maker Nicolas Appert won the prize in 1810 with a canning method still used to this day. Since then, the prizes for innovation multiplied in Europe and the United States, with much success.[7]

"Prizes can be the spur that produces a revolutionary solution," said a report by the McKinsey & Company consultancy. "For centuries, they were a core instrument of sovereigns, royal societies and private benefactors alike who sought to solve pressing societal problems and idiosyncratic technical challenges."[8] Prizes are also fundamental, Diamandis told me during our lengthy interview, for injecting society with the idea that something which seems impossible can indeed become a reality.

"The idea behind the prizes is that on the day before an invention is announced, it's a crazy idea," Diamandis told me. "If it wasn't a crazy idea the day before, then it would not be a great invention. So the question that I ask companies, organizations and governments, is 'do you have a place in your organizations where crazy ideas can be born?' Because if you're not experimenting with crazy ideas, with ideas that can fail, you will be stuck with small steps of continued improvement, but you will never invent something new. Prizes are, precisely, mechanisms to boost crazy ideas."[9]

Before the Ansari X Prize was offered for the development of a reusable space craft, no one believed that was possible and therefore no company was investing on that idea. But the prize lured a number of people into the ring. And after Allen won it, half a dozen aerospace companies were created to push the project forward, with investments that topped $1 billion.

In 2010, when the Deepwater Horizon, a British Petroleum semi-submersible drilling platform, created an ecological disaster in the Gulf of Mexico, no one believed that the existing systems for cleaning up oil spills at sea could be improved, Diamandis said. Several organizations, including Diamandis' X Prize, joined forces to offer a prize to whoever invented a better way to clean up the spill. "The results of the competition were spectacular. The winning team managed to quadruple the efficiency of the existing technology," Diamandis told me.

Skeptics point out, and with some reason, that prizes are often less an incentive to innovation than thinly veiled publicity campaigns by companies, or even sophisticated efforts to pay less for good ideas. It's also true that prizes are not a substitute for the basic research required to invent new products or improve existing ones. Nevertheless, prizes are an effective way to wake up interest in solving challenges, stimulate the largest number of talented people possible to turn ideas into reality, and create a culture of innovation. The advantages offered by prizes far outstrip the limitations pointed out by critics.

WE MUST ACCEPT AND LEARN FROM FAILURES

One fundamental key to creating a culture of innovation is to foster the idea that failure is often a prelude to success. Children must be taught from an early age that the most famous entrepreneurs in the world stumbled several times before they succeeded, and that the failure of a company does not mean the failure of the entrepreneur. Perhaps schools should teach the example of Facebook's purchase of the WhatsApp instant messaging system in 2014, for a remarkable $19.5 billion.

The two young Silicon Valley men who created WhatsApp —Brian Acton of the United States and Jan Koum of the Ukraine— had failed in a number of earlier attempts to become billionaires. Acton had applied for a job with Twitter in 2009 but was turned down. True to the Silicon Valley culture, he not only did not try to hide his failure but announced it publicly on his Twitter account. "Got denied by Twitter HQ. That's ok. Would have been a long commute," he wrote.

But the most amusing thing was that months later, Acton applied for a job at Facebook and was also rejected by the company that would pay him $19.5 billion five years later. Acton again announced his rejection on Twitter: "Facebook turned me down. It was a great opportunity to connect with some fantastic people. Looking forward to life's next adventure." I wonder how Facebook's human resources director felt five years later, when the company bought WhatsApp. "The Facebook human resources chief should be trembling. The joke cost him $19.5 billion," the *El País* newspaper in Spain wrote the day Facebook announced the purchase of WhatsApp.

That's a funny story, but it's only one of the thousands of examples of enterprises that fail more than once before they succeed. The examples mentioned in the first chapter —Thomas Alva Edison, who failed in more than 1,000 attempts before inventing the light bulb, or Alexander Graham Bell, whose invention of the telephone was rejected by the company today called Western Union —are a few more. And there are many others, like Henry Ford, the pioneer of the auto industry and founder of the Ford Motor Company. Ford first started a company, the Detroit Automobile Company, that went bankrupt. And that was not his only failure. He called his successful vehicle the Ford Model T because he had started with the Model A and failed with all his models until he got to Model T. But he was never intimidated by the taunts of some of his peers, who joked that he was wasting his time and would be better off to spend his time trying to develop "a faster horse." Ford used to say that the important thing was to embrace risk and do audacious things, even though many people would see that as madness.

PRIZES FOR FAILURE?

Silicon Valley's biggest secret is that it managed to create a culture where the fear of losing out on an opportunity is bigger than the fear of failure. Professor Baba Shiv put it this way in an article for the *Stanford Business School News*: "What is shameful to these people is sitting on the sidelines while someone else runs away with a great idea." In that spirit, and to try to change the culture of fear of failure in Latin America and Spain, Singularity University in 2014 was launching several prizes in Buenos Aires, Mexico City, Monterrey, Madrid and Barcelona for "entrepreneurs who take risks," independently of their success. "Our objective is to celebrate and recognize the people who take big risks, including those who fail, because failure is punished in the majority of these cultures. We want to reward risk, which is part of the creation of any successful new company," Salim Ismail, in charge of international relations at Singularity University, told me.[10]

That's an excellent idea. We will have achieved a culture of innovation on the day that our entrepreneurs talk about their failures with the same ease and optimism as the co-founder of WhatsApp showed after he was rejected by Twitter and Facebook. Societies that punish failure must be changed into societies with collective admiration for entrepreneurs who take risks, regardless of the results of their projects.

SECOND SECRET: FOSTER EDUCATION FOR INNOVATION

The deficit of human capital dedicated to innovation in the region
—in other words, the shortage of engineers, scientists and technicians— is dramatic. And the reason is no secret: the majority of Latin American university students study liberal arts or social sciences.
Latin America's educational systems are still anchored in 19th Century schemes that turn the study of math and sciences into pure tor-
ture. Furthermore, young people entering the university tend to be
more attracted to careers that address the worst problems of their
societies, which helps to explain why Latin America is producing so
many economists and so few engineers or scientists. Whatever the
explanation, the fact remains that while Finland and Ireland have 25
graduates in engineering per million people, Chile has only eight,
Mexico has seven, Colombia has six, Argentina has five and the rest
of the region has even fewer.[11]

How do the more advanced countries stimulate the study of math,
science and technology? In many cases, by playing games. That's no joke.
I remember that when I asked Bill Gates during an interview for his
suggestions on how to persuade more young people to choose careers in
science and engineering, he replied that primary schools must radically
change the way in which they teach those subjects. "They have to offer
projects that are fun for the children," Gates said. "For example, design a
small submarine, or a small robot. The children should understand that
science is a tool for doing something that they want to do, and not a
desert they must cross to perhaps find a good job once they cross it."[12]

In some countries, like Singapore, primary schools select the best
math students at a very early age and channel them into technical
schools. During a visit to a primary school in Singapore some years
back, I saw how teachers, instead of asking students to do abstract math
calculation, asked them to calculate the distance of a free kick in soccer,
or the distance between musicians on stage at a rock concert. At the
secondary school level, the most successful countries make sure that all
their schools have modern science laboratories so that students can learn

in the most fun manner possible. The key, according to several studies, is to make science and engineering fun, and not something abstract understood only by the most brilliant students. At the university level, many countries, like Finland, also limit the number of students who can study certain careers, so that they can decide how many scientists and bachelors in medieval literature graduate each year.

Eugenia Garduño, director for Mexico and Latin America for the Organization for Economic Cooperation and Development —the club of developed countries that administers the PISA tests to 15-year-old students all over the world— told me that by the time students reach secondary school it's already too late to encourage them to study for science or technical careers. That must be done starting in pre-school. "Already in pre-K, the students' tendencies are starting to appear," she said. "That's why it's crucial that, even before the children start school, they are involved in science activities, especially girls and students from poor families, the two groups most vulnerable in math and sciences."[13] Countries that created pre-school programs to attract these two groups to math and science, and which send their best teachers to the schools that most need them, are achieving the highest increases in the PISA tests, she added.

WE MUST TEACH HOW TO PROCESS INFORMATION,
NOT JUST CONVEY IT

In the era of Google, when we can access information about virtually anything on the Internet, our schools no longer need to convey knowledge. Instead, they have to teach students how to process information and encourage creativity. Harvard education expert Tony Wagner says in his book, *Creating Innovators,* that the principal objective of schools should no longer be to prepare youths for university, but to prepare them to innovate. "What we know is increasingly less important, and what we can do with what we know is increasingly more important. The capacity to innovate —the ability to solve problems creatively or turn new possibilities into realities, and skills like critical thinking and being able to communicate and collaborate with others— are much more important than academic knowledge," said Wagner.[14]

For Wagner, innovation can be taught in schools. The key is that teachers, instead of rewarding students based on the knowledge they acquire —that is, what they "know"— reward them based on their capacity to analyze and solve problems and learn from their failures. "In most high-school and college classes, failure is penalized. But without trial and errors, there is no innovation," Wagner wrote.[15] Wagner recalled that Amanda Alonzo, a high school teacher in San Jose, California, whose students have won a number of science prizes, once told him that "one of the most important things I have to teach my students is that when you fail, you're learning." Wagner concluded that the schools doing the best job of preparing students for the 21st Century economy are those that reward them for what they study as well as their capacity to solve problems, work in teams, persevere with their projects, take risks, learn from their mistakes and are not discouraged by their failures.

Wagner's other key recommendation is that schools and universities should emphasize interdisciplinary thinking. "The university system today demands and rewards specialization. Professors earn tenure based on research on narrow academic fields, and students are required to declare a major in a subject area... But the most important thing educators can do... is to teach that problems can never be understood or solved in the context of a single academic discipline," Wagner wrote.[16] The best universities are those that allow students to build their own interdisciplinary careers, such as robotic medicine or medical engineering. At Olin College, for example, students create their own career tracks, like "Design for Sustainable Development" or "Mathematical Biology." And that's what university education will be increasingly like in the future.

WE MUST CHANGE THE LENS FROM CHILDHOOD

To start thinking in an interdisciplinary way and create revolutionary innovations —or disruptive innovations, as many call them—

263

we have to change the lens through which we see things. And many innovation gurus suggest that the key to promoting innovation among children is to teach them to ask the right questions. Instead of asking them to solve specific problems, the gurus say we must teach them to reformulate the problem as a broader question: What's the final goal?

In their book, *The Solution Revolution*, William D. Eggers and Paul Macmillan provide a perfect example of how reformulating a question can help us to see things in a different way. If we ask how we can improve schools, we are limiting our minds to how to improve an education system made up of brick buildings, classrooms, blackboards and desks. But if we refocus the question on our goal, and ask how we can improve the education of our youths and prepare them for the labor market of the future, we will achieve much more creative solutions, they argue.

"This last question opens a range of possibilities that may or may not include traditional education as we know it," the authors argue, adding that it also leads us to consider possibilities like distant education or the "flipped classes" made popular by Salman Khan. "If you think about how to solve a problem in terms of existing solutions, you are limiting the potential solutions to a defective status quo."

The same happens in other settings. If a company asks how it can sell more, it is limiting its thinking to how to improve the products it makes, speed up its distribution networks or improve its marketing strategies. But if it asks how it can increase revenues and contribute to society, it will expand its field of vision dramatically and find new products or services that it might have never considered. In the same way, if we ask how we can move forward in our jobs, we are limiting ourselves to a narrow number of possibilities. It would be better if we ask ourselves what we can do to satisfy our economic needs, improve the quality of our lives and be happy.

Another way of changing the lens through which we see things, suggested by Luke Williams in his book *Disrupt*, is to replace our working hypothesis with one that is intentionally wacky. To do this, Williams suggest turning our hypothesis upside down. For example, in the case of how to improve our schools, with bricks, classrooms, blackboards and desks, Williams suggests we ask ourselves what would happen if we educate our children without any of these elements. Just like when we reformulated the question to focus on our final goal, turning a traditional question upside down can open our eyes to revolutionary solutions, he says. Whatever the formula, what's clear is that one of the keys to creating a culture of innovation is changing the lens through which we see things —like a test at the eye doctor's office. In our schools, companies and governments, we should routinely encourage the analysis of problems from different angles by raising different questions. Many times, the secret is in the question.

THIRD SECRET: REPEAL LAWS THAT KILL INNOVATION

As we pointed out in the opening pages of this book, most Latin American countries and many nations across the world need to simplify the procedures for opening or closing companies, adopt laws that enforce respect for intellectual property and modify bankruptcy laws that punish business failures excessively. In the new world of productive innovation, where companies are launched and re-launched, and constantly die and are re-born, governments must make it as easy as possible to open and close companies.

Although some countries, like Chile and Mexico, have reduced their bureaucratic hurdles to opening new companies, many others remain among the champions of red tape. Argentina requires 14 steps to register a new company, Brazil and Ecuador require 13 and Venezuela requires a remarkable 17 steps, which generally require several months and bribes to government officials, according to the World Bank.[17] Facing such hurdles, and the costs of bribes paid to "speed up" the red tape, it's no coincidence that many Latin American business people never launch their projects or start them in the underground economy.

And unless we add laws that protect intellectual property with sufficient vigor, incentives for innovation will have even less impact. The higher the fear that one's ideas will be stolen, the lower the incentives to try to turn it into a reality. In many of our countries, authorities not only do not combat intellectual piracy but sometimes turn a blind eye to it. The giant La Salada black market in the Buenos Aires province of Argentina, the Tepito market in Mexico City, the San Andresito markets in Bogotá and Cali in Colombia and the La Bahía market in Guayaquil, Ecuador, all sell pirated music, movies, video games, computer programs, clothes and even pharmaceuticals at rock bottom prices.

Many people who shop in those black markets see it as an inoffensive bit of naughtiness which, in the worst of cases, affects only multinational companies that already make a lot of money. But few understand that intellectual piracy affects not only foreign companies but also local enterprises. In many cases, it discourages potential innovators from even trying to start their projects, and discourages potential investors from supporting them, because of the possible competition from pirated products.

BANKRUPTCY LAWS THAT PUNISH FAILURE

One of the principal hurdles to innovation mentioned by many of the entrepreneurs I interviewed for this book is the rigid bankruptcy laws in most of our countries, which make it almost impossible for innovators who fail in one project to try a second or third time. In many Latin American countries, the laws turn entrepreneurs who declare bankruptcy into social pariahs, who cannot launch any new business, sign checks or even keep their personal property.

That's profoundly different from the legal frameworks in countries that promote innovation. In the United States and most other industrialized countries, the laws allow a company that declares bankruptcy to open a new company on the same day. U.S. laws also make it difficult for creditors of failed companies to seize the personal property of owners or members of the board of directors —something common in many Latin American countries. The Latin American legal tradition has its logic— to bar managers from plundering companies. But it also can lead to absurd situations, like barring business people from launching a new enterprise until the liquidation of their companies is completed, a process which can take decades.

"In Argentina, it is hard to fail," Emiliano Kargieman, the Argentine who is producing nano satellites that could revolutionize the aerospace industry, told me in an interview. "To shut down a company is physically and economically demanding. You wind up in court for years, and the process is terrible. I have friends who moved to other countries, because they didn't want to go through that again. It discourages people from starting a company. Failure should be easy. Not only must we increase the birth rate of new companies, we must also increase the death rate of companies. The important thing is to be able to fail as quickly as possible, so you can get up and start again."[18]

Countries that promote innovation tend to support reorganizing companies instead of liquidating them, and have extremely quick processes for settling bankruptcy cases. Some industrialized countries have special courts for speeding up reorganizations or bankruptcies and some, like South Korea, allow the process to be done online. In Singapore, the average length of a reorganization, liquidation or bankruptcy is eight months, while in Finland it's nine months. In contrast, the average is five years and three months in Ecuador, four years in Brazil and Venezuela, two years and seven months in Argentina and one year and seven months in Mexico, according to World Bank statistics.[19]

"In many Latin American countries, we have legislation from the days when bankruptcy was a crime," World Bank expert Augusto López-Claros told me in an interview. "In Chile, which just reformed its bankruptcy laws, if you declared bankruptcy until recently you could not even write a check. You were marked for life, you were a social pariah. You failed once, and you failed forever. In the United States and other countries, failure is an opportunity. Look at American Airlines. It reorganized, and that allowed it to merge with U.S. Airways and come out stronger."[20]

"OUR COUNTRY PERSECUTES PEOPLE WHO ARE DOING POORLY"

Martin Migoya, co-founder of Globant, an Argentine company that produces software for Google, Linkedin and DreamWorks and has nearly 3,200 employees in Argentina, Colombia, Uruguay, Brazil, Great Britain and the United States, is one of the super-successful business people who are campaigning to change the bankruptcy laws in Argentina in order to boost innovation. "Our country punishes, it really persecutes, people who are doing poorly. The guy who is doing well rises and the other is buried, when in fact the two results should be much closer," Migoya said in an interview in Buenos Aires.[21]

Like most successful innovators, Migoya failed several times before he succeeded. "Before I started Globant, when I was young, I started two or three things and did badly in all of them," he recalled. When he was 21, shortly before graduating from electronic engineering, Migoya and a friend —one of Globant's current partners— created a synthesizer-like electronic box that allowed musicians to synchronize various instruments. But the idea did not take off and the two youths realized, after approaching several music shops, that there wasn't much demand for the device. During that process, however, the friends discovered that the micro corrugated cardboard they needed for the devices was difficult to buy. Office supply shops told them they did not know where to find that type of cardboard. So the young men changed course and started to sell micro corrugated cardboard. But that company did not succeed either.

Several years later, Migoya and his partners started their success story when they started Globant in 2003 with a very simple formula: take advantage of the low cost of labor in Argentina at the time to develop software and sell it abroad. In 2014, they registered with the U.S. Securities and Exchange Commission (SEC) and raised $58 million with an initial public offering. But Migoya and his partners were lucky to have failed when they were younger, in small projects that did not require them to declare bankruptcy. Had they been forced into bankruptcy, it's likely that Argentine laws would not have allowed them to rise again and create a company like Globant.

FOURTH SECRET: STIMULATE INVESTMENTS IN INNOVATION

It's no secret that the countries that invest more in research and development usually patent more inventions and put more new products on the market. The country that leads the world in its percentage of investment in research and development, Israel, spends 4.3 percent of its Gross Domestic Product (GDP) in this sector. It's followed by Finland with 4 percent, Japan with 3.3 percent, the United States with 3 percent, Germany with 2.8 percent and France with 2.2 percent, according to the Organization for Economic Cooperation and Development (OECD). In comparison, Brazil spends 1.2 percent of its GDP on research and development, and the rest of the Latin American countries spend less than 1 percent of their respective GDP on that sector.[22]

The second big problem behind investments in innovation in Latin America is that the biggest part of the money comes from government —through public universities— and not from private enterprise, which knows the market best. But in countries with the most success in innovation —Israel, Finland, the United States and members of the European Union as well as rapidly advancing countries like China— the biggest part of their investments in research and development comes from private enterprise. While nearly 70 percent of all U.S. investments in the sector comes from private enterprise, in Argentina it barely reaches 21 percent, while in Mexico it's 43 percent and in Brazil it's 46 percent, according to the Organization of Ibero-American States (OIS).[23] In Latin America, the people who make the decisions about when and where to invest in innovation are often government functionaries who have little or no knowledge or experience in the development of potentially marketable products.

THE ROLE OF COMPANIES AND UNIVERSITIES

According to the OIS, the meager collaboration between the private sector and universities in Latin America is due in large part to a "clash of cultures." While many emerging countries' universities see themselves as producers of pure knowledge, uncontaminated by commercial interests, private enterprise sees itself as dedicated exclusively to increasing its profits. Although this is starting to change, many Latin American professors and researchers consider it more prestigious to write an academic paper on some theoretical issue than to collaborate with private enterprise to invent a new technology or a new product. In the most innovative countries, universities have even created private companies to co-register patents with professors, researchers and private enterprise.

When I visited Hebrew University in Jerusalem, I met the directors of Yissum, a university enterprise that contacts every professor every few months and asks if they have any new discoveries that can be offered to the private sector. If the answer is yes, Yissum handles the paperwork for registering the patent at the international level —a long and costly process — and finds private companies or investors interested in the project. And if the project turns into a commercially viable product, profits are split— 40 percent each for the professor or researcher and the university and 20 percent for the university lab that participated in the project.

In that system, the professors who generate patents are the stars of their universities. Yissum has already registered 8,300 patents for Hebrew University for about 2,400 inventions, many of which were bought by companies like IBM, Bayer, Merck or Microsoft. Shouldn't the universities in Latin America be urgently creating their own versions of Yissum, knocking on the doors of their professors every six months to ask if they have some invention that can be patented?

VENTURE CAPITAL

The third great challenge in promoting innovation is to encourage the growth of venture capital funds, people willing to risk their investments in startups or companies just starting out that have a great potential to fail. Luis Von Ahn, the Guatemalan who founded the Duolingo company for free online language courses, told me he managed to raise $40 million from venture capital for his project in the United States, something he would have found difficult if not impossible in Latin America.

"The venture capital companies that invested in Duolingo knew they had a 95 percent chance of not recovering their money because the chances that a technology startup will fail are about 95 percent. But that's precisely the idea of a venture investment," Von Ahn told me. "They invest with the idea —and this is what's missing in Latin America— that if they invest in 100 high-risk startups, 95 of them will fail but the other five may be the next Google or the next Twitter. And those five will pay for the rest of their investments, and make a lot of money."[24]

Von Ahn used the example of Facebook's purchase of WhatsApp in 2014. When the deal was announced, all the media reported that Facebook had paid a whopping $19.5 billion to the two company founders, but few pointed out that the venture capitalists who invested in WhatsApp also made fortunes on the deal. "Venture capitalists know they are never going to earn $19.5 billion investing in restaurants, so they elect to invest in technology startups, even if they are very risky," Von Ahn told me. "We have to create that culture of venture capital in our own countries, because the mindset of many investors in Latin America is 'I'll give you the money, but you have to guarantee me that we will recover 100 percent of the investment.' In contrast, venture capitalists know that most projects will fail but they don't care because they know that with one big project that succeeds they will make more profits than with any other investment."[25]

And how do we create venture capitalists?, I asked him. Von Ahn admitted that's not easy, but said that perhaps governments could offer fiscal incentives for those types of investments. That would not be a bad idea. Venture capitalists are one of the engines of Silicon Valley, and one of the key factors in most successful innovation ecosystems.

THE COLLECTIVE INVESTMENTS OF CROWDFUNDING

Fortunately, there are other novel sources of investment, like crowdfunding, which allows innovators to raise funds through individual contributions from thousands of small investors on websites like Kick-starter.com. Innovators with little access to bank loans are increasingly financing their projects thanks to this system for online fund raising.

That's the case of Rafael Atijas, a young Uruguayan who invented a three-string guitar that helps children learn how to play the instrument, whose traditional six-string version is too complicated for small children. Atijas' story highlights the possibilities enjoyed by innovators today: He invented his string guitar in Uruguay, raised funds in the United States through Kickstarter.com, started to manufacture them in China, warehouses them in the United States and now sells them in 30 countries, mostly the United States, Japan, Canada, Great Britain and New Zealand. And he does it all from his laptop in Montevideo, Uruguay.

How did he do it, I asked him. Atijas, who earned a marketing degree in Uruguay, told me he invented his three-string guitar while earning master's degree in Integrated Marketing at New York University in New York City. To graduate, he had to write a thesis with a business plan for a new product. In effect, he had to invent something and develop a plan for turning the idea into reality. Looking for an idea, Atijas, who is also a musician, found it during a visit to his six-year-old niece. "I knew I had to find something in music and industrial design, the things that I really like. And I got the idea when I saw my niece trying to play a typical guitar for children, which are just small versions of regular guitars. I thought of creating a guitar with three strings that would allow children to play and listen to the notes much more easily."[26]

After earning his master's, Atijas returned to Uruguay, approached an industrial design company and invested $90,000 —$45,000 from Uruguay's Innovation Agency and the rest from his savings, relatives and friends— to contract for prototypes, designs and everything related to the development of the three-string guitar. But the money was not enough to start production, so he posted his project on Kickstarter.com in March of 2011. Atijas fixed a goal —required by Kickstarter.com— of $15,000 in one month. People ordered the guitars with their credit cards, on the understanding that if the project failed and they did not receive their three-string guitar, the purchase would be canceled and their money would be returned. To Atijas' surprise, he received $65,000 in the first month. "It was incredible," the young Uruguayan told me. "I spent the days watching the Kickstarter page on the computer, clicking 'refresh' and watching how the contributions added up."[27]

Later, and still from his laptop in Uruguay, Atijas search AliBaba. com, a massive directory of factories in China, for one that could produce the guitar. He selected one that seemed to be the best, flew to China to personally confirm the factory was not a fraud and ordered the first samples. With the $65,000 he had raised on Kickstarter.com, he ordered 600 guitars, shipped 400 to people who bought them on Kickstarter and sold the rest for $150 a piece on Loogguitars.com. In the next two years, Atijas and his partner, who also manages the company from his laptop in Montevideo, sold 3,500 guitars in 30 countries.

When I spoke with Atijas, he had just posted a new product on Kickstarter.com, an electric version of the three-string guitar, and raised $70,000 in one month. He is currently developing new instruments, such as a piano and drum kit for children. And his entire company was built without bank loans or venture capital.

FIFTH SECRET: GLOBALIZE INNOVATION

Increasingly, innovation is a collaborative process —often done in public, like the cases of Jordi Muñoz, Bre Pettis and the "makers" and scientists like Rafael Yuste— that requires working in close contact and real time with others working on similar projects in other parts of the world. To achieve that, education and research must be globalized, something that has started to happen —better late than never— in countries like Chile and Brazil but not in most of Latin America.

In contrast to Sinagapore, China and other Asian nations, the majority of Latin American countries do not allow foreign universities on their territory and have no agreements for joint degrees with the best universities in the first world. What's even worse, many Latin American universities do not require more than a basic knowledge of

English. Whether we like it or not, English has become the lingua fran-ca of science and technology all over the world. The Chinese, despite the communist system and different alphabet, have made giant progress learning English since the government declared the "internationaliza-tion of education" as one of the key goals in its five-year plans. More than a decade ago, China decreed the mandatory teaching of English in all schools, four hours per week, starting in third grade. The impact has been immediate, which I confirmed during a recent trip to China. Contrary to what I found during a previous visit 15 years ago, when I could not communicate with anyone on the street, today many youths in large Chinese cities can communicate in English.

Partly because of their increasing proficiency in English, China, South Korea, Singapore, Vietnam and other Asian countries with dif-ferent political systems are sending many more students to study science or technology in U.S., Canadian, European and Australian universities that require fluency in English for admission. According to the "Open Doors" report by the Institute of International Education, U.S. uni-versities had 235,000 students from China in 2013, 97,000 from India, 71,000 from South Korea, 45,000 from Saudi Arabia, and 20,000 from Vietnam, but only 16,000 from Mexico, 11,000 from Brazil, 7,000 from Colombia, 6,000 from Venezuela, 2,500 from Peru, 2,400 from Chile and 1,800 from Argentina.[28]

Another study of student flows around the world, and not just the United States, showed similar results. China had 441,000 students abroad, India 170,000 and South Korea 113,000. In comparison, the United States had 51,000, Mexico 26,000, Brazil 23,000, Spain 22,000, Argen-tina 9,000 and Chile 7,000, according to the UNESCO's Global Education Digest for 2010. The study also showed that 3.5 percent of South Korean university students and 1.7 percent of China's were studying abroad, while only 1 percent of Mexican students and 0.4 percent of Brazilian and Argentine university students were enrolled abroad.

How does one explain that South Korea, with a population less than half the size of Mexico's, has four times more students in U.S. universities than Mexico, the Latin American country with the highest number of university students in the United States? And how to explain that Vietnam, a communist country with a different alphabet, has more young people studying in U.S. universities than Mexico? The first explanation is that the Asian countries, after seeing China make its successful turn to capitalism in 1978 and reduce its poverty at a rapid pace, dove full force into the global economy while we in Latin America sat on the sidelines, clinging to 19th Century nationalist and statist ideologies. The second explanation, pointed out by several U.S. university presidents I interviewed, is much more simple: many Latin American students are not sufficiently proficient in English to pass the language exams required by U.S. universities.

WHY DO WE APPLAUD THE GLOBALIZATION OF SOCCER AND NOT SCIENCE?

As I wrote in my column titled "Latin America needs a Messi in Science," Latin American countries should embrace and take maximum advantage of the globalization of science, just as they do with soccer. We saw during the last World Cup that soccer is one of the world's most global activities. Almost all the players on Latin American national selections play abroad, and gladly return home to play for their teams. And that doesn't just happen with soccer powers like Argentina or Brazil, whose stars have been playing in the best European leagues for a long time. It also happens with smaller countries, like Costa Rica and Chile.

Those two small countries managed historic performances in the last World Cup in large part because their players had experience competing in the European leagues against the best in the world. The Costa Rican team, which played in the quarter finals for the first time in history, included players with clubs in Spain, the United States, Belgium, Norway, Germany, Switzerland, Denmark, Netherlands and Greece. Out of its 11 starting players, only two did not play abroad.

The globalization of soccer helped countries without a great soccer history to compete head to head against the best, without any self-doubts. Costa Rica beat Italy and tied with England in 2014, unthinkable results just a few years earlier. And Chile beat Spain. England, Spain and Italy were eliminated by much smaller rivals. In most Latin American countries, there is now a generalized acceptance that the globalization of soccer helped to improve the quality of their players. Why not accept the same premise for scientists? Why do we often criticize the "brain drain," a 19th Century concept, instead of taking advantage of the new phenomenon known as "brain circulation?"

In the globalized world of the 21st Century, the most successful countries will generate a "brain circulation" that benefits both the source countries and the receiving countries. Just as China, South Korea and other emerging powers in technology send a higher percentage of their students to universities abroad, Latin American countries must encourage their most promising scientists to work with the leading scientists in the world —and return home periodically to teach or collaborate with research projects— just as soccer players on national selections do every four years for the World Cup. With more "brain circulation," our scientists will be more competitive and we will have more chances of creating a new Steve Jobs —or a Messi for science or a Neymar for technology.

STUDENT PROGRAMS IN CHILE, BRAZIL AND MEXICO

Fortunately, some Latin American countries are getting their act together. In 2008, the first government of Chilean President Michelle Bachelet created a $6 billion fund to award 6,500 annual scholarships for postgraduate studies in the United States and other countries with the best universities in the world. In 2011, Brazil followed suit with an ambitious program called Science Without Borders that proposed sending 100,000 graduates in engineering, science and technology to study abroad. Science and Technology Minister Aloizio Mercadante announced that under the new program, the government would award 75,000 scholarships, and the private sector another 25,000, for studies toward master's and doctorate degrees "in the best universities in the world."

THE FIVE SECRETS OF INNOVATION

And in 2013, the Mexican government announced its own mega-project for student globalization called *Proyecta 100,000*. The program aimed to expand Mexico's 16,000 students in U.S. universities to 27,000 by 2014, 46,000 in 2015 and so on until it hit 100,000 in 2018. In other words, the Mexican government hoped to have a total of 319,000 Mexican students in U.S. universities. Around the same time, U.S. President Barack Obama launched his "100,000 Strong in the Americas" campaign, designed to increase the number of Latin American students in U.S. universities to 100,000 by 2020.

Although it remains to be seen whether these programs will meet their goals —in fact, most are currently advancing at a slower pace than planned— the good news is that at least some countries have accepted the need to globalize education and put their scientists and technicians to work in the principal centers for research and innovation around the world.

It's true that some of the Latin American scientists and engineers who leave to study abroad will not return. However, as we have seen in China, India, South Korea and other countries with large numbers of students abroad, even those who remain in the United States help to accelerate the development of their native countries as either investors, entrepreneurs, professional visitors or collaborators in scientific projects. The secret is that their native countries must give them the opportunity to do that. They have to change what used to be called a "brain drain" into a "brain circulation" and even a "brain gain" for developing countries.

COUNTRIES WILL COMPETE FOR TALENT, NOT LAND

Chile and Brazil also recently launched programs to import innovators —literally. That's not a joke. Both countries created economic incentives to attract young entrepreneurs from around the world, embracing the idea that the countries with the strongest progress now compete for talent, not territories. Just like the best technology minds are concentrated in Silicon Valley, Chile and Brazil want to create their own enclaves for technology innovation.

Brazil launched a program in 2013 that offers domestic and foreign technology entrepreneurs nearly $100,000 in government assistance, plus free office space and business, legal and accounting advice. The public-private program called "Startup Brazil" expects that up to 25 percent of the companies benefiting will be owned by foreigners whose managers will have residency visas. The operations manager of "Startup Brazil," Felipe Matos, told me that 909 companies applied for the first round of 50 awards, including about 60 from the United States. Curiously, the United States was the foreign country with the highest number of applications.

"We want to attract interesting minds, and people who can help us become more competitive," Matos told me.[29] When I asked why a young U.S. entrepreneur would want to move to Brazil, one of the countries with the highest bureaucratic barriers to opening and managing a business, Matos answered, "There's a lot more room to grow in Brazil than in mature economies. Brazil is the biggest consumer market in Latin America. It has 80 million Internet users, and is just beginning to buy things online."

In Chile, the government program "Startup Chile" was launched in 2010 to attract exclusively foreign entrepreneurs, principally in the Internet sector. The government offers $40,000 to each entrepreneur, as well as a work visa and free work space. More than 7,200 applications have been received from more than 50 countries and people with an average age of 27, and 670 have been selected, I was told by the program's executive director, Horacio Melo.

Out of the 670 startups selected when I spoke with Melo, more than 160 were from the United States. The program focuses exclusively on attracting foreigners and does not oblige them to remain in Chile. After spending six months in the country and launching their companies —as well as meeting other requirements such as sharing their experiences with local entrepreneurs and speaking at universities— beneficiaries can return to their home countries or go anywhere they want. About 30 percent remain in Chile, Melo told me. When I asked how he manages to persuade a U.S. entrepreneur to launch a startup in Chile, Melo told me, "We accept startups at very early stages, when they are still too risky for angel investors in the United States. They come to Chile so they can test their hypothesis, validate whether that hypothesis functions, and reduce the risks for potential investors."[30]

Obviously, "Startup Brazil" and "Startup Chile" are still too young to aspire to creating new Silicon Valleys in Latin America. But, like the plans to increase scholarships for graduate studies abroad, they will help to create the kind of circulation of talent that greatly helped China, India, South Korea and other emerging countries in recent decades. The number of their foreign applications also show that the idea of attracting foreign creative minds to Latin America is not so crazy.

THE REASONS FOR HOPE

Fortunately, Latin American and many other regions of the emerging world don't lack the talent, creativity or audacity to do something new. Latin American countries, for instance, are far from being stagnant societies afraid of experimenting with the unknown. Several of them have been at the forefront of issues such as the election of women presidents —that backfired in many cases, but that's another story— conditional subsidies for school attendance, the mass purchase of school laptops, gay marriage and the legalization of marijuana. Some of those decisions have not had a happy ending, but they could only have come out of dynamic societies open to experimentation. And that is a good sign.

Many Latin American cities are already at the forefront of urban innovation. The Colombian city of Medellín was selected as the most innovative city in the world in a 2013 contest organized by *The Wall Street* Journal and CitiGroup, beating out competitors like New York City and Tel Aviv. Twenty years ago, Medellín was known as the world capital of cocaine. But in just two decades, with a strategy of "urban acupuncture," designed to carry out first-world projects in less developed neighborhoods to integrate them to the rest of the city,

Medellín managed to reduce its homicide rate by nearly 80 percent and become a much more livable and prosperous city.

As an example, in 2011 Medellín inaugurated a giant escalator, almost 400 meters long, in one of its poorest and, until recently, most dangerous neighborhoods. The escalator, in six sections, connects Comuna 13, on a steep hillside, to a metro station and the rest of the city. Until 2011, the 140,000 residents of Comuna 13 had to walk up about 350 steps, almost the height of the tallest skyscraper in New York, to reach their homes, making it almost impossible for them to work in the city.

Buenos Aires, Lima and Guayaquil have carried out equally novel improvements. The government of the Argentine capital installed a free WI-FI system in all public schools, and in 2014 announced it was moving its offices to a super-modern building in Parque de los Patricios, one of its poorest neighborhoods. The municipal government already had created a technology park in the neighborhood, and offered economic incentives to companies and universities to move there. The design of the new building was assigned to the studio of Lord Norman Foster, a world-famous architect who designed the German parliament and the Beijing airport, among many other projects. Lima and Guayaquil, just a decade ago among the ugliest cities in Latin America, have become tourist centers thanks to new shoreline boulevards that changed their faces overnight.

And in Mexico City, there have been fascinating urban experiments such as the health clinics established in metro stations —where 5 million people pass through every— that can perform blood, urine, and HIV tests. The clinics, in key intersections of the metro lines, have helped ease overcrowding in hospitals and prevent diseases.

"They have come from China and many other countries to see our metro clinics, and they all say, 'How marvelous!'" the Federal District's Health Secretary, Dr. Armando Ahued, told me.[31] "The clinics can do 19 types of laboratory exams to detect the 66 most common diseases, and we do it for free for those covered by the government. People can have blood drawn, and come by the next day to pick up the results."

At the personal level, there's a surplus of examples of successful Latin American innovators like Gastón Acurio of Peru, Jordi Muñoz of Mexico, Emiliano Kargieman of Argentina, Alfredo Zolezzi of Chile, Luis Von Ahn of Guatemala and others we have highlighted in this book. There are many others, in Colombia, Venezuela, India, and other Latin American, Eastern European and Asian countries, as distinguished or more, not included in these pages for reasons of space and because I chose to focus on some of the innovators who are least known and are doing the most original work.

Many of them, it's true, are succeeding outside their native countries. Our great challenge now is to create ecosystems favorable to innovation —a culture that promotes creativity, that celebrates innovators, admires entrepreneurs and tolerates their failures— so that many more of them can flourish in their own countries. It can be done, and quickly, because there's a surplus of talent and because the steps to achieve it —like the five secrets we just listed— have been tested and proven in other parts of the world.

The proof is in plain sight. There are countries with all kinds of different political systems —from the communist dictatorship in China to the rightist dictatorship in Singapore, or the democracies in South Korea, Taiwan or Finland— that have prospered much more than Latin American countries in the past 50 years because they bet on education and innovation. Those countries are registering more and more patents for new products, which bring in more and more revenues and reduce poverty at a faster clip. It's time for us in Latin America, like them, to jump head-first into the era of the knowledge economy and realize that the key choices of the 21st Century will be neither "Socialism or Death," nor "Capitalism or Socialism" nor "Government or Market," but rather something much less ideological: be creative or stagnate. Or, to put it in more dramatic terms, innovate or die.

Notes

PROLOGUE

[1] Luisa Kroll, "Bill Gates Says There is Something Perverse in College Ratings," *Forbes*, January 31, 2013.

[2] World Bank and the International Finance Corporation, Doing Business 2013, 2013.

[3] Andrés Rodríguez-Pose, "Los parques científicos y tecnológicos en América Latina: un análisis de la situación actual," InterAmerican Development Bank, June, 2012, 19.

1. THE COMING WORLD

[1] World Bank/International Finance Corporation, Doing Business 2013: Smarter Regulations for Small and Medium-Sized Enterprises, 2013.

[2] Richard Florida, "Cities are the Fonts of Creativity," *New York Times*, September 15, 2015.

[3] Richard Florida, speech to the 22nd EBN Congress, Derry-Londonderry, Northern Ireland, May 29-31, 2013.

[4] *Ibid.*

[5] *Ibid.*

[6] *Ibid.*

[7] Barack Obama, State of the Union Address, Feb. 12, 2013.

[8] Gonzalo Martínez, lecture delivered at Singularity University, Palo Alto, California, March 11, 2013.

[9] Matthew L. Wald, "Just don't call it a Drone," *The New York Times*, February 2013.

[10] *Ibid.*

[11] Jordi Muñoz, interview by the author for *Oppenheimer Presenta*, CNN, April 2013.

[12] Brad Templeton, interview by the author, Palo Alto, California, March 2013.

[13] Chunka Muy, "Fasten Your Seatbelts," *Forbes*, January 22, 2013.

[14] *Ibid.*

[15] Tim Hume, "Heal Thyself: The 'Bio-inspired' Materials that Self-repair," *CNN*, February 22, 2013.

[16] *Ibid.*

[17] World Economic Forum, "The Global Information Technology Report 2014", http://www.weforum.org/reports/global-information-technology-report-2014.

[18] Daniel Kraft, interview by the author, Mountain View, California, March 2013.

[19] Jonathan Cohn, "The Robot Will See You Now," *The Atlantic*, March 2013.

[20] Tina Rosenberg, "Turning Education upside Down," *The New York Times*, October 9.

[21] *Ibid.*

[22] Sir Richard Branson, interview by the author for the *Oppenheimer Presenta* program, *CNN*, May 31, 2013.

[23] Brad Stone, "Bill Gates on His Foundation's Health and Education Campaigns", *Bloomberg*, August 8 2013. http://www.bloomberg.com/bw/articles/2013-08-08/bill-gates-on-his-foundations-health-and-education-campaigns.

[24] Peter H. Diamandis and Steven Kotler, *Abundance: The Future is Better than What You Think*, (Free Press, 2012), 9.

[25] Charles Kenny and Justin Sandefur, "Can Silicon Valley Save the World?" *Foreign Policy*, July 2013, 74.

[26] Peter H. Diamandis and Steven Kotler, *Abundance: The Future is Better than What You Think*, (Free Press, 2012), 304.

[27] World Bank, "World Development Indicators", http://wdi.worldbank.org/table/4.2.

[28] WIPO, "U. S. and China Drive International Patent Filing in Record-Setting year," www.wipo.int, March 13, 2014.

[29] *Ibid.*

[30] U. S. Patent and Trademark Office, "Patent Counts by Origin and Type, Calendar year 2013," March 2014, www.uspto.gov.

[31] Andrés Oppenheimer, "Who's winning, who's losing innovation race", *The Miami Herald*, March 27, 2014.

[32] Nicola Perra, interview by the author, Northeastern University, May 2013.

[33] *Times Higher Educativa*, "The World University Rankings 2013," http://www.timeshighereducation.co.uk/world-university-rankings/compareuniversities.

[34] QS Ranking of World's Best Universities, http://www.topuniversities.com/university-rankings/world-university-rankings/2013.

[35] Jiao Tong University, Shanghai, China, "Ranking of the best universities in the world," http://www.shanghairanking.com/ARWU2013.html.

[36] RICYT, chart "Graduados en educación superior", 2014, www.ricyt.org/indicadores.

[37] Andrés Oppenheimer, *Basta de historias*, (Debate, Mexico) 17.

[38] Organization of IberoAmerican States, "Ciencia, tecnología e innovación para el desarrollo y la cohesión social," 2012, 35.

[39] *El País*, "América Latina ocupa los últimos puestos del informe sobre educación", *El País*, Spain, December 4, 2013.

[40] Bain & Company, "The Great Eight", 35, http://www.bain.com/publications/articles/eight-great-trillion-dollar-growth-trends-to-2020.aspx.

[41] Vivek Wadhwa, interview by the author, Palo Alto, California, March 2013.

[42] Herbert N. Casson, *The History of The Telephone*, (A.C. McClurg, 1910) 58-59.

[43] Arthur Reston, "Wilbur & Orville Wright: A Chronology," 69, http://history.nasa.gov/monograph32.pdf.

[44] Shelley Carson, "The Unleashed Mind: Why Creative People are Eccentric," *Scientific American*, April 2013.

[45] CBS, *60 Minutes*, interview with Elon Musk, June 3, 2012.

[46] *Time* magazine, "The Secrets of Genius: Discovering the Nature of Brilliance," *Time special edition*, 2013.

[47] *Ibid.*

[48] *Ibid.*

[49] "The Regional Distribution and Correlates of an Entrepreneurship-prone Personality Profile in the United States, Germany and the United Kingdom", *Journal of Personality and Social Psychology*, April 2013.

2. GASTÓN ACURIO: THE CHEF WHO GIVES AWAY HIS RECIPES

[1] *The Economist*, "The Peruvian Gastronomic Revolution, Continued," February 22, 2014.

[2] Gastón Acurio, interview by the author, Miami, February 2013.

[3] Sociedad Peruana de Gastronomia, report, 2013.

[4] According to the Ipsos/Apoyo 2012's national poll of reasons to be proud, 53 percent of peruvians chose Machu Pichu; 45 percent prefer gastronomy; 42 percent, natural resources; 34 percent, arts and culture; 32 percent, natural landscapes, and 30 percent, history.

3. JORDI MUÑOZ AND THE "MAKERS" MOVEMENT

[1] Chris Anderson, *Makers: The New Industrial Revolution*, (Crown Business, 2012), 147.

[2] Jordi Muñoz, interview by the author, April 2013.

[3] Rosa Bardales, phone interview by the author, May 2013.

[4] Jorge Muñoz Esteves, interview by the author, May 2013.

[5] *Ibid.*

[6] Chris Anderson, *Makers: The New Industrial Revolution*, (Crown Business, 2012), 146.

[7] *Idem.*

[8] *Idem.*

[9] Chris Anderson, *Makers: The New Industrial Revolution*, (Crown Business, 2012), 148.

[10] *Ibid.,* 149.

[11] *Ibid.,* 150.

[12] *Ibid.,* 150.

[13] Jordi Muñoz, e-mail to author, May 2013.

[14] Chris Anderson, *Makers: The New Industrial Revolution*, (Crown Business, 2012), 108.

[15] *Ibid.,* 110.

[16] *Ibid.,* 109.

[17] *Ibid.,* 114.

[18] *Ibid.,* 114.

[19] *Ibid.,* 116.

[20] Matt Haldane, "U.S. Slowly opening up commercial drone industry" *Reuters*, Aug. 8, 2013.

[21] Raúl Rojas González, interview by the author for *Oppenheimer Presenta*, CNN en español, April 2013.

[22] John de Leon, interview by the author, Miami, April 2013.

[23] Chris Anderson, *Makers: The New Industrial Revolution*, (Crown Business, 2012), 170.

[24] *Ibid.*

[25] Jordi Muñoz, interview by the author, April 2014.

4. BRE PETTIS AND NEW INDUSTRIAL REVOLUTION

[1] Bre Pettis, interview by the author, Brooklyn, August 2013.

[2] *Ibid.*

[3] *Ibid.*

[4] Abraham Reichental, interview by the author, July 2013.

[5] Eric Savitz, "Manufacturing the Future: 10 Trends to Come in 3D Printing", *Forbes*, July 12, 2012.

[6] *Ibid.*

[7] Vivek Wadhwa, interview by the author, Mountain View, Ca., July 2013.

[8] Charles Hull, phone interview by author, July 2013.

[9] *Idem.*

[10] *Idem.*

[11] University of Pittsburgh, "Entering a New Dimension: 4D Printing," September 30 2013, http://www.news.pitt.edu/news/entering-new-dimension-4d-printing.

[12] Ben Rooney, "If You Think 3D Printing is Disruptive, Wait for 4D Printing," *The Wall Street Journal*, July 30, 2013.

[13] Ben Rooney, "Still Hype Around 3-D Printing for Consumers, Says Report," *The Wall Street Journal*, October 4, 2013.

[14] Rakesh Sharma, "Will UPS Succeed in Popularizing 3D Printing", *Forbes*, August 2, 2013. http://www.forbes.com/sites/rakeshsharma/2013/08/02/will-ups-succeed-in-popularizing-3d-printing/.

[15] Carlos Fresneda, "Impresoras 3D con un nuevo uso metálico", *El Mundo*, Spain, October 16 2010.

[16] *Idem.*

5. RAFAEL YUSTE AND THE BRAIN MANIPULATORS

[1] Dr. Rafael Yuste, interview by the author, New York City, August 2013.

[2] Barack Obama news conference, White House, April 2, 2013.

[3] Rafael Yuste, phone interview by the author, December 2013.

[4] Rafael Yuste, interview by the author, New York City, August 2013.

[5] Charles Q. Choi, "Experiment Lets Man Use his Mind to Control Another Person's Movement", *The Washington Post*, Aug. 29, 2013.

[6] Rafael Yuste, phone interview by the author, December 2013.

[7] *Ibid.*

[8] *Ibid.*

[9] *Ibid.*

6. PEP GUARDIOLA AND THE ART OF INNOVATING WHILE WINNING

[1] Staff report, "Hay que respetar el mundo de cada persona': Guardiola," *El Tiempo*, Colombia, April 30, 2013.

Josep Guardiola, "Guardiola y la importancia de la táctica," conference in Buenos Aires, Argentina, posted May 7, 2013 on YouTube, https://www.youtube.com/watch?v=0ujt7kNzai0.

[3] Staff report, "Hay que respetar el mundo de cada persona': Guardiola," *El Tiempo*, Colombia, April 30, 2013.

[4] Staff report, "La vida del Pep Guardiola al descubierto", capítulo 1, Penya Barcelonista de Lisboa, http://penbarlis.blogspot.com/2009/03/la-vida-de-pep-guardiola-al-descubierto.html, March 28, 2009.

[5] Guillem Balagué, *Pep Guardiola: la biografía*, (Editorial Córner, 2013), 61.

[6] Staff report, "Hay que respetar el mundo de cada persona': Guardiola," *El Tiempo*, Colombia, April 30, 2013.

[7] *Ibid.*

[8] Guillem Balagué, *Pep Guardiola: la biografía*, (Editorial Córner, 2013), 72.

[9] Staff report, "Guardiola, absuelto de acusación de dopaje en Brescia," *Marca.com*, Oct. 23 2007. http://archivo.marca.com/edicion/marca/futbol/internacional/es/desarrollo/1049308.html.

[10] *Ibid.*

[11] Guillem Balagué, *Pep Guardiola: la biografía,* (Editorial Córner, 2013), 103.

[12] Staff report, "El humilde Pep," *La Nación*, Argentina, Dec. 28, 2013.

[13] Josep Guardiola, "Guardiola y la importancia de la táctica," conference in Buenos Aires, Argentina, May 7, 2013, posted on YouTube, https://www.youtube.com/watch?v=0ujt7kNzai0.

[14] Carlos Murillo Fort, phone interview by the author, November 2012.

[15] *Ibid.*

[16] Josep Guardiola and Fernando Trueba, "Conversaciones de Pep Guardiola y Fernando Trueba," posted on YouTube, May 18, 2012, https://www.youtube.com/watch?v=cPrdgWwbGMQ.

[17] Josep Guardiola, "Sentirlo," *El País*, Spain, March 2, 2007.

[18] Josep Guardiola, "Guardiola y la importancia de la táctica," conference in Buenos Aires, Argentina, May 7, 2013, posted on YouTube, https://www.youtube.com/watch?v=0ujt7kNzai0.

[19] *Ibid.*

[20] Javier Mascherano, "Pep Guardiola: el triunfo de un gentil liderazgo," *La Nación*, Argentina, Jan. 31, 2013.

[21] Josep Guardiola, "Guardiola y la importancia de la táctica," conference in Buenos Aires, Argentina, May 7, 2013, posted on YouTube, https://www.youtube.com/watch?v=0ujt7kNzai0.

[22] Jimmy Burns, "Barca: A people's Passion," (Bloomsbury 2009) http://www.jimmy-burns.com/books/football-books/barca-a-peoples-passion/.

[23] Rob Hugues, "Barcelona Changes Jerseys and its Values," *The New York Times*, Sept. 27, 2011.

[24] Staff report, "Cruyff: lo mejor para el FC Barcelona es que vuelva Pep Guardiola", *Mundo Deportivo*, Spain, April 16, 2014.

[25] Jorge Valdano, "Guardiola es como Steve Jobs," Eurosport interview, published YouTube, Nov. 15, 2012. https://www.youtube.com/watch?v=TfAe5rBr1zo.

7. BRANSON, MUSK, KARGIEMAN AND THE ART OF REINVENTING ONESELF

[1] Sir Richard Branson, *Losing my Virginity* (Crown Business 2011) 31.

[2] Sir Richard Branson, interview by the author, May 2013.

[3] *Ibid.*

[4] *Ibid.*

[5] *Ibid.*

[6] *Ibid.*

[7] Sir Richard Branson, *Losing my Virginity* (Crown Business 2011) 31.

[8] *Ibid.*

[9] *Idem.*, 45.

[10] *Idem.*, 50.

[11] *Idem.*, 55.

[12] Sir Richard Branson, interview by the author, May 2013.

[13] *Ibid.*

[14] Sir Richard Branson, *Like a Virgin: Secrets They Won't Teach You in Business School*, (Portfolio/Penguin 2012).

[15] Sir Richard Branson, interview by the author, May 2013.

[16] Sir Richard Branson, *Losing my Virginity* (Crown Business 2011), 68.

[17] *Idem.*, 74.

[18] *Idem.*, 77.

[19] *Idem.*, 92.

[20] *Idem.*, 102.

[21] *Idem.*, 190.

[22] *Idem.*, 192.

[23] *Idem.*, 203.

[24] *Idem.*, 215.

[25] *Idem.*, 220.

[26] Sir Charles Branson, interview by the author, May 2013.

[27] Patt Morrison, "Elon Musk of SpaceX: The Goal is Mars," *The Los Angeles Times*, August 1 2012.

[28] Staff interview, Elon Musk, *Esquire*, October 1 2008.

[29] *Idem.*

[30] Justine Musk, "I Was a Starter Wife," *Marie Claire*, September 10, 2010.

[31] Elon Musk, interview by Scott Pelley for *60 Minutes*, CBS, June 3, 2012.

³² Patt Morrison, "Elon Musk of SpaceX: The Goal is Mars," *The Los Angeles Times,* August 1 2012.

³³ *Ibid.*

³⁴ *Ibid.*

³⁵ Sir Richard Branson, *Losing my Virginity* (Crown Business *2011)* 410.

8. SALMAN KHAN AND "FLIPPED SCHOOLS"

¹ Salman Khan, Skype interview by the author, Mountain View, Ca., October 2013.

² *Ibid.*

³ *Ibid.*

⁴ Salman Khan, *The One World School House,* (Twelve 2012), 76.

⁵ Virginia Heffernan, *"Education Needs a Digital Age Upgrade"*, *The New York Times,* August 7, 2011.

⁶ Salman Khan, *The One World School House,* (Twelve 2012), 80.

⁷ *Idem.*, 169.

⁸ Salman Khan, Skype interview by the author, Mountain View, Ca., October 2013.

⁹ *Ibid.*

¹⁰ *Ibid.*

¹¹ *Ibid.*

¹² *Ibid.*

¹³ *Ibid.*

¹⁴ *Ibid.*

¹⁵ *Ibid.*

¹⁶ *Ibid.*

¹⁷ *Ibid.*

¹⁸ *Ibid.*

¹⁹ *Ibid.*

9. ZOLEZZI, VON AHN AND THE SOCIAL INNOVATORS

¹ Alfredo Zolezzi, phone interview by the author, December 2013.

² *Ibid.*

³ *Ibid.*

⁴ Guillermo Scallan, interview by the author, January 2014.

⁵ *Ibid.*

⁶ Alfredo Zolezzi, interview by author, December 2013.

[7] *Ibid.*

[8] *Ibid.*

[9] Nicolas Alonso, "La revolución de Zolezzi", *Qué Pasa*, Chile, January 2, 2014.

[10] Alfredo Zolezzi, interview by the author, January 2014.

[11] *Ibid.*

[12] Paula Cardenau, interview by the author, January 2014.

[13] Beatriz Pellizari, interview by the author, January 2014.

[14] Muhammad Yunus, interview by the author, for *Oppenheimer Presenta*, CNN en español, September 2013.

[15] *Ibid.*

[16] *Ibid.*

[17] Fernando Fabre, interview by the author, January 2014.

[18] Enrique Gómez Junco, inteview by the author, January 2014.

[19] Luis Von Ahn, interview by the author, March 2014.

[20] *Ibid.*

[21] *Ibid.*

[22] *Ibid.*

[23] William D. Edgers and Paul MacMillan, *The Solution Revolution: How Business, Government, and Social Enterprises are Teaming up to Solve Society's toughest Problems* (Harvard Business Review Press, 2013), 10.

[24] *Idem.*, 11.

[25] Staff report, "World Giving Index," *Charities Aid Foundation*, 2013.

10. THE FIVE SECRETS OF INNOVATION

[1] Thomas Friedman, "Need a Job?: Invent it," *The New York Times*, March 30, 2013.

[2] U. S. Department of Labor, Bureau of Labor Statistics, *Employee Tenure Summary,* ", (Sept. 18, 2012). http://www.bls.gov/news.release/tenure.nr0.htm.

[3] World Bank, *Latin American Entrepreneurs: Many Firms, but Little Innovation*, (2014). http://www.worldbank.org/content/dam/Worldbank/document/LAC/LatinAmericanEntrepreneurs.pdf.

[4] Organization of Ibero-American States, *Ciencia, tecnología e innovación para el desarrollo y la cohesión social,*" (2012), 34. http://www.oei.es/documentociencia.pdf.

[5] *Idem.*, p. 35.

[6] Andy Freire, interview by the author, April 2014.

[7] Peter H. Diamandis and Steven Kotler, *Abundance: The Future is Better than You Think*, (Free Press, 2012), 219.

[8] *Idem.*, 221.

[9] Peter Diamandis, interview by the author for the *Oppenheimer Presenta* program on CNN and Foro TV, May 2014.

[10] Salim Ismail, interview by the author, February 2014.

[11] World Bank, *Latin American Entrepreneurs: Many Firms, but Little Innovation,* (2014). 18, http://www.worldbank.org/content/dam/Worldbank/document/LAC/LatinAmericanEntrepreneurs.pdf.

[12] Andrés Oppenheimer, "Gates: Latin America Needs better Schools", *The Miami Herald*, April 8, 2008.

[13] Eugenia Garduño, interview by the author, April 2014.

[14] Tony Wagner, "Educating the Next Steve Jobs", *The Wall Street Journal*, April 2012.

[15] *Idem.*

[16] *Idem.*

[17] World Bank, Doing Business 2014, 233 and 234.

[18] Emiliano Kargieman, interview by the author, August 2013.

[19] World Bank, Doing Business 2014, 233 and 234.

[20] Augusto López-Claros, interview by the author, October, 2013.

[21] Martín Migoya, interview by the author, Buenos Aires, Argentina, March 2013.

[22] Organization of Ibero-American States, "Ciencia, tecnología e innovación para el desarrollo y la cohesión social," (2012), 34. http://www.oei.es/documentociencia.pdf.

[23] *Idem.*, 35.

[24] Luis Von Ahn, interview by the author, March 2014.

[25] *Ibid.*

[26] Rafael Atijas, interview by the author, February 2014.

[27] *Idem.*

[28] Institute of International Education, International Students: Leading Places of Origin, 2013, http://www.iie.org/Research-and-Publications/Open-Doors/Data/International-Students/Leading-Places-of-Origin.

[29] Andres Oppenheimer, "La apuesta tecnológica de Latinoamérica", *El Nuevo Herald*, June 15, 2013.

[30] *Ibid.*

[31] Armando Ahued, interview by the author, March 2014.

Acknowledgments

A very special thanks to Romero Britto, one of the most successful artists in the world, who suggested the idea and personally designed the image of Albert Einstein on the cover of this book. "To illustrate a book on innovation, creativity and genius, nothing better than a face of Einstein," he said. Britto himself is a living example of a successful creator and entrepreneur, an artist who could have easily filled a chapter in *Innovate or die!*

Born into poverty, the son of a single mother who had 12 children —three of them died at birth— Britto moved to Miami at the age of 22 and started selling his paintings, joyful and full of life, on the streets of the Coconut Grove neighborhood. He soon placed some of his paintings in an art gallery in a shopping center, but his career took off after one of his designs was selected in a contest for an Absolut Vodka label. From then on, his designs have been bought by brands like Mini Cooper, Audi, Swatch, Movado and Hublot and his paintings, sculptures and painted objects —produced in his Miami studio, which employs about 100 workers— now bring in revenues of up to $80 million per year, according to some estimates.

When I asked him for the secret of his success, he said it came spontaneously. "I like to be surrounded by pretty things, that make me feel good. And what I did was to create a universal language of things that make people feel good," he explained.

This book benefited enormously from the assistance of Cristóbal Pera, editorial director of Penguin Random House in Mexico, who offered invaluable suggestions for improving the original manuscript. Pera is an exceptional editor, the kind all writers want for our books. He is a man of extraordinary warmth, always ready to help with anything. And he has an eagle eye for missing paragraphs, superfluous words and concepts that can be improved.

Another person who supported me at all times and served as my guide in the world of science was my wife, Sandra Bacman, to whom this book is dedicated. A PhD in biology and a scientific researcher at the University of Miami's Neurology Department, Sandra helped me to really understand what some of the scientists I interviewed for this book had explained to me —some with more luck than others.

Finally, my thanks as always to my editor at *The Miami Herald*, John Yearwood, whose recommendations always improve my texts; to Cynthia Hudson and Eduardo Suarez, CNN executives who kindly allowed me to use TV studios to interview some of the innovators I include in this book; my attorney, Thomas Oppenheimer, one of the best lawyers in Miami; my agent at ICM, Kris Dahl; colleagues Ismael Triviño, news producer for Oppenheimer Presenta on CNN and Foro TV, and Annamaría Muchnik, Angelina Peralta, Bettina Chouhy and Malen Nousari; and my good friends like Ezequiel Stolar and several others who encouraged me to explore good ideas —and discard others— during the research for this book.